"Morning Glory"

Diary of an Alien Abductee

By
Gloria Ann Hawker

Write to Print

P.O. Box 1862
Merrimack, NH 03054

Gloria Ann Hawker

Library of Congress Control Number: 2001096420

Morning Glory Diary of an Alien Abductee / Hawker

ISBN 0-9714272-3-2

COVER ART: Chy Montana / edited by Electric Wigwam
AUTHOR'S PHOTO: Peggy Williams with Kim Jew Photography

Printed in the United States of America
Publishing Services Provided by:

Write to Print

P.O.Box 1862
Merrimack, NH 03054
www.writetoprint.com

Address All inquires about this book to:
Gloria Hawker
P. O. Box 14779
Albuquerque, NM 87191

ACKNOWLEDGMENTS

I owe a debt of gratitude to my husband, Fred, without his patience, understanding and insightful support throughout my "secret-life experiences" enabled this book to become a reality. Michelle, without your expertise, knowledge of computer programs was put to the test in your correctness to seeing a reality come true. Your labor of love is deeply felt. Thank you dear one. Kathryn, your understanding and belief in the truth of my story promoted this book. Your persuasion and push were there when I wanted to shelve the manuscript because reliving the truth was hard. Thank you for being the dearest of friends.

Sylvia with your interest and credence in my story, thus you accepted the responsibility of being the editor of "Morning Glory". Sylvia, my deepest appreciation for your labor of love comes from within my soul.

Juanita, Helen, Susan, Linda, Kathryn, Christine W., are the kind souls who gave of their time to trudge through the drafts of the manuscript and provided editorial comments and suggestions, and Chy, a talented lady who designed the cover of "Morning Glory". I extend to each of you a heartfelt gratitude for your dedication.

A special person who helped me find my way through this traumatic life I owe a wealth of gratitude. Mr. Budd Hopkins, don't ever give up in your belief in your work and your care and love of each human alien abductee. You bring reality of truth of the unknown facts to each of us. My family and I owe a special thank you to Mr. Michael Lindemann, who believed in my story and initially made the first contact on my behalf to Mr. Budd Hopkins. Christine M. you were there for my family and me with your knowledge and guidance throughout the years.

Gloria is a valued friend. I knew she was an alien abductee but I had no idea what the substance of her "other-worldly" experiences involved, that was her private area and I respected her silence. Now, Morning Glory tells the story.

Under the cover of a normal, unpresupposing, middle-class housewife and mom, Gloria dares to lead us into unthinkable territories where all conventional expectations are violated. She presents us with all the things that frighten us the most. She is relentless. She has no mercy. Who can live with so much fear and yet manage to keep on track with their everyday life while they are living a nightmare?

Morning Glory tells of one woman's journey of cosmic and self discovery. Gloria is real. She's authentic. She's courageous and yet, she's afraid of her own shadow. Who among us can't relate? No matter how you read her, Gloria will get to you!

Susan L. Barclay

MORNING GLORY.....The beauty of this delicate trumpet shaped flower that produces in its uniqueness vibrant colors of blues, purples, whites, and pink that grow on a fast-growing vine with weedy tendencies. Sucking up the summer rays, these **MORNING GLORIES** shine and express their beauty as they open in the warmth of the morning sun and close quietly at the end of a long day.

Why then am I compared to and called by different friends of who do not know of each other "**MORNING GLORY**"? Perhaps I am found to be as such as this delicate flower? This delicate flower with its weedy vine, which extends far beyond and outward, toward the universe and its universal alien beings?

Such then I shall name my book.....**"MORNING GLORY"**, Diary of an Alien Abductee

NOTES FROM THE EDITOR

I first met with Gloria Hawker on a Sunny Afternoon at her home in Albuquerque, New Mexico. That initial meeting was to be one of many we would have over the course of this book.

My first reaction to her story was one of overload. I have always lived by the "Star Trek" creed that anything is possible in the galaxy; but the events I was hearing about were anything but "friendly" visitors making "first contact" from outer space! For the next three days, I actually wondered if this woman was a nutcase or a true victim.

In the weeks that followed, I began to realize that Gloria had indeed, been victimized by the Others. As her story unraveled, I began to feel a deep compassion for her and for all those who have been abducted.

However, there is also another scenario to this story, and that is that Gloria has actually been helped by the Others at times in her life. I can't help but wonder if perhaps they do have a higher, albeit ulterior motive. I do know one thing for certain; my "Star Trek" fantasies have been radically altered since beginning this journey with Gloria. I am no longer certain of the benevolence of those Beings who travel the universe, whether known to humans or not.

I do encourage the reader to draw his or her own conclusions after reading this fascinating account. It will certainly give the reader many things to think about. It may even possibly change the reader's perceptions and beliefs about what is really "out there."

Sylvia F. Adamska
April, 2001

Table of Contents

PART I

ALIEN ABDUCTIONS

AND SO IT ALL BEGINS...

My name is Gloria. The story I am about to tell you is true. The memories are mine. There are some who will believe that my experiences could not possibly have happened. I am here to tell you that they have indeed happened to me over the last twelve years. I am writing about these events to help others come to terms with what may be happening to them. If I can help just one person who has been through what I have been through, then writing this book will have been worth it. I have no reason to lie about what I have experienced. You may believe it or not; but if you find yourself identifying with what you are about to read, know that you have my compassion and support in what you are living with.

WE THOUGHT IT WAS A HOT AIR BALLOON
THE WHITE LIGHT

September 19, 1988 Labor Day Weekend

This holiday weekend included just another normal Sunday. My ritual began in the kitchen, preparing a large breakfast for everyone. My husband Fred, drove a taxicab all night. He would come home from work tired, hungry, and impatient to get six or seven hours of sleep. After breakfast, our 15-year-old son Brian, daughter Michelle, age 12, and I, would go to Mass at Risen Savior Catholic Church. After Mass, I would come home and do the laundry, the ironing, or maybe go grocery shopping.

I always prepared a large dinner on Sunday. It seemed to be the one day I was not running Brian and Michelle to

1

soccer, football practice, or other extracurricular school functions. Our meals during the week were eaten at a time that was convenient for them.

Sunday was also special because our daughter, Vanessa, who attended the University of New Mexico, would come to spend the day with us. Brian and Michelle would entertain themselves with quiet games, so as not to disturb their father, or go outside to play with friends. On that particular Sunday, Brian was interested in a book about the movie, *Star Wars*. He protested when I told him to get some homework done. "Why do I have to finish homework, Mom? Tomorrow is a holiday."

Michelle followed in her older sister's footsteps. She was the second "socialite" and tomboy in our family. Since noon, the doorbell had not quit ringing, as her friends called for her to go out and play. I noticed she was not as active as usual. She seemed somewhat sluggish, indicating to me that she might be getting ill. It was unusual for her to stay inside. Many times when she was sick, I would have to force her to stay in bed or in the house until she got well. Almost nothing kept this child from her rough, outside games of soccer and football.

Michelle's life revolved more around her friends than around her studies. However, as the day wore on, she seemed to feel better and before I knew it, she was outside with her friends.

As afternoon moved into early evening, dinner dishes done, it was soon time for Fred to trot off to his taxi-driving job. I felt somewhat apprehensive about that evening. I had the misfortune of possessing some psychic abilities that we discovered a month after our oldest child was born. I say misfortune, because my premonitions always had to do with some devastation resulting in death. There was no time of day or night when I would not be shown visions of misfortune happening to others.

I had experienced the demise of a taxicab driver within the last month, through a psychic vision. I did not want Fred to go to work that night. Fred left for work dejected, not because of my feelings, but because he would much rather have stayed

2

home with his family that evening. All my premonitions had been correct in the past and I felt the inevitability of the evening to come. Fred was gone and Vanessa had returned to the dorm, as she had other things to attend to.

I have never liked being by myself at night. I have always experienced this unsettling fear when left at night to be the sole parent. I have never understood why I detested being alone at night.

Soon, a feeling of intense anxiety came over me. This type of fear had grabbed at me and plagued my adult life ever since I could remember. I should have been used to staying by myself at night; after all, doesn't one's age and experience play a large part in overcoming fear? No, it does not. I was still the "fraidy cat" I had been as a child.

When Fred and I got married, he was in the Air Force. I knew he would not always be home at night. Blinded by young love, I attempted to become a strong, well-adjusted Air Force wife.

Reflecting back on those early years when Fred worked nights at the base, I remember dreading bedtime. I would lay wide awake as some unimaginable presence dominated my very being. Every little unfamiliar noise I heard would find me curled up in our large bed, shaking with fright. After what seemed like forever, I would drift off into a light sleep. The morning sun never rose soon enough for me, and it was useless to pretend that I was well-rested the next day.

I kept these mental wanderings a secret, as intimidating as they were, so as not to instill this fear in our children. I never sought help for this problem. I tried to resolve it within myself but fear continued to be a part of my life, engulfing my nights as the years went on.

After Fred left the Air Force, he worked as a sales representative for various computer companies. Once again, I found myself living with the fear of being alone at night when he was out of town on business. Each time, the anxiety would engulf me as night fell.

During that time, I had the responsibility of being both mother and father to our four children. I repeatedly told myself to be strong and get over my fear of being alone at night, for the sake of our children. I could not allow them to see or hear me crying and shaking in my bed at night. One would think you would feel safe with others sleeping in the same house, even if the others were small children; but for some reason, I was afraid for our children as well. I had never felt this way as a child or adolescent. Why now? I had no insight as to what had brought on this particular fear of nighttime.

I began to react with anxiety, striking out verbally at my husband when he would return home from his business trips. Finally, Fred decided to start his own computer business. My fear lessened, but was still there. I dreaded the hour when he would tell me he had to go away on business.

After Fred and Vanessa left that Labor Day Sunday evening, I called Michelle into the house to get ready for our weekly visit to my parents. They lived six miles away in the Valley. I felt I needed the distraction of a visit to rid myself of the premonition of danger.

Thankfully, nothing unusual took place that night. The trip was rather mundane and we returned home about 9:30 p.m. Michelle was not feeling well again. She had a temperature, so I sent her upstairs to get ready for bed. I told Brian to get ready for bed as well, but said he could read if he wanted to.

I went into the laundry room and gathered up folded clothes that were ready to be taken upstairs and put away. I had re-checked all the doors, making sure they were securely locked. I made certain all the lights were off downstairs. Walking up the dimly lit stairway, arms loaded with a full laundry basket, I entered Fred's and my bedroom first.

I don't know why I didn't turn on a light in the bedroom. I suppose I felt the dim light in the hall was sufficient. Michelle and Brian had their bedroom doors closed. Entering the dark room, I walked to the armoire, located on the

4

east wall, next to the open balcony door. I had left it open because the weather was very warm that time of year. As I opened the armoire door, something caught my eye through the open balcony door.

To my amazement, I noticed a large, bright white light. I thought it must be a hot air balloon trying to go over the mountains or land on our street. I closed the armoire and went outside on the balcony to watch the unusual flight of a hot air balloon at night. I wanted to see if it would go over the Sandia Mountains or land on our street.

A week prior to the Balloon Fiesta Albuquerque hosted ever year, as many as 400 hot air balloons would arrive for balloon events. The balloonists would make practice flights during the days before the Fiesta, although it was rare for them to fly at night.

So I found the sighting unusual, especially for a balloonist to attempt going over the Sandias in the dark! If that was the pilot's intention, I figured the winds must be right for him to even attempt flight over the mountains. However, it seemed to me, he should be higher up than he was or he wouldn't make it. Maybe he intended to land on the street close to our home.

The balloon I watched was in the sky to the southeast of our home. Our house was located on the largest corner lot of our street.

As I stood there listening for the sound of the propane burner and waiting to see if the balloon would actually take flight or land, I suddenly realized there was no flame coming from the burner that carried hot air into the envelope of the balloon. I also noticed that the balloon was not moving. Could the pilot be in trouble?

I was excited. I wanted to share all these goings-on with Brian and Michelle, just in case the balloon did land near our house. We could then go out and help the pilot and his chase crew wrap the balloon, as the children had done in the past. I ran into the house greatly excited, hollering for Brian and Michelle to come to the balcony and watch the hot air balloon.

I told them I thought the pilot might land near our house, and that he was very close to us now.

Brian and Michelle ran out of their bedrooms and rushed to the balcony. We stood there together, listening for the sound of the propane burners, for about fifteen minutes. The balloon simply remained aloft and motionless. We all wondered if the pilot was in trouble.

After awhile, we began to think this was not a hot air balloon at all. We wondered if maybe it was an experiment by the military, such as a new top-secret airplane.

Our ideas became sillier and our conversation grew more comical. As a joke, I said, "Well, maybe it is an alien aircraft!" We all laughed about that and Brian said, "Mom, you are crazy! I'm going to bed!!" It made good sense for all of us to do that so we went back inside.

I finished putting away the folded clothes and got ready for bed. Just before I got into bed, I decided to have one more look outside to see if the object was gone. As I took a last look, it was apparent the object had not moved an inch. It was in the exact same spot as before. I continued to wonder what the object might be.

Michelle had heard me open the balcony door and called out to me, asking if it was still there. Before I knew it, she was outside with me again. We both looked at the round object that had a large white light.

Michelle felt more feverish and should have been in bed. However, she begged to stay for just a few minutes, promising to go quietly to bed and stay there. Because of her persistence, I let her stay up awhile longer.

I stood by the open door trying once again to figure this thing out, binoculars in hand. Suddenly, there seemed to be something wrong with my binoculars. I could no longer see the large white light. It seemed to have disappeared! In its place, I saw five or six smaller white lights that appeared to be where the large white light had been. The small lights were all in a circular pattern!

I was so engrossed with this development that I was startled to find Michelle standing next to me. I had forgotten she was there, but was comforted by her presence. We took turns looking through the binoculars. I noticed that as soon as she pointed the binoculars toward the object, the large white light would go off and the small white lights would appear again. It was as if they were small windows with light shining through. How could that be?

Michelle handed the binoculars back to me and the same thing happened again. We traded the binoculars between us two or three times with the same results each time.

We went back into the house. Michelle thought we should phone Grandma and Grandpa to find out if they could see anything unusual toward the direction of our home. I enticed Brian to come out and look through the binoculars while we waited for my parents to answer the phone. Their response was negative. They didn't see anything from their house six or so miles away.

When Brian and Michelle used the binoculars as she and I had done, they saw the same light changes Michelle and I had seen. I noticed that it was 10:30 p.m. Brian began to sing the theme from "Twilight Zone" --- 'doo-do-doo-do' --- telling me he was seeing "little green men" and "Maybe it's a UFO, Mom!" I said, "Yeah, Brian, right. Just because I made a joke earlier. You know there's no such thing!"

Brian then remarked that he was going back inside to stay. He told us to go ahead and watch THAT DUMB THING and stated that if there was ANYTHING, he'd hear about it tomorrow. He said he was plumb tired and watching was a waste of his time! "Night," he said as he went inside to bed.

Michelle and I stayed outside looking through the binoculars. As before, every time we shifted the binoculars to our eyes, the circular lights would come on. I then suggested to Michelle that we go to Brian and Debra's balcony. Their balconies were located on the southeast side of the house. I thought we might have a better vantage point there.

"Morning Glory" Diary of an Alien Abductee

After observing again, using the binoculars in the same way, I began to think very seriously as I stood on the larger connecting balcony, that this might be something from Sandia Base or Kirtland Base. It appeared to be high up and perfectly still as I looked straight up at it.

Michelle and I went back into my bedroom. I thought Vanessa might still be up, so I called her at the sorority house. I explained to her what we had been observing and asked her to go outside and look in the direction of our home. But again, just as with my folks earlier, Vanessa saw nothing unusual.

My folks called back to suggest I call the TV stations, as they may have received reports from others who had seen the object. I checked the time again. It was 11:00 p.m. I hesitated to call the television stations, but did so anyway. I called KOAT (channel 7) and KOB (channel 4) and explained to them what we had been looking at since 9:30 p.m. I asked if they had received any reports on it. Evidently, they thought I was a big jokester, as I overheard much laughing about "this lady on the phone." One person said, laughing, that he would go and get his binoculars and look at the area if I would describe the main streets he needed to look toward. I felt very foolish. The man on the other end of the line said no one had called in any type of reports of a white light object or whatever. Then he began to laugh even more. I felt foolish and did not call any of the other TV stations or radio stations. I could not call any of our neighbors, because it was too late at night. I went back to Brian's room and asked him if he wanted to look at this thing again. He responded, "Go to bed, Mom."

By now, I was experiencing anxiety and much nervousness about this object and just needed to know something about it. My dad called back twice as Michelle and I kept vigil on this thing. We kept running back and forth from the east bedroom balcony to the south bedroom balcony in our daughter Debra's room. The unidentified light remained in the same position. Every time we looked through the binoculars, the large light would go out and the smaller lights would come on.

8

Michelle was burning up with fever, so we went into my bedroom and I took her temperature. After medicating her, tucking her into bed, and reassuring her of her safety, I told her that we would probably hear about it in the morning on the radio or TV, or in the newspaper. I explained to her that the "thing" was not hurting us. I felt we both needed to get some rest. It had been an exciting night. Michelle did not know how uneasy I was feeling about this whole thing.

By then it was close to 1:00 a.m. I tossed and turned and could not get to sleep. I felt very restless. With Michelle's high fever and her feeling uncomfortable, she was soon in my bedroom again, standing at the side of my bed. "Can we look at it one more time, Mom?"

We both went back outside. The object was still there. I told Michelle to get back into the house. She scanned the night sky through the screen door. She asked me, "What is 'round' over Sandia Crest that sparkles with blue, orange, green, and purple blinking lights?"

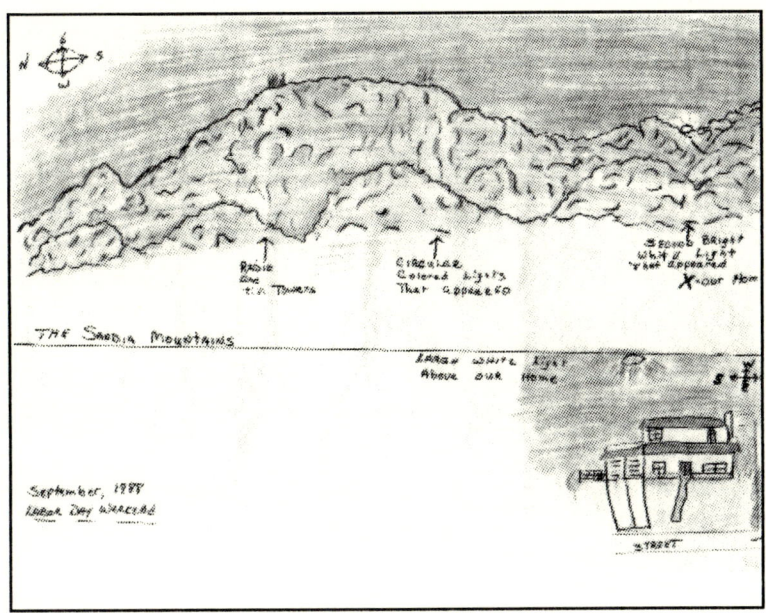

The White Lights

I asked her to repeat what she had said. Then I asked for the binoculars so I could see what she was looking at. I knew there were radio and TV towers located on the crest of the Sandia Mountains. The towers had red lights on them, so I really did not know what she was looking at until I saw the same round, blue, orange, purple, and green flashing lights above the Crest. The small, round colored lights seemed to be surrounding the restaurant (atop the Crest) as well.

The restaurant was about two miles south of the radio and TV towers. There were six lights! Dear God, what was going on? Now we had the large, round white light by our house, and these other small colored lights as well, over the Crest. The individual colored lights did not move either.

I am not a good estimator of distances, so I could not tell how close the lights were to the restaurant, or how high up they were. I also could not estimate distance or height of the large white light above our home. Michelle and I stayed up another thirty or forty minutes just watching both sets of lights.

Finally, I'd had enough. Michelle was feeling warmer and we both needed to get some rest, so we went back to bed again. I was certain we would hear all about it in the morning. Michelle and I went back to her room where we talked to each other for a little while longer, until she fell asleep. Then, I went to bed and covered myself tightly with all my blankets. I still could not sleep. Brian was sound asleep. I kept getting out of bed to go to the open balcony door every five minutes, then every ten minutes, and finally, every half hour, just to check. The round flashing lights remained in the same position over the Crest. The light above us still had not moved.

At 3:00 a.m., I promised myself this would be the last time up to look. I felt very irritated and very uncomfortable by then. I got out of bed. Looking straight out the open door, through the screen door, directly in front of me, but lower in the mountainous hills, was another white light! OH MY GOD.

I wished Fred or Vanessa was home. Now, I was scared. What was going on? Just then, I didn't think it was Kirtland Air Force Base or Sandia Base doing any kind of experiments. Or were they? I had three unidentified things to look at. I thought to myself, "Watch the light to see if it moves. See if any of them move."

September 20, 1988 Labor Day Weekend

I do not remember going back to bed last night, but morning came and I was in bed. I woke up with the blankets tightly wrapped around my body. The time was 6:30 a.m. and Fred was not home from work yet. I got out of bed. I ran to the door to check for the objects in the morning sky, hoping to see what we had actually been looking at. There was nothing in the sky as I searched outside the house.

I put on my robe and went to get the newspaper to see if there was any mention of the object. I scanned the paper quickly. There was no news at all about the object and lights we had observed. Filled with anxiety, I turned on the radio. No news there, either, so I turned on the TV. Nothing was said about what we had seen.

The telephone rang. It was my dad calling. He was curious about what we had been looking at the night before. He wanted to know if we had found out what it was. He and Mom had been up looking at the TV to see if there was any news about it.

My dad suggested I call the airport because they might have tracked it on their screens. He said maybe the people in the FAA tower would have information on the object.

I called the airport. A man answered the telephone and identified himself. I was nervous about asking for information, so I did not hear his name clearly when he identified himself. I asked if they had picked up anything unusual on radar the previous night, or if anyone had reported anything unusual in the eastern sky.

I then told him the story of our sighting, giving him the times of the events. He listened intently, then gave me a phone number to call. He asked me to call and tell my story to the person who answered the phone.

After dialing the number, I wanted to be sure I would remember the name of the person I was going to speak with. A man answered the telephone. I was so nervous, I asked him his name twice, and still did not get it correct. I heard Bill or Bob, so that is what I wrote down. I told him I had just called the airport tower and spoken to a man about what my children and I had witnessed during the night.

He did not seem to be very interested in what I had to say, but listened, then began to ask me questions. He repeatedly quizzed me about the size of the objects, how bright the lights were, the times we had seen the objects, and the colors of the small round objects. After he obtained this information, he asked my name, age, and the location of our home. Very quickly he said to me, "Consider this documented. And don't talk about it."

Before I could ask any questions, he hung up! I was stunned, thinking this definitely had to do with the military. I wondered why I should not talk about it. I still did not have my questions answered and now was even more curious about the phenomenon.

I cannot explain the feelings I experienced at the time. I could not believe that man would not answer any of my questions about what we had seen. Why had he been so secretive?

When Fred got home I must have had a quizzical look on my face. Immediately, he asked me what was wrong. We sure had a story to tell him! I did not answer him as I was pursuing my own thoughts.

It dawned on me that Fred always had the radio on in the taxicab. I had hoped he would walk through the door with much anticipation and excitement about the events of the previous evening. I waited to hear his story about a lighted object that not only he, but many others as well, had seen during the night.

It did not happen. As the minutes passed, Fred again asked me what was wrong. I suddenly felt overwhelmed, tired, and very much confused. I needed him to confirm, with an exciting news story, what we had seen last night. I became sad when I realized he had no story to tell.

Brian began to tell his dad about how Mom and Michelle were up all night looking at aliens. He was laughing about how crazy we were. Brian thought this was a great, amusing story. I knew that, because of Brian's joking, this was going to be a hard story to tell; but with Michelle having witnessed the very same unusual things, hopefully, Fred would believe me. Our great tale was then told.

Fred has always played devil's advocate in our family. His explanation was that either Sandia Base or Kirtland Air Force Base was conducting some kind of experiment and that the Bob or Bill person could not reveal secret information to us. He said the possibility of this was good, since the military bases conducted many of their experiments at night. I could not settle for his explanation. Michelle and I knew there was something very different about the whole situation. We just could not put our finger on it.

With the exception of three of our neighbors, the people living on our street were not very friendly. I knew the children better than any of their parents. This was unusual for Albuquerque, as the previous neighborhoods we had lived in were like family to us. Therefore, I did not feel as if I could ask my neighbors if they had seen the large round lights or the smaller colorful lights Michelle and I had observed the night before. They would probably have thought I was an unusual sort of person.

Michelle and I stayed close to the TV and radio during the day to listen for much awaited news of our adventure. The event we witnessed never made the news.

When Monday evening came, Michelle and I anxiously began to search the sky to see if we could find any more of the bright white lights. We saw nothing unusual as we scanned the eastern sky. Around 9:30 p.m., we went outside again to look. We did not see anything unusual, but something appeared to be "wrong." I could not immediately identify the problem.

Then I realized that the four radio and TV towers located on the Crest were not lit up with their usual glowing red lights.

The tower lights were off! Looking south from the towers toward the restaurant, we saw that the restaurant lights were also off. This was very unusual because those lights were always on.

Michelle said, "Look, Mom! There are some airplanes up there!" Sure enough, we watched airplanes circling around the restaurant on the Crest. We were quite sure we also heard a helicopter.

We watched the airplanes for some time. I normally went to bed at 10:00 p.m. The activity was still going on at the top of the mountain when I went to bed that night.

September 21, 1988 Tuesday

I again made phone calls to close friends and family to see if anyone else had seen the beautiful lights. The answer was no, but they would look in the eastern sky, just out of curiosity.

Michelle, Brian and I spent Tuesday evening in the same manner, looking through the binoculars. That night, we again saw the round, flashing, beautiful colored lights in shades of peach, blue, and green. They flashed brilliantly.

As on the previous night, they did not appear to be moving in any direction. I was excited that the lights were back up in the sky. I quickly got on the phone to my folks and gave them specific directions on where to look for the lights. They could not see them. Feeling dejected, we went to bed while the objects continued to flash their beautiful colors in the eastern sky.

Michelle and I had not slept well the last couple of nights. I felt very restless and experienced anxiety about being alone in bed. I felt an unusual anxiety or concern about what exactly, Kirtland or Sandia was experimenting with. Was it something that would hurt us? Sometime after 2:00 a.m., sleep overcame me.

14

THE ILLUMINATING WALL

September 22, 1988 Wednesday

September 22nd was just another normal Wednesday morning, as it had been for the last several months. Fred called to let me know he would be working late into the morning. The time was a little after 7:00 a.m. Brian and Michelle seemed to be in "slow-motion mode." I worked at Bernalillo County Hospital part-time as a Clerical Specialist in the Medical Pool Department. I had to be there by 8:00 a.m.

All hospital employees were assigned parking spots in different areas of the massive lots surrounding the large university hospital. My assigned spot was located in the northwest area "M" parking lot, several blocks from the hospital. The hospital incorporated a shuttle bus for patient use. The shuttle bus drivers would see employees walking in the morning or late evening, and would offer us a ride, dropping us at the closest point to our destination. The drivers did this out of compassion and concern for our safety. I had to walk across another small parking lot designated for patient use only, then down or up two flights of concrete stairs, depending on the time of day. The drivers had told me that they would go out of their way to drop me off or pick me up near those stairs.

On that particular Wednesday morning, I arrived at my usual time and drove to my assigned parking slot. Though my morning seemed to be going smoothly, I was puzzled about the weird occurrences of the previous Sunday through Tuesday. I realized I had to put aside my thoughts and feelings about the incident. I had a job to perform and had to be able to do it well.

I settled into my routine as I got out of the car, made sure the doors were locked, and began walking toward the concrete stairs. I thought about how much I loved my position in the medical department. I always felt very professional at work. I dressed in a professional manner because I knew I would be working with patients, nurses, neurologists, and neurosurgeons. I had chosen to wear my favorite shoes that morning. Even though they had a three inch heel, they were very comfortable, and complimented the outfit I wore.

The stairs had ten steps in each section. I took the first step down. I was carrying a folder, so I was careful going down to the first landing. As I put my foot onto the first step of the second set of stairs, I suddenly felt a powerful force hit my back. The force was so strong, I could not stop myself from falling. I thought someone had been running and accidentally pushed me, but was also there to catch me. I tried to grab the railing but was unable to do so. I didn't know what had happened!

When I awoke, I found myself lying at the bottom of the second set of stairs facing a large concrete wall. My body was in severe pain. I lay there, dazed and incoherent. I had no idea what had just happened to me. A young lady was kneeling over me and telling me not to move. I did not know which part of my body hurt the worst. I thought she was the person who had accidentally pushed me and made me fall. She was so frightened, she began to holler for help. A young man ran up and he was just as frightened as she was. I was very embarrassed about my skirt being up around my thighs and about these people seeing my exposed thighs. It wounded my vanity to be lying there hurt and confused about what had just occurred.

I listened to their conversation. They both said they had been walking toward me and had both witnessed my fall. They told me that it was as if someone had pushed me and that I actually "flew" above and down some of the stairs. The lady said she saw me hit the large concrete wall.

The young man said he would run to the hospital and get help if the shuttle did not come in a few seconds. He then quickly left to get help. I wanted to sit up but the lady held me down. I tried to move my legs and realized neither one would move. I cried to her that I needed to sit up and she helped me to do so.

Not realizing the extent of my injuries, I somehow dragged myself to the bottom step and just fell over on her. The lady helped me to remove my shoes because having them on caused excruciating pain in my feet. It seemed to be an eternity before help came. At last I heard her say that the shuttle was coming and that she was going to flag it down.

She then ran for the shuttle, yelling at the top of her voice. The lady driver radioed the hospital for help. Soon I saw her familiar face looking down at me. Help arrived, along with the young man. An employee emergency crew, hospital supervisors, and investigators surrounded me. By then, twenty people were looking at me and working on me. It was a bit hard to take. As I was strapped to the gurney and put into the employee ambulance, I hoped I had said thank-you to the young man and lady who had come to my aid. I hoped I would remember their names.

In the emergency room, many nurses and doctors worked on me. They asked question after question. I finally passed out. Everything just went black and everyone faded away. When I woke up, my parents were by my side. I later learned that my husband and daughter could not be located and the hospital had found my parents' phone number and called them.

I had a large knot on my head. I had back and neck injuries and severe injuries to my legs and feet. My legs and feet were so swollen that the x-rays were unreadable. I remained in the emergency room until 4:00 p.m. The doctors decided to release me and I was told to go home and stay in bed. I was given Tylenol for the pain. Because of the extensive damage to my legs, I was directed to take the stronger Tylenol. There were imminent suspected problems that could occur which could be damaging to my nerves and muscles. It was believed that stronger pain medications would only cover up any effects of these suspected problems.

I was not to get out of bed even to use the bathroom. The doctors expected me to be bedridden for the next six weeks. I was instructed not to walk. I had to stay off my legs, and keep

17

them elevated higher than my heart. My legs were bound with wrappings that were used for sprained legs. The diagnosis was sprained legs and feet.

I wondered why I was being released when it took male nurses to lift me very carefully into the car. It also did not make sense to the nurses and some of the doctors who had taken care of me, that I was being released. When we arrived home, it took three men to carry a 105 pound lady up the stairs to my bed.

Fred had come home from work and gone to bed without any knowledge of my accident. He had a terrible surprise when I was brought home. He was unable to stay and take care of me and left for work at his regular time. My parents stayed with me until Brian and Michelle were ready for bed. During the night, the pain in my legs became even more excruciating. My right foot turned completely to one side.

This experience marked the awakening of an unexplained journey that would turn my whole world upside down for years to come. I was about to experience new discoveries and have encounters with an unknown species. I was about to experience things that were so unimaginable, they did not even exist in my realm of life.

September 23, 1988 Thursday

Thursday morning when Fred came home from having worked a double shift, he found me in tears because of the intense pain. After making sure Brian and Michelle had gotten off to school, he carried me down the stairs, put me into the car, and took me to the hospital.

The orthopedic doctors took more x-rays and examined my legs and feet. They asked more questions, then returned to the conference room to confer with other orthopedic doctors. There now seemed to be an acute underlying problem that the top orthopedic doctors and surgeons were diagnosing. They came to look and move my legs and feet; especially the right foot that turned inward.

18

Fred would not tell me what the doctors discussed or what was going on with my legs and feet. Eventually, we were told I might need surgery. The hours passed and the orthopedic doctors and surgeons decided that, for the time being, I was to be put on a stronger dosage of Tylenol for pain. My legs would be wrapped with more padding to give them support.

After spending most of the day in the emergency room, I was again released to go home. The doctors now had a better idea of what had happened to my legs. I had broken a bone on the front of my right foot, severely sprained my right leg and ankle, and severely sprained my left leg. In both legs, every muscle and nerve had been pulled. As a result, the muscles and nerves had become entangled with one another.

I had also suffered a concussion as a result of the fall. Along with the bumps and bruises, I had possibly injured my spine and re-injured my neck. I was immediately nicknamed "elephant legs" because the new brown wrappings around both legs were quite huge.

Fred, tired from lack of sleep, had to leave for work soon after we arrived home. My parents had come again to help me. It was now definite that I would be in bed for six weeks. Both legs had to be elevated. My toenails had to be checked constantly because of a serious problem that could arise. If my toe nails turned blue, that would indicate a blood circulation problem in my legs.

I had a low tolerance for medications, and as a result, felt doped up by the stronger Tylenol. I preferred not to be on any type of medication. Family and close friends came to visit with me that evening. After everyone left, Mom and Dad made sure Brian and Michelle were in bed. They locked up the house and put whatever I would need in close proximity to me. Before they left, I asked them to leave the balcony door open and make sure the screen door was locked. It was somewhat warm that evening.

Because I was feeling so drugged from the Tylenol, I felt no fear of being alone that night; but the recurring thought of

19

not being able to do for myself devastated me. I wondered what I would do if there was an emergency and I couldn't get to Brian or Michelle. Their welfare was on my mind.

In spite of the heavy medication, I was still unable to close my eyes and go to sleep as easily as I had thought I would. I seemed to be experiencing a restless anxiety. I was safe and comfortable and therefore, should have had no reason to feel anxious. I tossed and tried to turn my upper body to get more comfortable.

Time went by…10:30 p.m.….11:00 p.m. Fred had made a second phone call that evening to see how I was doing. He called frequently. By 11:30 p.m. I finally felt as if I had control over my anxiety, and could just close my eyes.

I had noticed that my legs seemed to have no feeling in them. I had been instructed by the doctors to keep them elevated and straight on the pillows at all times. This made lying on my back in the same position even more uncomfortable. I had been in bed for the last two days with my legs propped up on three or four pillows.

I was in no mood to accept this type of existence for the next six weeks! I was a workaholic. I never sat still. I always had to be doing something. I enjoyed cooking, baking, gardening, walking, and family activities. These things were my enjoyments in life. Lying in bed that night, I wondered if I would ever be able to experience any of those activities again.

I had finally reached the point where I was feeling somewhat more restful. I was just about ready to close my eyes. I remember lying on my back, staring toward the north bedroom window, looking at the beautiful colors being projected on the northwest wall between the bathroom door and the window. The panels of blue, purple, orange, and peach did not register in my mind, but seemed instead, to relax me even more. I enjoyed the reflecting colors that bathed the entire wall for an unknown amount of time.

All of a sudden, as I lay there in bed, I began to think I was hallucinating. These "things" were coming toward me! Something was not right.….These "things" were not human!

Someone help me! Something was coming through the wall. There were five...five...I didn't know what they were...Oh my God....they were coming toward me, toward the bed!

Illuminating Wall

I screamed loudly. Why weren't Brian and Michelle coming? I screamed louder still. Oh my God, they were at my bed. Oh my God, two of them were at my side. I told myself to get up, roll over, get away, get away. I couldn't move. I couldn't move. Bright light. There was bright light, white bright light. Help me, someone, please help me! One was standing by my bedroom door. I told him, "Don't you dare go down that hall! YOU LEAVE THEM ALONE, DO YOU HEAR ME? LEAVE THEM ALONE!!!"

He had his hands on my head. I told myself to move, turn my head quickly. Leave me alone! I tried hard to turn my head, and at the same time, realized that three more of these "things" were doing something to my legs. I was terrified, so terrified! It felt as if I could not breathe. This "thing" was rubbing my head! I had to get away.

21

What a horrible dream I was having! He was doing something to my hair and forehead. The hands were not

"Leave Me Alone!"

human hands. Oh! Those fingers! I was screaming and trying to move my head. I couldn't move my body. There was too much confusion! I think I must have passed out.

September 24, 1988 Friday

To my amazement, when I awoke, it was morning. I welcomed the bright sunlight shining into the bedroom, the early morning sunlight of a brand new day. Suddenly, I was back in the middle of a very confusing, thoroughly horrible night. I didn't know what had happened, and yet, I did know what had happened. I was literally shaken up, confused, and scared. It had to be the medication. There was no other explanation. The medication had caused me to go through that frightening hallucination! That was the only sound and reasonable explanation I could come up with.

I noticed that my legs were off the pillows. My legs hurt. They hurt badly. The bedspread was on the floor. The sheets and remaining blanket were in disarray, as if someone had had a fight in the bed. The hallucination had been so real! I couldn't explain it. Why had I dreamed something so terrible? Those "things" I saw didn't exist.

Why then, was I so upset and confused? The anxiety of it all caused me to shake. I kept telling myself over and over again, "I need to get control of myself and do it now!" My head hurt so much! I experienced a strange sensation throughout my body. It was all so unreal; but I was convinced it had happened. What was it? Why had the dream felt so real? It was so unbelievable. I did not understand.

The medication. I promised myself I would not take another one of those pills! Why had I dreamed of something that was not human, and so unlike us? The eyes had been very large...large and black. Their heads had been...large. They were short, whoever I had imagined them to be.

These were some of the fearful thoughts and questions I wrestled with over and over again that morning. I gained some insight but no answers. All I wanted to do was erase the hallucination from my mind, but I found that impossible to do.

I was so confused and distressed, I assumed the only answer was that the hallucination had been caused by the medication I took. I had never experienced an hallucination before. Why, at that point in my life, would I suddenly begin to hallucinate?

I realized that I had not been asleep when I saw the wall illuminating with the very same colors Michelle and I had seen in the round objects over Sandia Crest. Why and how had those colors come into my bedroom? What were those strange beings who had come through the wall? I had been awake. It had not been a dream! Could I have been awake and had hallucinations like that?

Suddenly, I thought of the children. How could I have forgotten them? Were Brian and Michelle all right? I heard them stirring in their own rooms, and before I knew it, Michelle was in the bedroom with me. Not wanting to frighten the children, I waited to see if they would say anything about an unusual dream or experience during the night.

Neither of them said a word. It seemed I would have more time to reflect on the events of the prior evening!

Fred came home from work before my parents arrived to be with me for the day. He had immediately come upstairs to check on me. Fred always added his extra touch by babying me when I was ill. That morning was no exception. I was upset because he had not been at home during my traumatic experience. He had not been there to hold me close and make my terrible hallucination go away.

Fred was very tired. He'd had very little sleep since my accident. I did not want to bother him with my horrific experience of the night before. I waited until after he had eaten breakfast and was lying in bed, before telling him the events of the previous night. He was incoherent and unresponsive as he listened to my story. I was not even sure he heard what I was saying.

My mother came into the bedroom to take care of my morning needs. I did not want to alarm her, so I said nothing of the night's events. I was so tired and very restless. I had thought sleep would come after having breakfast, but it did not.

My sister, Linda called to say she would come over to help Mom and spend some time with me. She asked if there was anything she could bring me. She must have heard something different in my voice because she questioned me. "Gloria," she said, "is it the pain, the medication?" She continued to interrogate me until I told her about the vivid hallucination I'd had. I was embarrassed, and told her that I did not understand it myself. She listened intently to my story and was very concerned about me. Finally, she said, "Gloria, I'm going to bring you a book that I have read. I want you to read this book."

Linda showed up about two hours later. After greeting our mother, she came upstairs to the bedroom. She had her hand behind her back as she stood in the bedroom doorway staring at me. She explained by saying she just needed to check me out before she showed me the book she had brought.

Linda noticed how shaken up I was and she brought the book closer so I could look at it. It was a pocket-sized book. When I looked at the cover, I wanted to jump right out of the bed. I had a violent reaction to the cover of the book she showed me. Linda saw my reaction and asked if the picture of the alien looked anything like what I had seen coming through the wall the previous night. I was in a state of shock! On the cover was a picture of the beings I had seen! The title of the book was Communion written by Whitley Strieber.

We discussed the entire incident of the previous night. Linda asked me many questions. She asked if we had seen the white and colored lights anymore. I told her we had seen the round colored lights the previous Tuesday night.

Linda left the book for me to read. I found it to be interesting "fiction." At the time, I believed that ours was the only world in a small universe and that there were no other species comparable to humans. I basically had no interest in that particular subject, and therefore, no knowledge about it. I had maintained this belief as a child and had carried it into adulthood. Even when I watched "alien" movies on TV, they were nothing more than fictional stories to me. I never gave them a second thought once they were over.

As disturbing as the picture on the cover of that book was, I still could not accept what had happened the previous night. I was convinced the events were simply hallucinations. Certainly there were no other species living in our universe!

I did know one thing, though; I never, ever wanted to go through such a fearful and unexplainable hallucination again!

I was determined to quit taking the medication. That afternoon, after my mother had stopped watching to make sure I took the pills, I literally rolled off the bed. Catching my legs with my hands, I maneuvered myself to the floor. From the nightstand next to the bed, I grabbed the medication bottle and painfully dragged myself to the bathroom.

I intended to dispose of the pills that had caused my hallucinations, by flushing them down the toilet. I was not ever going to experience another horrible "dream" like that again. That day, I chose the lesser of two evils: to endure the pain rather than to have something scare the living hell out of me. There was enough stress and fear in my life. I certainly did not need to add any more!

My sister Linda was reading the *Albuquerque Tribune* (the evening newspaper) when she came across an article dated September 22nd in the "Letters to the Editor" section. She was very excited when she called to ask me if we got the Tribune. I told her we did not. Linda then began to read the article to me over the phone. The article read:

"DID ANYONE SEE THE WONDERFUL THING IN THE CITY SKY SUNDAY?"

A wonderful, exciting and unexplained thing happened over the skies of northeast Albuquerque in the pre-dawn hours of Sunday morning, September 18th.

The news media all missed it! I called every one of you that would answer, starting at 5:15 a.m. You immediately called Kirtland Air Force Base, who said probably just some nut.

Is the Albuquerque media so controlled by Kirtland that they will not have the guts to question them?

What my family and I saw over Albuquerque is a remarkable story. I will not recount it in this letter, I have suffered enough of your laughter and humiliating attitudes for one day.

Come on, news media, use your telephone polls. Or are they reserved for the important questions like which NFL game to watch on Sunday?

To my fellow citizens who witnessed the events of Sunday morning: We are not nuts! Contact your favorite newsroom numbers. Tell them we want to know what we saw, not what the government wanted us to see.

S. Hardy
Albuquerque

Clipping from the Albuquerque Tribune

I was ecstatic to hear confirmation that someone else had seen the white light. Linda brought the newspaper over to me. I called the *Albuquerque Tribune* to see if I could locate this Ms. Hardy. I found out that, as a rule, the Editor of the column could not give out phone numbers or addresses. This policy protected those who wrote in to the column. He did tell me that her first name was Sandy. He asked me to leave my name and phone number. He said he would contact Sandy, give her my phone number and tell her that I wanted to speak with her regarding her article. Sandy Hardy never contacted me.

During the weeks I was bedridden, Michelle found two other books at the public library to educate us on the subject of UFOs. As we looked through those books, we found drawings of unidentified flying objects - or "flying saucers" as we called them.

The first book did not help us because we were trying to locate nighttime pictures of "saucers" with white lights, hoping to identify what we had seen. To our dismay, we found no information that satisfied us. While we were not sure exactly what shape our object had been, we had an idea that it was round, because of the effect of the small white lights that came on when we had looked through the binoculars. The lights had appeared in a circular shape.

The author of the other book Michelle had found was unknown to me. Not having been interested or educated on the subject of aliens or UFOs, I did not know who Budd Hopkins was. The title of his book was The Incredible Visitations At Copley Woods. The book caught my interest and I began to think about the possibility of other strange beings in our universe.

After finishing Budd Hopkins' book, I picked up Communion and re-read it. As I compared the two books, I finally began to realize that my "hallucination" that Labor Day weekend was no hallucination at all. It had merely been a horrible dream - a dream that felt very real and very life-like.

I asked myself how I could possibly have been dreaming when I had not even been asleep! How could such an ungodly thing ever happen to me? And if there really were "different" beings out there, why would they bother me? I could think of no reason why they would. So how was I going to cope with this awful "happening?"

Having rid myself of the medication, I decided I would no longer experience an event like that again. Little did I know, when I made that decision that my journey was just beginning.

HYPNOSIS SESSION

August 22, 1994

On August 22, 1994, I underwent hypnosis to discover more about my experience with the five Greys that had come through the illuminated bedroom wall. The hypnotherapist was Mr. Valdez. The following is an account of what that session revealed.

I knew I saw something black and odd looking that had to do with the Greys. I saw the small Grey to the far right, next to the bedroom window, carrying a black box.

The left side of the room did have a very bright, white light that illuminated just the left side of the room and the left side of the bed. The Grey set the small black box at the end of the bed next to my injured left leg. Two of the Greys worked on my left leg and possibly the right leg also. Another Grey worked on me around my left hip or stomach. Another Grey did something to the front of my head. He rubbed his hands through my hair. He may also have done something to my nose and eyes.

I saw the other Grey standing next to the door that led into the hallway to Brian and Michelle's bedrooms. That Grey left my bedroom. I was sure he went into Brian's and Michelle's bedrooms.

I was paralyzed from the chest down. I was able to move my head from side to side, and able to move my eyes. I tried to scream but could make no sound.

Eventually, I learned that when you scream, the Greys have a way of controlling the sound of your voice so that your screaming cannot be heard.

There were two Greys working on my legs. Through hypnosis, I saw one of the Greys lift up from my leg, something resembling a long, empty intestine type tissue. It was filled with a substance that had evidently come from my body. The substance appeared to be bright red intermixed with shades of orange and peach. The substance appeared to be in layers throughout the tissue.

The intended purpose of this substance will be revealed further on.

Next, the Grey carried the tissue to the black box and put it inside.

I do not know what the Grey did with Brian and Michelle, or what the other Grey did to my stomach or hip.

For the next four days, I continually smelled menstrual blood. No one else seemed to smell the odor. I had not had a menstrual period since my hysterectomy in 1984.

I was confused by this experience and questions flooded my mind. How could I smell menstrual blood when I did not have a uterus? I had been left with only one ovary as a result of the hysterectomy in 1984.

Why did the Greys work on me while I was lying in bed, in my own bedroom? Why did they not take me to their ship for those procedures? The answer to that question is still unknown.

Before our third meeting, Mr. Valdez confirmed to me that he had a client, a young man, who had been with another man on Sandia Crest around 12:30 a.m. on Sunday, September 19, 1988. They had been in their car at the Crest parking lot when a large, round object with a bright white light came from the eastern sky and approached them while they sat frozen in their seats.

The object appeared to be investigating them as it circled the car a couple of times. I was not told how long the object remained there or if the men were abducted. Mr. Valdez was trying to find out if either of them had been abducted. I also was not told what time the two men left the parking lot at the Crest. Hearing the story of the two men at the Crest from Mr. Valdez, confirmed what we had seen that night.

October, 1988

The days passed quickly as I recovered from my injuries, but the nights dragged on endlessly. I had apparently learned to sleep with one eye open and one eye closed (if you call that sleeping). I had become much more aware of any unusual noises I heard. Even the sounds of the house settling in the night would wake me up.

The instinctive reaction to these noises would set my insides to shaking with fear of the unknown. If I had thought my first episode of intense fear was bad, what I experienced in the weeks to come was far worse! Many a night I was too terrified to even close my eyes and relax. I had no desire to see those beings again - not even in the context of a horrible dream.

I would lie in bed, constantly praying to our Lord for protection and safety, not just for me, but for Brian and Michelle as well. I somehow knew that our daughters Debra and Vanessa were safe, and I also knew that God was protecting Fred.

As the weeks went by, I seemed to be recuperating as well as could be expected. I had begun my countdown to the day when I would be able to leave the prison of my bed and not ever return to it. I'd had plenty of time to think about the strange and frightening occurrence. I still had many questions but no answers. The more I tried to understand and reason it out, the more I began to feel as if my life had been turned upside down by those "characters" that had invaded my realm.

Eventually, life became somewhat normal. I had no other hallucinations or bad dreams. With only one more week to go, the expectation and sheer excitement of being able to get up from my bed encouraged me.

My main concern was if I would be able to walk again. The doctors had already told me I was going to be on crutches for some time while I learned how to walk again. The following week, I would begin physical therapy every other day.

Those six weeks of being disabled made me more compassionate toward those who are permanently disabled from disease, illness or an accident. I soon learned how to accommodate my needs from day to day and to do for myself. Having learned to crawl and drag myself around did not bring down my self image or my pride. I saw it instead, as a large step in not having to depend upon others for the normal things in life that all of us take for granted. I found it particularly frustrating not to be able to get around under my own power at times - like when those five beings had entered my bedroom that fateful night. It was inconceivable to me that I had not been able to protect my children and myself.

With the week nearly over, I began to anticipate the joy of being freed from my bed. Michelle and Brian would come into the bedroom to talk or do their homework on the bed while I read or did various projects.

On that particular evening, Brian went to bed early. Michelle was still up around 10:00 p.m., but was also ready for bed. The weather was still warm, so we kept the balcony door open until the children went to bed. As Michelle went to close the balcony door, I heard her say in a shocked voice, "Mom! They're back! There are six of them now."

I asked her who was back? She told me that the lights were back, the colored lights, but in a different place! I crawled out of bed and dragged myself to the door. I stretched to see if I could locate the colored lights. As before, the lights were over the Sandia Mountains, but appeared to be traveling south, toward the Manzano Mountains.

We looked out the door for some time before realizing that the lights were not traveling, but stationary. The blue, purple, peach, and orange colors the objects emitted were so sharp, we were certain that someone beside ourselves would be able to see them.

In an attempt to convince not only myself, but Michelle as well, that the objects were Sandia Base or Kirtland Air Force Base experiments, I told her we were not going to worry about them. We both went to bed.

Because of what I had experienced five weeks prior, I was restless until 2:00 or 3:00 a.m. I turned off the light and

32

tried to relax. I began to experience feelings of anxiety and fear. Seeing the round lights had upset me. I was angry because I could not rest. I closed my eyes and seemed to sleep.

I do not know what made me open my eyes and look at the bedroom ceiling. I saw a very bright, round, white light about two inches in diameter, continually circling the bedroom ceiling. As I watched the light travel the circumference of the ceiling, many thoughts entered my mind. I knew then, that the beings were coming back. I knew they were for real this time. I allowed my imagination to take over, and suddenly, the worst was there with me. I did not hear them or the stranger, come into the house. Was this going to be another fearful hallucination?

I became as stiff as a board, not even breathing, moving only my eyes to locate the source of the light. I felt an unknown presence in the room and I was thinking, "Oh no... he is standing at the open door to our bedroom."

The door to the hallway was located on the same south wall as the head of our bed. I laid there quietly because I knew some stranger had come into the house and I had not heard him come in. "He" was standing in the doorway shining a light before making his move. I laid there waiting, my imagination scaring the hell out of me. I did not even want to breathe. Hearing my own breath frightened me more. I decided not to breathe so I could hear "his" breathing.

I heard no movement or other breathing. Feeling brave, I regained my composure and slowly turned toward the open door. I saw no one standing there. I became even braver and decided to crawl out of bed toward the open door. I quietly tried to find something in the darkened room to protect myself with.

I crawled out of bed. No one attacked me, but the light was still going around and around. I looked down the hall, and saw no movement. I heard nothing unusual. Everything was quiet. Something told me not to turn on the lights, and to make sure the balcony door was locked. I thought maybe someone was out on the balcony trying to get in.

Quietly, I crawled around the end of the bed, my body shaking with every movement. I reached the door and looked through the sheer curtain in both directions. I saw no one. I heard no footsteps. I sat on the floor trying to figure out where the light might be coming from. I crawled to the north window and again, saw nothing.

Still feeling a presence, I crawled back to the nightstand and turned on the light. I fell asleep with the light on. I awoke early in the morning and turned off the lamp.

When Fred arrived home from work, I told him about the round colored objects Michelle and I had seen again. I asked him if he too, had seen them. His answer was "no" and that it was probably some experiment that the bases were conducting. I also told him about the white light that had circled the bedroom ceiling for hours, and about the presence I had felt in the bedroom and the hallway. Fred was so tired that he appeared to be disinterested.

The round, bright white light invaded the bedroom many times after my original sighting, although I don't remember how *often* it appeared thereafter. Many a night, I would watch its uniqueness until I fell asleep. It seemed that the light would appear every time Michelle and I saw the colored objects.

I began to feel as if the small white light was somehow taking care of us while Fred was at work. At the time, I did not know that it had any connection to the Greys. I still do not know the reason why the light circled my ceiling. However, I soon found it somewhat comforting, as it would put me to sleep at night.

The sixth week finally arrived and with it, the most difficult part of my recovery began. It was frightening to have to learn how to walk again, but it felt so good to be standing straight, even though I had to use crutches.

The ice therapy baths twice a day were as unwelcome as the horrific nightmares I had begun to have. The ice baths had to be at freezing temperatures. I was told that the football players were put through this form of therapy to heal their sprained feet and legs.

My doctor told me, "no pain, no gain." What was good for our UNM Lobo team had to be good for me if I was going to get well as soon as possible. However, it was not the doctor's feet and legs that were being put into freezing water twice (and sometimes three times) daily!

The therapy progressed and new therapy was added each week. I found that I was walking better and was much more mobile as long as I had those crutches.

THE REAPPEARANCE OF THE COLORED AND WHITE LIGHT

Fred had an evening off, which was very good. Dusk turned into a dark, unusually warm evening for that time of year. Michelle was outside playing with her friends. She came into the house yelling that she saw one or two of the colored round lights. We investigated the lights again. Fred was outside and also witnessed the lights for the first time. As we looked through the binoculars, we found ourselves wishing that we had a telescope to be able to view them even better.

Michelle remembered that the parents of her friend, who lived about four miles away, owned a telescope. She called her friend and spoke with the parents. She told them we wanted to look at the moon and stars, and could we borrow the telescope? They said yes, we could borrow it. Fred and Michelle went to pick it up.

When they returned, we discovered that the telescope could not be used because of a missing electrical cord. There was also another device that went on the telescope that we did not know how to use. In the end, we shared the binoculars and scanned the eastern night sky.

At the time, we were living quite close to the Sandia Mountains. I began to scan the sky from the southeast to the northeast. While doing so, I accidentally moved the binoculars

down from the top of the Crest and caught sight of an unusual
light.

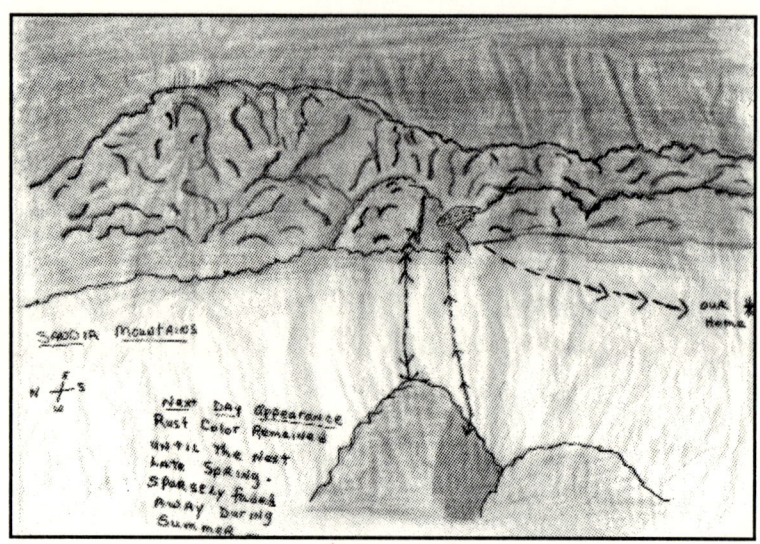

Rust Color on the Mountain

The light was away from any of the homes in that area.
I adjusted the binoculars for clearer vision and gasped in horror
and excitement. Unbelievable was the only word I could find
to describe what I was looking at. I quickly gave Fred the
binoculars, and watched his disbelief and awe at what he was
seeing. Then Michelle looked through the binoculars. What we
saw was a round object. Fred and Michelle also agreed with
what I had seen.

We got into the car and drove to the main highway,
traveling north, to see if we could locate the object. The area
where we thought the object was located, was approximately
three to four miles from our home. We did not find it though,
so we returned home and went up to the balcony. The object
was still there. We never saw it leave the area that night. We
took turns during the night to watch it. Eventually, I was the
only one up, keeping an eye on it. Finally, I gave up and fell
asleep.

Early the next morning, we went out on the balcony to look in the direction of the object. To our amazement, it was in a canyon that was not visible from the highway. From the balcony, looking toward the mountain, there was a large hill that made up one side of the canyon. A small hill on the south side, and not all the way up, looked as if it were burnt. It was a dark rust color. The rust color remained in that area until late the next summer. My sister and I had planned to hike into the area, but I was unable to walk very far or climb, because of my injuries from the accident.

Again, there was no news coverage or talk of anyone else having seen the object.

ANOTHER MILESTONE FOR ME

November, 1988

Several weeks passed and I eventually left the crutches behind. Once more I was able to walk on my own, though I was still unable to drive. Many nights would go by when Michelle or I would go out onto the balconies to search the skies for colored round lights or the large white lights. Several times we saw the colored round lights, either to the southeast of our home (toward the Manzano Mountains) or between the Sandias and the Manzanos. Once we counted at least twelve round colored lights.

I called the University of New Mexico Observatory to ask if they had any telescopes that visitors could use on their own. I had hoped the person I was speaking to would understand that I wanted to view anything that might interest me. I was told that there were some telescopes that were available for personal use. We did not really think we would have another opportunity to view the colored objects, but the time came sooner than we expected.

I was not yet allowed to drive the car on the evening we saw the colored lights again. I phoned my Dad to see if he would drive us to the University Observatory. Michelle, my

Dad and I shared our mutual excitement. At last we would be able to find out exactly what the objects were.

When we arrived at the Observatory, we were disappointed to find out that there were no telescopes we could personally control. On the Observatory patio were six privately owned telescopes of different sizes. Those telescopes were all directed toward the southern sky. We asked the owners if their telescopes could be turned toward the east for viewing. We were told they could not turn their telescopes. The owners had been instructed by the director to set their telescopes on the southern skies.

I found and spoke to the director in charge that night. I told him about my phone call to the Observatory earlier that evening. He told me I had been misinformed about private use of the telescopes. All the telescopes on the patio were privately owned. The students who shared their own telescopes with the public had to follow specific directions. We were dismayed at finding this out, but managed to enjoy the evening anyway.

The UNM Observatory has a very large telescope, complete with domed ceiling that opens to the sky for viewing. There were many people at the Observatory that night, and the three of us waited at least 45 minutes on the stairway of the larger telescope. We were very excited because we had never looked through a telescope large enough to view planets and constellations. Experiencing the closeness of the universe was an astronomical event for us.

We were about fourth in line when the three young ladies who directed and controlled the large telescope said they needed to close the dome because it was late. We stood there watching as the huge silver doors were closed.

Not long afterward, we again ventured out to the Observatory. The round objects were visible on a night when Fred was not working. As soon as we saw the objects, we went down to the University Observatory. We hoped that, by chance, the telescopes would be turned toward the east. As we entered the area, we went directly to the stairs and got into line. Already, the line was long. As we got closer to the large telescope, we were surprised to learn that it was turned to view the western skies over Albuquerque. When it was our turn, we were astounded at the view of the planet and billions of stars not visible to the naked eye. What a magnificent and glorious wonder it was! Our naiveté in trying to learn about the round objects had led us to further knowledge of the universe and its never ending vastness. It also reinforced our belief that we were not alone in that huge, dark vastness.

For a period of six months, we watched the night skies and observed our beautiful, reflecting, colored lights in the eastern sky above the Sandia and Manzano Mountains. Many times, we would get into the car and just drive south to see if we could locate and see the objects up close. We hoped to possibly witness a landing of the objects at Sandia Base or Kirtland Air Base.

However, the objects always seemed to be stationary, and never moved from their given area on any particular night. Some evenings we would see what appeared to be small airplanes circling the objects.

During that time, Michelle and I noticed that we both experienced a heightened fear and anxiety about going to bed and getting to sleep at night. Brian, however, displayed a quiet, non-caring attitude about the whole thing.

Fred had asked me to start documenting the various phenomena that occurred in our home, including the illuminating wall and the "visitors." I kept all of my hand written documentation in a folder, not realizing what I would do with it some day. After all, who would believe me anyway?

As the nighttime paranormal activity increased, my feelings and emotions expanded to the point that I began to feel somewhat "crazy" in the sense of meaning "insane."

I was experiencing more psychic ability, which I hated. It always had to do with someone's demise in becoming either quite ill or dying. Death surrounded me. I saw train wrecks, airplane crashes, fires, tornadoes, and hurricanes, always knowing, seeing, and being with the person or people before or right as the event was happening. I experienced the abduction, sexual cruelty and eventual death of one young woman who was in her twenties. At a later time, I experienced the abduction and death of another woman in her late forties.

Because I was seeing and knowing what was going to happen, I felt a responsibility to help, find, and redirect people's lives so they would live. Unfortunately, I did not always know the location of the incident. Some of those horrible occurrences happened in different countries all over the world. I felt there were people I could have helped locate before their eventual deaths.

I could no longer deal with my intensified psychic abilities. Not knowing how to handle the visions just brought more fear into my life. I prayed constantly to Our Lord to take the ability away from me. I felt as if I was living and being with each of those humans, some as young as babies, others, older adults.

In each case, I knew when and how death would come to them, before it happened. I sought the help of a minister who was very close to me. Eventually, the minister told me that what I was "seeing" was the "devil's work" and to just keep praying.

To present date, my psychic abilities have diminished somewhat.

THE LADY IN BRIAN'S BEDROOM

Spring, 1989

Late one evening, I sent Brian and Michelle upstairs to get ready for bed. It had been over half an hour since I had heard any noise coming from either of them. I thought they must already be in bed. I had not yet finished my task in the kitchen when Michelle began to holler at me from upstairs. She was very excited and disturbed. She wanted me to go upstairs right away. I hollered back to her to "let me finish what I am doing, and I will be up." She said "No! Come up now!"

I procrastinated because I wanted to finish what I was doing so I could lock up the house and get to bed myself. I was very tired that night. I yelled back up to her "Just a minute. Let me finish here!" Evidently, she did not hear me yell, as her bedroom was some distance from the kitchen.

Michelle came running down the stairs and into the kitchen to get me. She was impatient, very agitated and nearly screaming at me, saying, "Mom! Mom! There is a lady in Brian's room!" She was very insistent. She was also frightened and repeated that sentence to me as she grabbed my arm tightly and dragged me out of the kitchen, through the dining room, to the large entry way, and up the stairs. Then, in almost a whisper, she told me to be very quiet and listen.

We walked down to the end of the hallway. For some reason, we were stopped about a foot away from Brian's closed bedroom door. I don't remember trying to immediately open Brian's bedroom door. It was as if something had stopped us right where we were standing and we could not go any further. Michelle whispered to me, "Do you hear the lady talking to Brian, Mom?"

Yes, I did hear a female voice. At first I thought he had his radio on, but as I listened more closely, I heard Brian responding in short sentences, as if he were having a conversation with the female. I could not understand what the female voice was saying to him. It seemed as if she was asking him questions, because of the way he was responding. He answered the lady in a quiet and rational voice. I could not hear very well what the conversation was about.

I suddenly realized that Michelle and I were practically lying down on the hallway floor. I could not recall how long we had been lying on the floor. I seemed to have changed my mind about wanting to go into Brian's bedroom. I no longer felt an urgent need to enter his room. I thought it strange that I didn't react more quickly, especially since I was hearing a female voice in his room!

Brian's bedroom also had an outside door leading to a shared balcony off his older sister's room. It was possible that someone could have climbed up to the second story balcony. There was a high wall that surrounded the balcony. Our Shasta travel trailer was parked very close to the exterior wall of the house below the balcony on the south side. If someone intended to enter our home, they would have to be lifted from the top of the trailer by someone, or they would need a short ladder to get over the surrounding wall.

I thought about this, as I was "forced" to lie there in the hallway with my daughter. It was so unlike me to simply lie there when I suspected a stranger was in one of my children's rooms. I also had the distinct feeling that an unknown presence was nearby, or that something was wrong.

When it became quiet in Brian's room, I was "released" by whatever force had held Michelle and me to the floor. No one "told" us we could get up; we simply arose and automatically headed directly into Brian's room.

The anticipation of what I might find was somewhat frightening. The only thing on my mind was whether Brian was in bed, and if so, was he was okay? I quickly walked to his bedside, while listening for the radio. The radio was not on. Brian was asleep!

I woke him up and asked who he had been talking to. What lady had he been speaking to? Had he fallen asleep with his radio on? He sleepily told me he had not spoken with anyone. He had not left his radio on because he'd wanted to go to sleep immediately. He said no one was in his room.

Since Brian seemed to be okay, I checked the outside bedroom door. It was locked. I opened the balcony door and Michelle and I went out to see if we could find anything unusual. The large wrought iron gates were closed. I looked for indentations on the roof of the trailer to check if anyone had tried to come into the house that way. I found nothing wrong.

We came back into Brian's bedroom and locked the door to the balcony. We left his bedroom door to the hallway, open. I thought it unusual that Brian did not wake up as Michelle and I carried on our conversation outside his doorway. I then went across the hall to Debra's bedroom and checked in her closet, under her bed, and made certain her outside balcony door was locked as well.

I thought about the events of the evening as I tried to fall asleep. I was skeptical as to why I had not reacted sooner in getting into Brian's bedroom. I could not understand why it seemed that Michelle and I only went as far as the bathroom just north of Brian's bedroom. I eventually fell asleep with many unanswered questions about what had actually transpired that evening.

DISCOVERY OF THE TRIANGLE SORE

I awoke early the next morning and lay in bed reflecting on the previous evening. I brought my left hand up from under the blankets and turned it over. On my left hand, below the ring finger and below the knuckle, I noticed a very strange sore. It had not been there when I went to bed the evening before. The sore appeared to be infected. It looked like a strange burn, but I did not remember burning myself there.

I examined the sore more closely. It was not a cut either. It appeared to be a weird burn, but it did not hurt like a burn. What amazed me the most was its triangular shape. I could not remember what I might have done to that part of my hand to have caused the odd- shaped burn. The burn mark was outlined in deep red. The skin on the inside of the triangle appeared puffy, and a lighter shade of red. The skin within the triangle looked as if Saran Wrap had been placed over the sore. It was actually an ugly sore.

Brian and Michelle had awakened and were stirring in their rooms. Brian came into my room wondering why his bedroom door was open. I told him I had left it open the night before. I questioned him about my being in his room with Michelle, to check on him. He did not remember anyone - especially me - having spoken to him.

That morning, Michelle and I teased Brian about the lady being in his room the night before. He became upset with our teasing. We then told him of the female voice we had heard coming from his room, and how we had only been allowed to go as far as the bathroom in the hallway. He did not believe us.

I medicated the sore on my left hand with different burn ointments and antibiotics. After a couple of days, the sore looked just as it had when I'd first discovered it. I noticed no change in the sore's consistency. I began using other salves for burns on the sore, but it did not change in either size or color. It did not hurt or itch the way a burn or cut would have.

One week later, when I was cleaning the middle hall bathroom, Michelle came in and stood by me. She raised her left hand in front of me. I gasped as I saw that she too, had the same triangular-shaped sore! Hers was the same size as mine, outlined in dark red, with the same odd skin texture and redness.

I asked her when she had burned herself and how it had happened. She said she did not remember burning or hurting herself, but that the sore had appeared on her hand the day after we'd heard the lady in Brian's room.

I then showed her the sore on my own left hand. She asked what kind of medications I was putting on my sore. I told her what I had been using, but that the ointments did not seem to be working. I began to medicate her "burn" in the same manner.

Two weeks passed. Michelle and I still had the burns on our hands. Apparently, the ointments were having no effect on them. The burns appeared to be the same as the first day we had noticed them.

The third week, a friend of ours who is a registered nurse, suggested we put vitamin E on our sores. She was just as puzzled over the sores as we were. The strange thing was, we could not tell her where or how we had gotten the sores on our hands.

By the fourth week, our friend suggested we go to the doctor. She asked me if I had tried covering the sores after putting the ointments and vitamin E on them. I told her I had not covered them, but began to use gauze and tape to cover our sores.

By the fifth week, Michelle and I finally began to see some changes in our triangular-shaped burns. It took a couple more weeks after that before they began to fade. The skin did not peel, the burns simply began to fade away while the outline of the triangle remained a little darker. The faded imprint remained on my hand for many months after the initial burn healed.

Some years later, a UFO investigator informed me, after seeing a drawing of my hand and the triangular mark, that many UFO abductees have that particular marking somewhere on their bodies. It is put there by their alien abductors.

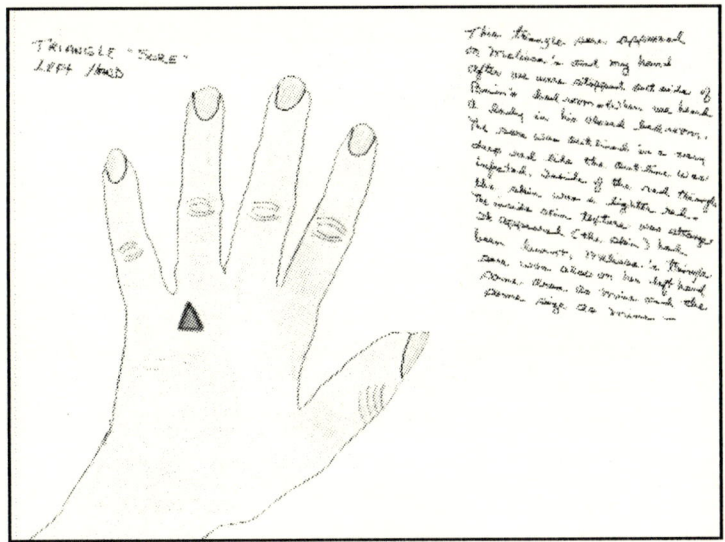

The Triangle Sore

THE MYSTERIOUS STONES

The week after we heard the Lady in Brian's Room, I went in there to clean. I found six triangular, bluish stones on the bookcase in his room. The stones were beautiful. They varied in color from turquoise to light blue, to dark blue.

I had never seen that shade of blue before. The quality and sharpness of the blues were quite striking in different lighting. I noticed, as I picked up and examined the stones, how perfectly cut and polished they were. Each one was a perfect triangle. I turned them around, upside down, then set them back down on the bookcase.

I asked Brian where he had obtained the beautiful stones. He said to me, "What stones?" He did not know what I was talking about until I actually showed him the stones. He then told me that he did not know where they had come from.

Brian had been a Cub Scout and had worked his way through Boy Scouts. He had been working on the Order of the Arrow. I assumed he had found them someplace while camping, or that he had traded them for something of his own, with one of the other scouts.

Brian seemed to be disinterested in the stones, so I placed them on top of his bookcase in a certain pattern, just to see if he would disturb them. The stones remained in the same pattern until they completely disappeared one week after I discovered them! Brian had no knowledge of their disappearance. I checked the areas where they might have been tossed or hidden. The stones were never found in his room or in the garbage.

The stones may not have been in any way related to the UFO phenomena. Their discovery, the timing of their discovery, and their uniqueness has always remained a mystery. However, I felt that there was a connection between the "Lady in Brian's Bedroom" and the beautiful triangular stones.

A NEW BEGINNING??

In October of 1989, I accepted a full-time position at University Hospital Mental Health Center, in the Department of Programs for Children and Adolescents. I was a Clerical Specialist V. I was Secretary to a variety of psychiatrists, psychologists, and social workers.

In September of 1990, the bankruptcy which we had dreaded for the previous three years, was finalized. We were forced into bankruptcy because of a large computer company that had defrauded us. Our home was taken away from us. The validity of the bankruptcy procedure was later questioned by the authorities with regard to misconduct and mistreatment by the lawyers who took everything we had. Unfortunately, the investigation did us no good. We had lost everything.

We experienced another trauma and new beginning when we moved into a large townhouse. Six months later, we moved again, to get Brian and Michelle back into the designated school district we preferred. We then moved into the townhouse we presently live in, which is in close proximity to the Sandia Mountains.

After that final move, I began to think I would finally be rid of the horrific "dreams" I had been experiencing. I believed the cause of my "dreams" to be stress, sadness, and the many unhappy times that had come our way. We had nearly lost one of our children in a toboggan accident while we were going through bankruptcy procedures.

In the early part of 1991, Fred went into business for himself. He obtained a large contract at Honeywell Aeronautics Division. Travel was not a requirement of his new position, and he was able to quit his evening job of driving a taxicab. He also taught at Albuquerque Technical Vocational Institute. Our lives seemed to be more relaxed and easygoing. Once again, we were a normal family.

AN UNKNOWN SURGERY?

One Saturday, three months after moving into our first townhouse, I was cleaning the downstairs bathroom. I stood on the commode to clean the lights above the mirror. The commode seat gave way and I fell to the floor. I re-injured my right ankle.

I hobbled around at work and at home for two days before going to the doctor. As I was sitting in the radiologist's office, waiting to be released to go back to my doctor's office, the radiologist who'd read my x-rays came out to ask if I'd ever had surgery on my right foot. I told him no, I had never had surgery on my right foot.

My primary-care doctor informed the radiologist that I had previously injured both of my feet and legs, but no surgery had been performed. The radiologist was very insistent and argumentative about the fact that I had, in fact, had surgery on my right foot. He said he did not believe me when I told him I'd never had foot surgery.

I spoke to the radiologist about the extensive injuries I had sustained in 1988. He said what he was seeing was not from the broken bones of previous injuries, but from a surgery that was performed recently on the bones in my foot and the surrounding area!

When my primary-care doctor got the x-rays about an hour later, he viewed them with me and pointed out the area of concern. My primary-care doctor was just as astonished to see the site as I was. He said, "Yes, that particular area of the foot did appear to have had surgery done to it."

He reminded me that he had known me for many years, and knew I had never had any foot surgeries. He also noted that, to look at my foot, there was no scar tissue evident from a surgery. My doctor said he could not explain this. His current diagnosis was that I had again, severely sprained my ankle and would be put into a cast. I was put on crutches for six weeks.

The fifth week I was in the cast, I began to have very sharp pain in my leg. It swelled, and I experienced numbness around the toes. The entire leg became very cold. At first, the doctor could not diagnose what was happening to the leg. He removed the hard cast and put my leg into an air cast. Further x-rays revealed nothing else. Time went on and the pain became unbearable as the other symptoms worsened.

My primary-care doctor (Dr. G. Davis) sent me to see Dr. P. Stern, an orthopedic doctor. More x-rays were taken with no positive results. After consulting with his partner, the orthopedic doctor had an idea of what the diagnosis might be.

He wanted me to make an appointment immediately, to see Dr. David Bankston, M.D. Dr. Bankston was researching a type of dystrophy known as reflex sympathetic dystrophy.

The initial appointment was set up for an entire afternoon so that Dr. Bankston could put me through various tests at Anna Kaseman Hospital.

While waiting for the test results, the orthopedic doctor sent me to see a neurologist. The neurologist tested me for post-polio syndrome and nerve damage. I received the test results from Dr. Bankston within the next couple of days. The four doctors who were caring for me at that time did not think I had post-polio syndrome, even though I'd had polio when I was twelve years old. All doctors agreed that the diagnosis was reflex sympathetic dystrophy. Excruciating pain is one of the symptoms of reflex sympathetic dystrophy.

They put me on very strong pain and anti-inflammatory medications. The pain became even more severe. Dr. Bankston decided on a therapy that would put me in the hospital a total of nine times over the next six months. I was to be anesthetized with an epidural that would paralyze me from the waist down. I would receive relief from the pain for about two weeks at a time. Because a person can only have eight or nine of these treatments, the patient eventually learns to accept and live with the pain.

In my case, the pain never went away. In fact, it increased, and the leg began to atrophy, a new symptom that again led my doctors to believe that the reflex sympathetic dystrophy had awakened the post- polio syndrome.

In May of 1991, Dr. Sherman, who was the only polio doctor in Albuquerque, diagnosed me with post-polio syndrome. I was put into a sturdy leg brace that soon became a part of my body for the next few years.

When one has reflex sympathetic dystrophy and post-polio syndrome, the body goes through symptoms of freezing. Winter became my most dreaded season, as I could not stay warm. I had to learn to dress differently and wear a lot of cotton undergarments with wool top clothing. Summer was not as bad, but I still had to wear cotton undergarments, even when the temperatures were in the 90's. My challenge was to stay warm in an air conditioned office where my boss would not respond to my complaints about extra cold air.

I had always been a physically active person. I simply could not accept the prognosis of ending up in a wheel chair. I set out to do something about it. I spoke with Dr. Sherman, the polio doctor, about different activities I might be able to do. He suggested, as an experiment, that I try swim therapy at a facility with an in-house doctor and a swim therapist.

After some investigation, Dr. Sherman discovered that the Arthritis Foundation would work with me. He was not too keen on the idea, but said he would follow my progress closely and that we should give it a try. Dr. Sherman also asked if he could use my treatment as an experiment that might benefit his other post-polio patients.

At the Arthritis Foundation, the water in the swimming pool was kept at 92 degrees. After consulting with the Arthritis Foundation's specialist, Dr. Sherman agreed to a trial period of therapy for me. I had two sessions per week, lasting 1 ½ hours each. I met and made many new friends with various arthritis problems. They helped me learn the rigorous exercises.

The water aerobic exercises were very strenuous and made me tired. I would go to water exercise at the end of my workday at the University. I would then go home to dinner, which Fred had prepared, exhausted and in pain. Normally, Fred would have gone to work before I got home. He was teaching at Albuquerque Technical Vocational Institute, part-time.

As a result of therapy, I did grow stronger, which surprised my six doctors. During a 2 ½ year period, I struggled with many highs and lows because of my disability. There were many times when I was ordered to bed for a week at a time, and literally put to sleep for the entire week. Medications or injections were used to relieve the excruciating pain. But my fight continued. I was determined to win.

As time went on, I experienced more highs than lows as the muscles strengthened in my legs and the nerves and blood vessels began to cooperate with each other. The pain began to subside somewhat.

A sad change took place in the last month of 1993. A new therapist came on board at the Arthritis Foundation and new aerobic exercises were introduced. After a two week period of the new exercises, I had to take a week off to recover from devastating pain. I began a routine of one week for exercise and two weeks off until the pain began to dominate my life again. I felt as if I had indeed lost the battle. Living through that low point in my life brought back past memories of an illness I had been afflicted with at the age of twelve.

The school principal had called my mother and told her I was very ill and having bad pain in my legs. She asked that someone come get me. I remembered my Dad walking into the principal's office to take me home. I tried to walk out of the school, but because of the pain in my legs and back, he had to carry me to the car. I became very weak and was put to bed immediately. I cried because the paralyzing pain became so intense. I could no longer move my body.

Shortly after that episode, I had no memory of anything else until I woke up approximately one week later. There was a chiropractor sitting by my side. The hour I woke up, I remembered a dream I had when I was asleep. I clearly remember that dream to this day.

The dream was about a game that is played outdoors with two people. It was a game my brother and I always played. The game was called "Annie, Annie Over the House." The game was played by throwing a ball over a pitched roof house to each other, and points were made. In my dream, I was in the front yard, ready to run and catch the ball as it rolled off the pitched roof. But I could not catch the ball and it flew behind me. I turned around to pick up the bouncing ball, and as I looked up into the northern sky, I saw a very bright, white, round light that seemed to be traveling toward me. I hollered as loud as I could for my brother to come to the front yard. He

51

quickly ran around to the front yard, and I showed him the bright white light as it came closer to us. I don't know what happened after we saw the very bright, white, round light. I do know that we just stood there, watching as the light retreated in the same direction it had come from.

I awoke from a state of unconsciousness. I felt as if I had just been asleep. I thought maybe what I had experienced was not a dream but an actual event. I felt very confused by the fact that I was lying in bed and an older, white-haired man was sitting next to the bed. I did not recognize him, and I did not seem to know what he was doing in my bedroom.

I was afraid to make any noise. I closed my eyes but kept peeking until my mother came into the room. I could not tell my mother about the dream until a day later. I may have told my brother though, because he and I were quite close in age, and we were "buddies."

When I regained consciousness, I experienced severe back pain. As I lay in bed, I remember being afraid to move because I did not want my back to hurt. The chiropractor began to examine me by turning my body and having me turn my body from back to front. Then he had me lift my legs up from the bed, turn my ankles and wiggle my toes. This was all I could do. I was asked to sit up in bed and was also able to do that. The excruciating pain left my body. The chiropractor then turned my legs to the edge of the bed and helped me to stand up. I found that I could not stand by myself.

Two days later, when the chiropractor again made his home visit, I had a secret surprise for him. I had been standing on my own and taking a few walking steps. This surprised everyone. From that point on, I grew stronger. I could not walk for long periods of time as that caused devastating pain in my back and legs. I was very limited as far as physical activities. It was hard for me not to be able to go out and run, or roller skate, or ride my bicycle, or keep up with my brother while playing.

After several weeks of being home bound, I returned to elementary school. It was difficult for me to go back to school wearing a brace. I was outfitted with special "boots" that had steel inside the shoes. Many of the children teased me about them. I soon grew to hate my "new" shoes.

During the next few years, I developed into a shy, quiet girl who felt like an outcast because of her "brown army boots." I was also teased about my skinny legs. Not only did I feel different from the other children because of my ugly shoes, I also felt isolated by my inability to participate in the physical games everyone else had fun playing.

The one-mile walk to school and back home each day produced severe leg pain. My mother learned how to do my physical therapy at home. Twice a day, she diligently exercised my legs. I saw the chiropractor and the orthopedic doctor twice a week. I could not understand why they constantly inflicted so much pain on me.

Over the years (as the story was told to me later), our regular medical doctor said I would die from my unknown disease. The disease I had would soon come to be known as polio. The doctor said there was no use putting me in the hospital. There was nothing the doctors could do for me. My mother's chiropractor heard about my symptoms and came to stay with me, professing that he was not going to let me die.

My healing came from a Baptist family who lived on the next street. The father of that family was a preacher. The day I regained consciousness, Mr. and Mrs. Salmon came to our house to tell us that their family had stayed up all night praying for me. They said I would get well and live. Our Lord answered their prayers.

I questioned the dream I'd had. Was my survival actually Our Lord's healing hand, or had an unknown alien species done something to bring me back from near death? Because of my love for God, I knew He had intervened on my behalf.

When I experienced low points in my adult life, after being diagnosed with post-polio syndrome, I would reflect back on that childhood memory. Every time I thought I'd lost the battle, I would become that small ten year old child who fought back with determination to win her dream of not being different. I once again became the child who struggled to regain her ability to resume physical activity. I was the child who willed herself to grow stronger, not only in health, but in mind and spirit. Once again, I was the little girl who at last overcame the peer pressure exerted by others.

As an adult, I became stronger and, with my Lord at my side, fought to regain my health. I was determined not to end up in a wheelchair. The memory of my childhood bout with polio gave me great inspiration to get up and get going again. It gave me the incentive to keep trying and never give up.

MISSING DOCUMENTS

In late 1989, I stopped documenting my strange dreams. I began my documentation again in the summer of 1991. Activity between the "strange beings" and the three of us, had been ongoing since 1988. I felt confident I could rely on my memories, rather than to go on documenting.

In 1991, strange phenomena occurred often. I once again began to document each occurrence from the short notes I had made for myself during the previous year.

In 1991, my notes disappeared. I accused not only my children, but also my husband, of hiding or destroying all my documentation. The entire family pitched in to search with me. We literally tore the house apart from one end to the other. The fact that they helped me try to locate my missing documents proved to me that they believed me and supported me.

Several times, my documentation disappeared. We never found the recorded audiotapes or written documentation I had made of the frightening dreams that initially made me feel "insane." With the love and support of my family, I was able to reconstruct the written and audio-taped material I'd lost. The family suggested I hide my documents in a place known only to me, which I did.

I would no sooner get caught up on the reconstruction of an experience, than the documentation would turn up missing. Someone did not want me to keep written or audio-taped records of my dreams. Whoever was taking my documents finally gave up in the face of my determination.

Some months later, when Fred was out in the garage, he discovered a couple of my audiotapes on the floor. They had been broken and the tape pulled out and completely destroyed. Fred and I questioned our children about the incident. We believed them when they told us they had no reason to take and destroy "their" evidence.

The reality of someone coming into our home to search for my documents made no sense to us. Why would a stranger have any interest in what I had written, or even know I was writing about my experiences?

A SHARED VISIT WITH MICHELLE

Summer, 1993

Michelle and I had several shared abduction experiences. This particular one took place in a mountain. New Mexico has many mountain ranges. We do not know which mountain range we were taken to, and we do not know if we were even in New Mexico. The landscape consisted of pine trees and bushes that can be found on any one of New Mexico's mountain ranges. The following summary, constructed from notes made afterward, describes one such experience.

It was nighttime. There was a full moon. It was warm outside. Michelle was wearing a long, large white t-shirt that she sleeps in. There was a young girl around the same age as Michelle, wearing a blue summer nightgown. A woman, who I believe was the mother of the young girl, was walking with me. We were coming from an unknown place, higher, off the side of a mountain or hill within a hidden canyon. I don't know where the Greys took us. I only remember walking down the side of a large hill or mountain with four Greys. The girls were in front of us. Two of the small Greys were on either side of Michelle and the young girl. Two more Greys were on either side of the girl's mother and me. There was a light source, other than the bright moon, coming from somewhere else. The other light source illuminated the area quite well so that we could see where we were walking. My guess is, so we would not stumble over small or large boulders.

The ground was not smooth dirt but mountain type "gravel" (small sharp pointed rocks). Stiff blades of sharp grass and brown pine needles also covered the mountain landscape. The ground was uneven.

Walking on a downward slope, the woman and I remarked to each other about our feet and how they were hurting. I did not realize until a few minutes later that we were barefoot. We did not even have socks or slippers on, making our climb down very difficult. The sharp rocks and grass dug into our feet. The woman and I walked close to each other, as did the girls.

My feet and legs were not the only part of my body that was hurting. My genital (vaginal) area was also painful. I thought the reason I was having such pain in my legs and genitals was because we were walking in mountainous terrain on a downward slope. I assumed the walking was affecting my post-polio syndrome, causing the pain to travel upward because I was walking without the brace I wore on my right leg.

I sensed that the woman and I were in quite a mental stupor. We both seemed unaware of where we were or what was happening to the four of us. We were helping each other walk down the mountainside. Our walk was slow and tedious as the rocks, grass and pine needles continued to cut into our bare feet. The girls were six to eight feet in front of us. I noticed that they were speaking to each other. They seemed to be able to make the downward journey much quicker than we could.

As we came over another small hill, I saw a silver object in the distance which I recognized as "their" spaceship.

It was sitting at the bottom of the canyon among the pine trees. I was so exhausted, I did not think I would be able to finish the walk down to the spaceship, if in fact, that was where the Greys were taking us.

Michelle turned around to ask me how I was doing, and if I needed any help walking. This was when the other woman began to assist me on our climb down. She seemed to be in a daze herself. As we got closer to the ship, I had a feeling we were going to be taken home.

I remember walking up close to the ship, but I do not remember going into it. I have lost the memory of how we arrived home and back in our own bedrooms. Somehow, we communicated with the small beings, but at that moment, I did not know how they communicated with us or we with them.

We did not know at the time, that the small beings were called Greys. The reason I said we may have communicated with them is because in my notes, I wrote that they were friendly toward us when speaking.

The Shared Visit

I also wrote in my notes that I did not recognize the woman and her daughter. That was an incorrect statement because I did recognize the woman, and seemed to have known her for many years. However, I did not know her name or where I knew her from at the time.

The woman was Hispanic and appeared to be at least a couple of years older than I was. She was about my height and weight and had fair skin. She had short black hair. Her daughter was about the same height and weight as Michelle. I believe their height, at the time, was four feet, nine or ten inches. The daughter also had long black hair down to the middle of her back, as did Michelle.

HYPNOSIS ON THIS EXPERIENCE WITH BUDD HOPKINS

March, 1997

I had an inkling that I had seen this lady and her daughter before, along with Michelle, on a ship, lying on individual tables. Through hypnosis, the following is what I found out:

I awake, lying on a familiar table in a familiar room. I know where I am, and I do not want to be there. I feel cold and my body is shaking. I hear some female cries and moans. I am able to move my head to either side. I look to my right and I see the black-haired lady that I know. She is lying on another table and she appears to be awake and is crying and moaning somewhat. I don't know if anything has been done to her or not.

Michelle is lying on another silver table to my left. I think she might be awake. Soon I hear her crying hard and can not make out what she is trying to tell me. I try to sooth her by telling her that it will be over soon, and that I am there with her. I repeat this several times to Michelle.

On Michelle's left, on another silver table, is the daughter of the black-haired lady. She is crying also. Before I know it, I am surrounded by at least four Greys. I become somewhat hysterical myself, and am not aware of what the Greys are going to do to me. I am quickly paralyzed again and cannot move my head. I don't think I have a voice at this time. I hear no other sobs coming from anyone.

I have my sense of feeling back because I am experiencing bad pain in my stomach area. I feel that something has bloated my stomach area to make it large. The pain is horrible. My whole stomach and lower part of my body are in extreme pain. I cannot see what they are doing to me. I am full of fear because I do not know what they are doing to me and my head is in an upward position. My eyes, I think, may be paralyzed because I cannot seem to move them.

I want to scream and cry out, or just die because of the fear and the pain. I am so afraid for Michelle. I don't want them to hurt her like this. I don't know what they are going to do to Michelle, and I pray that she cannot see what they may be doing to me.

I am able to think at this point, and feel what is happening to me. I realize that I have experienced the same pain before. The end result was when they thought it was time for me to see, they let me see.

What I saw that time, was a very small baby that one of the Greys held in his or her arms. I just saw the back side of this infant that was not moving, then they took it away. I had no idea that I had just had a baby, or what the baby looked like. It was very small.

How could I have had a baby? In 1984, I had a hysterectomy. My doctors had left my right ovary, as it was somewhat healthy and would supply the estrogen I needed. So evidently, I can still get pregnant, but how can I carry a baby since I no longer have a uterus?

Suddenly, there is no more pain. One of the Greys, whom I feel is a female, walks over to my right side and lays a very small, clean baby on its stomach, across my naked chest, close to my naked breast. The baby has the same color skin as mine, no hair at all, and is about maybe nine inches long. I don't remember if the baby cried or made a noise. Its body felt a little warm on my skin.

The mothering instinct takes over, and I stroke it's little body. This little baby's skin feels smooth and soft, just like one of our human babies. The baby's head, though, seems to be a bit larger than its body. I don't know if this baby is a male or a female.

After a seemingly short period of time, the female Grey takes the little baby away from me. I cry and tell her not to take it away from me because it is my baby! I try to grab the baby but am again rendered paralyzed.

As the female Grey lifts the baby off my chest, I am able to see that the baby's eyelids are closed. I think its face looks like them. I am very devastated.

When I look over toward Michelle to see if she is okay, I see Greys around her. I do not know what has happened to Michelle. There are no sounds coming from her. She is quiet and seems to be asleep and still. I fight to get up. I want to go to her, but I am paralyzed.

I don't know how long we have been laying on our tables. We have the familiar cream-colored, lightweight blankets covering our bodies. I don't believe I have my nightgown on at this point. The blanket is warm and the material feels smooth. It has a sponge-like texture to it.

A couple of Greys come over to each of our tables and get us up. They make us walk straight forward into another room. Michelle and I walk side by side, and we ask each other if we are okay.

At the far end of the room is a table with a small black box on it. One Grey takes me to the table to pick up the small black box. The black box is about eleven inches long by eight inches wide. I am told to pick up the box and carry it with me.

I reach for the box with my right hand and gently lift it up. I almost drop it because the box is heavier than I expected it to be. I quickly bring my left hand forward to help support the heavy box. I nearly drop it. The box seems to be heavier on one side because it tilts away from me. I do not know what is in the black box.

As soon as I balance the weighted black box, the Grey says for us to follow him. We are taken to another room that appears to be a very small auditorium. The room is dimly lit. Upon entering, I see what appears to be a lower level. Quickly scanning the lower level, I think there are about ten to fifteen Greys down there.

The anticipation of not knowing what is to occur next has me very nervous. I feel as if we are on a stage. The Grey that walked us into this darkened "auditorium" tells me to set the black box on a small square table. This table is not very high. I have to bend at the waist to put the black box down on it.

We four women are asked to circle the table that is located in the middle of the floor. We do as we are directed. Then we are told to hold hands. I hold Michelle's left hand and the right hand of the black-haired lady. I realize I am not the only one who is shaking. Our hands are trembling, but the warmth of holding another human being's hand, comforts me.

We try to whisper to each other, but discover that we are unable to speak to each other. Our voices seem to have disappeared. I really think we cannot move our mouths. So we try to communicate with our eyes and squeeze our hands.

Then we are asked to sit down on the floor and cross one leg over the other. As we sit cross-legged, we are then instructed to hold hands again. The left side of my body is toward the audience. I do not have full view of the audience. We are told to concentrate deeply on the black box. They need our full concentration on the black box. We are not to think of anything else but this black box.

I know I cannot give my full attention to the small black box. I know I am being coerced continually, by a voice in my head, to concentrate on the black box. I feel dominated and very much compelled to concentrate on the black box.

Passage of time does not seem to be a factor when you are with the Greys. How long we sat there on the cold floor, I don't know. It could have been just minutes or an hour.

I am told somehow, that they need my full concentration and energy on the black box, as the black box needs to pick up all of our energies. Our powerful energies will grow strong and flow through each of us and into each of us will transport.

Whatever that last sentence means, I do not know. I try to move my head. I quickly find out that I cannot turn my head. With my eyes, I try to look out into the audience by just moving my pupils to the left. I want to see the other Greys. I want to see their reactions to what we are supposed to be doing, or what is going to occur.

When you look at one unexpressive, motionless Grey, they appear to be the same copy of one another. Their large black, almond eyes just stare at you and your fright becomes even greater. Many thoughts are able to come into my spinning head when allowed to. I am thinking about what is in the small heavy black box and what it is supposed to do to us. What kind of test is this? Is something going to come out of the box and hurt us?

The auditorium is deathly quiet; I become very lethargic. The repetitive, controlled voice makes me think of the black box and what its contents may be. Something seems to embrace my whole being and I feel I am somehow being pulled into the black box! I cannot imagine my whole body being pulled through the small black box; but suddenly, I feel and see each of us being drawn into it. I do not understand how I see this.

Somehow, I see and feel our entire bodies being taken into the black box and pulled through to an unknown space. I seem to have landed on some kind of moving walkway in a darkened area. I am the first to be transported through this unit. My whole human body is intact as I slowly feel my feet on something moving.

I am now standing by myself, but yet I feel some kind of movement. I feel a hard push against my body as if someone is being thrown against me in the dark place. Michelle seems to have fallen against me.

A half-second can seem like an eternity in a frightening situation such as this. Just as quickly as Michelle and I were transported, the other mother and her daughter are now behind Michelle. Afraid to move our bodies in any given direction for fear of the unknown, we remain standing.

We cannot see where we are or where we should go for safety. Something is moving below us, which frightens us even more. We do not know where we are.

My thoughts are that we must be outside of something. Or are we still inside of something? Have our bodies remained in that auditorium? Are we having an out of body experience? If my body is not intact, then why can I feel Michelle's body so close to mine?

A voice in our heads tells us to turn our heads to the left. I turn my head to the left. In awe and amazement, I suddenly see what has not been there before! There seems to be some kind of construction composed of large, tall and various sized, pure gold buildings or some kind of tall columns. They are beautiful. A strong, bright light is shown upon them for us. There are many of the golden columns. Tall and short, wide and thin, they stand erect, next to each other, protruding from a black background. I don't know what they are or where we are. Where we were taken and what we were shown is unknown to me to this day.

Budd began to bring me out of hypnosis at this point. As I was being brought out of hypnosis...

The four of us are riding on the unit the Greys have us on. We are going through some kind of hallway that has light in it. Some Greys make their presence known to us and walk along side of us. Suddenly, one Grey communicates to us that we are to stand back.

A door opens up on what appears to be the landscape of our Earth. Yes, we are on land. We do not realize where we have been until we step out from where we were. We are standing on firm ground!

A whole eternity seems to have just vanished. I look up to the night sky and see a full moon. We are instructed not to turn around. We are told to just follow the other Greys. I discover I can move my head, so I quickly turn around to see exactly what we came out of. It is as if I am being allowed to turn and look.

I cannot immediately comprehend what I am looking at. We have just come out of the side of a mountain! I see a door, or what I think is a door, covered with rocks, dirt, and grass. I see it being automatically closed!

This "dream" presents many more questions than answers, as the answers were not discovered through hypnosis.

About one year before being hypnotized by Budd Hopkins, I found the black-haired lady and her daughter. I had gone to elementary, and possibly junior-high school with her. We had not been close friends in school, but would speak to one another. She finished her education at a well-known Catholic high school in Albuquerque. She also attended the Catholic church we attended at the time.

I know for a definite fact that this was the black-haired lady. To protect her privacy, I will not name her.

Once we had discovered each other, we spoke many times, yet never about the shared experiences I was so eager to ask her about. Each time we talked, there was a feeling of "knowing" coming from both of us. She seemed to know a lot about me in my adult life - more than I ever thought she should know. This is still is such a mystery.

Just as I was feeling more confident and wanting to approach her on the subject of certain experiences with her and her daughter, she disappeared from my life. I no longer know her whereabouts.

ANOTHER STORY WITH THE BLACK-HAIRED LADY AND HER DAUGHTER

This is really Michelle's dream. I remember very little of this dream. My daughter, Michelle, became very upset with me because I did not remember exactly what took place or what happened to us. She did not want to fill me in on the specifics. She wanted me to remember them myself. This event happened within six months of "A Shared Visit With Michelle". The month, day and time were not documented.

I remember being with the Greys, along with the black-haired lady and her daughter. We originally thought this episode occurred near dawn, but the more I searched my memory, the more certain I was that it was still dark outside.

Michelle and I realized we were sitting at a kitchen table in an unfamiliar kitchen. The kitchen we were in did not belong to anyone in our family or any of our friends. The black-haired lady was across the table. Sitting next to her was her daughter. We all sat at the table in a dazed, sleepy state, as if we had just awakened from a long sleep.

The black-haired lady recognized the fact that we were in her kitchen. She got up and flipped the wall switch to turn on the light. She and her daughter were wondering what Michelle and I were doing in their home and in their kitchen.

I had no idea whether we were in Albuquerque or not. I sat there in a stupor thinking, is this a dream or what? How did Michelle and I end up in this woman's kitchen, sitting at her table? Michelle and I were just as astonished as they were.

Over the kitchen sink was a large window. As the four of us sat there stupefied, we heard a strange noise. We did not know where the sound was coming from. The woman began to investigate. She looked around her kitchen and walked to a connecting door that led to another dark room. Sluggishly, she said she was afraid to go into that room.

I told her I thought the noise was coming from outside. I got up from the table and went to look out the window over the kitchen sink. There were white curtains hanging on the window. As I peered through the window, a dim light seemed to illuminate the outside area. Evidently, the kitchen was at the back of the house because I saw grass and bushes. I glanced upward. Not very high up, there was a silver, round object that I had seen before. It was hovering not far away, right in her backyard!

Michelle was standing right behind me when I hollered for them to come and look. There was another larger window on the same wall as the small window. Everyone ran over to it so they could see the silver object.

Light was being reflected onto or around the silver object. I thought it was about dawn. I don't remember what anyone said at that point. I felt very drugged and was not comprehending what was happening. This is all I remember of the dream.

The next morning before breakfast, Michelle came to me and asked if we had gone anywhere that night. She wanted to know if I'd had a bad or strange dream. I told her yes, I'd had another one of those strange dreams, but it had not been all that bad. She began questioning me about my dream. She asked if the black-haired lady and her daughter had been in the dream. I asked her, "Why all these questions?"

I wanted her to tell me what happened in her dream that was bad, because I didn't remember. I thought she would tell me immediately or at least confirm more of my own dream. Michelle would not give me any information about our shared visit or the occurrences that had frightened her. She wanted acknowledgement from me that we had shared an experience the previous night.

Michelle became upset and insisted I tell her about my dream. After I told her what I remembered, she was even more upset. There was a strange quizzical look on her face. I thought she was going to cry.

Michelle said, "Mom, there is more to this dream. Don't you remember? There is more to it than just sitting at the kitchen table with the lady and her daughter!!"

I told her I didn't remember anything else about the dream or even how we ended up in the black-haired lady's kitchen. At that point, Michelle became quite agitated that I did not remember anything further. She told me we had been with the "beings" again. She also stated that she was not going to tell me the rest of the story because she wanted me to remember everything! When I remembered, we would talk.

I literally racked my brain for the next week trying to remember. Michelle would come home from school and ask if I remembered what had happened that night. This continued to bother her for some time. I guess she finally gave up on me. I never could get her to talk to me about that particular dream, or about what had occurred that night.

EFFECTS OF THE DAY AFTER

Our abductions increased dramatically at the beginning of 1993; so much so in fact, that I could not keep up with my documentation. Michelle and I did not seem to share many abduction experiences after the episode with the black-haired lady. However, I always knew when she had an abduction experience, because of the "day-after syndrome" she experienced the next day.

From the very beginning of this life-shattering phenomenon, you undergo a personality change. Because of the intense fear, you think you have gone insane. You do not

66

understand what is happening. You do not understand the overwhelming fear and feelings of insanity.

When you first sit up in your own bed after an abduction, you are sometimes, able to fall back asleep. Mostly, that depends upon what the entities have done to you. When you wake up, your physical reactions might range from lethargy, to having your head spin and wanting to faint.

There are a variety of symptoms humans go through after an abduction. I myself have spent countless days just sitting in a chair trying to sort out in my mind what occurred. At times, I simply sat there staring blankly into space, my brain unable to even understand or comprehend.

There are symptoms you experience before an abduction as well. I was beginning to recognize the connection between those feelings or "symptoms" and the horrifying "dreams" I was having. Before nightfall, I would begin to feel agitated and nervous. I would have the feeling that something was wrong or that something was going to happen. I experienced fear of the dark and fear of certain rooms in my home.

THE FACE

1993

The day had gone smoothly and without incident; so there was no justifiable reason why I should have had such uneasy feelings that evening. As bedtime drew near, I found that I didn't want to be in bed, or even go to sleep. I got into bed and although Fred was holding me tight, I was not able to fall asleep. Restlessness caused me to toss and turn. At 12:00 a.m., I was still tossing and turning, but by then, I was so exhausted, I drifted off into slumber.

I awoke with the shocking realization that I was not in my own bed or bedroom! I looked around to see just where I was but I did not recognize anything in that unfamiliar area. My first impression, as I turned my head, was that I was in the hospital. There appeared to be curtains on either side of me. I thought I was lying on a hospital bed in an emergency-ward cubicle. But if I was in the hospital, why was it so quiet and dimly lit?

My back was hurting a lot for some reason, so I tried to turn on my side to get in a more comfortable position. I really just wanted to sit up and get a better look at where I was, or else get out of bed and find out what was going on. To my amazement, my body would not move. I felt paralyzed!

I noticed that none of my family members were there with me. I thought to myself, there must have been some kind of accident while we were sleeping. Fred and Michelle must also have been hurt. Maybe they were lying on the other side of the curtains.

As I lay quietly, I heard heavy breathing on either side of me. I didn't remember getting sick during the night or having been in a car accident or any other kind of accident that would have landed me in the hospital. I had no recollection of what might have happened to us.

I felt very uncomfortable, nervous, restless and fearful. I needed to know where I was and what had happened to us. I attempted to move my body again, but the more I struggled, the more useless it became.

The aggravation of it all produced more fear within me. If this was a dream I was having, I just wanted to wake up and put an end to it. Already, I didn't like where this dream was going!

I looked down at my body by moving my eyes. There was a light-colored blanket covering me. The blanket was very warm. I turned my head to the left and saw light coming through the curtain that separated me from either Fred or Michelle.

"Oh my God, I see an image. I think I see the being! I see two of them! I am not in a hospital! Oh my God, oh my God! I don't like this dream! I tell myself, I repeatedly yell at myself, "Wake-up, Gloria! Wake-up, Gloria!" I do not realize that there is no sound

coming from my mouth as I scream and rage. I move my head from side to side. I look away from the side curtain and direct my eyes toward the foot of the bed. What I see standing there is a being! He is just standing there looking straight at me!

I feel myself shaking violently. I scream as loudly as I can. I move my head back and forth in uncontrollable rage. I scream for someone to help me, and for the being to go away and leave me alone! I struggle more fiercely to free myself, but my body will not move. Through the haze of my fury, I feel certain the being hears me. He walks away and disappears.

I was breathing very hard, almost hyperventilating. I calmed myself down. I realized I was not lying on a bed at all, but on a table. As I lay on the uncomfortable table, I felt as if my whole body were freezing. I noticed that a brighter light had been turned on. I looked in the direction the light was coming from.

I saw the shadows of two beings on the curtains. They seemed to be doing something to someone on the other side of me. I heard struggling sounds coming from that area. That poor person, I thought to myself.

I saw the beings' shadows walk away. Then, before I knew it, their shadows actually grew larger, indicating that they were walking toward me! I could not control my shaking and hysterical rage. I began to whisper loudly to myself.

They're coming! They're coming! They're coming to get me! I have got to hide! I watch their shadows grow larger and larger through the curtain until suddenly, I see them at the end of the table!

I feel the inside of my body shaking furiously. My head is turning at fifty miles an hour as I scream even harder and louder. I see one of the beings walk up to my left side, close to my shoulder. I struggle even more to get away from him. My head no longer moves. Before I know it, he puts his head right into my face! All I see is his face! Onto my face! His face looks stern and very mean!

69

At that point, I really thought I had died. I can not explain the fear and terror of HIS FACE being in my face. I could not perceive then, what happened next. Everything in my sight went black except for a symbol that was shown to me by the Grey.

I did not understand how he managed to visually show me the symbol in my brain. I did not know what the symbol meant. I thought the being was telling me to "shut up and behave."

Suddenly, I heard a very loud noise I could not identify. It sounded as if something had hit the outside wall of our bedroom extremely hard, or as if something had hit the window very hard. Something made a horrendously loud noise that jarred me so much, I woke up, sitting in my bed, shaking. This was the end of the conscious memory.

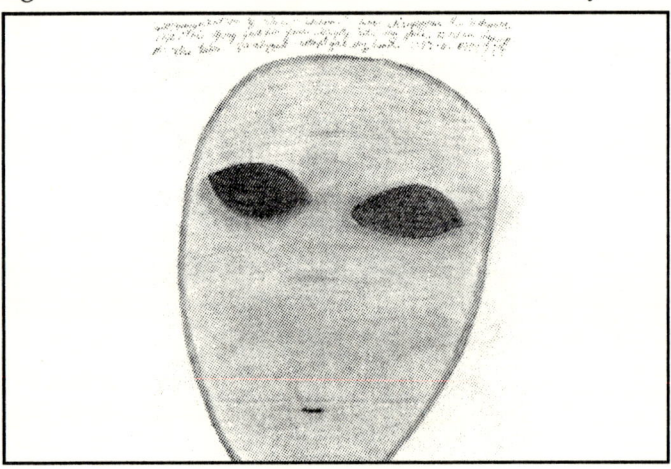

The Grey's Face

The next morning, I woke up in my bed. I spent the day sitting in a chair trying to put pieces of the dream together, trying to figure out what had really happened. Had this been another very real and terrible dream? I discovered that the aftereffects (feelings and symptoms) of an abduction were just as devastating as the dream itself.

For many years afterward, I believed the Grey had been telling me to "Just shut up and behave!" when he showed me that symbol.

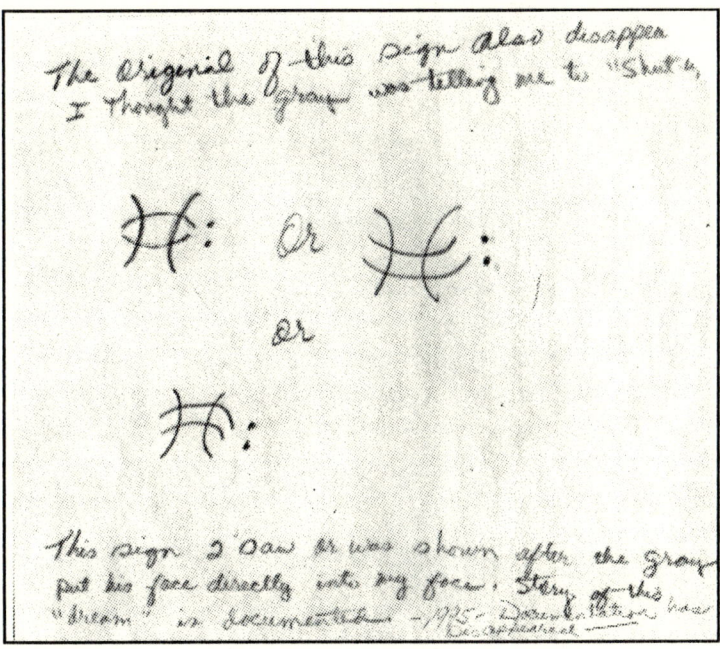

The Signs I was shown

Mr. Budd Hopkins did hypnosis on this experience. The Greys had put an implant into both my ears. An alien baby had been taken from me and the implantation of yet another hybrid baby was put into my body.

Only a few other people have been given the symbol I was given by the Grey. My symbol does have a meaning and at present, is under investigation. When Budd Hopkins hypnotized me on this dream, he had me draw the symbol for him. He questioned my drawing because he had never seen that particular symbol before.

Afterward, he made a trip to Australia, where he met with a male abductee whom he also hypnotized. This abductee had also seen a symbol during his experience. The symbol was similar to the one I had drawn for Budd. He had the male abductee draw his symbol also. When Mr. Hopkins returned home and compared the symbols, they seemed to be similar!

TWO SPACE SHIPS

1993

I quit my position at the University that year and had gone to work for Fred in his new business. Wednesday was my morning to go into the office late.

The day started out as usual that Wednesday morning. Around 10:30 a.m., I was ready to leave for work. I wanted to go to the office early, because Fred was going to Los Alamos National Laboratory on business.

I walked out the front door and closed it behind me. I was making sure the door was locked when I thought I heard a male voice tell me to look toward the mountains. I thought perhaps a man had walked up the sidewalk next to the garage and was speaking to me.

I looked but there was no one walking toward me now or when I went down our sidewalk to the driveway where my Mercury was parked. I ignored the voice. As I unlocked the driver's door, I again heard the voice tell me to look toward the mountains.

I didn't know where the voice was coming from, but it sounded very authoritative. I took a quick look and saw nothing. I thought the voice must just be in my head. It continued to repeat the same sentence to me as if it were demanding I do as it commanded.

I traveled my usual route to Montgomery Boulevard. At the end of our street, I made a left turn onto the street that curves and intersects at Larchmont and Calle de Carino. There was a stop sign at the intersection.

The strange voice I was hearing in my head no longer sounded male or female, but continued to be quite persistent. As I came to a halt at the stop sign, my car just quit running. I tried to restart the engine, but the car would not start.

The voice in my head became louder and very demanding. It commanded me to look up at the mountains. I looked. I sat there in the car, staring in awe, at something I could not believe I was seeing. I looked down at my lap, then up at the mountain again, just to be sure. Still, I was not certain of what I was seeing.

Up ahead, in the Sandia Mountains, there was a canyon directly in front of me. There were two silver-colored disks. I was looking at two spaceships, sitting there, side by side, in a high canyon.

I quickly scanned the neighborhood and the park across the street to see if any people were outside. I wanted someone to see those two spaceships! There were no people around.

Suddenly, I heard a crashing noise, as if someone had rear-ended my car. Then, I felt something enter my car from the top of the roof. As I turned my head, I thought I saw a small being sitting in the back seat. The being was visible for only a few seconds. Now, instead of hearing voices, I was actually seeing these beings and their ships in broad daylight!

The being seemed to be sitting directly behind me. I don't think it was my imagination, because the cushion in the back seat was indented, as if someone was sitting there. I also felt a very strong presence, like another person was in the car with me.

I must have sat at the intersection for at least fifteen minutes. I tried to open the car door to escape, but the door would not open. I was "told" to start the car. It would not start.

I tried the ignition a couple more times and the engine finally turned over. I did not realize my foot was so heavy on the gas pedal until the engine roared and the car began to race straight for the park. I quickly turned the steering wheel to the right and drove south toward Montgomery.

I wanted to go back home, but the car seemed to be driving on its own. I felt as if I had no control over the car. I thought if I held the wheel tightly and forced it, I could regain control and drive to a friend's house that was nearby. I would pick her up and bring her back to the area and show her the spaceships. I did not intend to show her the being in the back seat. I wanted to show her the spaceships.

The following events prove that I was not in control of my own thinking. Something temporarily took control of my mind and body.

When I reached the intersection at Larchmont and Montgomery, I could not stop the car at the stop sign. The car suddenly made a right turn and continued on. My usual route when traveling down Montgomery, is to get into the far right lane. Feeling as if I had no control over the steering wheel, the car automatically went into the left-turn lane. My hands were simply resting on the wheel.

I don't really know who had control of my car that morning. As I approached the intersection at Tramway and Montgomery, the traffic signal was red. My car careened through the red light and made another left turn onto Tramway Blvd, going south.

If I use Tramway (which is a rarity), I normally make a right turn at the intersection of either Commanche or Candelaria, heading west. My brain seemed to be affected in some way, as I felt dazed and emotionally numbed. I was not thinking clearly. It was as if something had taken over my mind too!

Just then, I "awoke" very quickly, and broke loose from the mind- control stupor and daze I was in. I began to repeat and say out loud, "You are not going to control me this way." I did not notice what I was saying until I began repeating the statement more loudly.

I immediately put my hands on the steering wheel and realized I was traveling faster than the posted 50 mph speed limit on Tramway. I was quickly approaching the intersection of Candelaria and Tramway. The steering wheel seemed to be under the control of someone else as I fought with the wheel to make a right turn onto Candelaria.

Thank God there was no traffic on the road at the time. Traveling at high speed and making a right turn at 50 mph was very frightening. I tried to regain my composure, but I was literally shaking in my boots.

Somehow, I was finally able to slow the car down. I felt I had regained control of my vehicle. However, when I approached other cars or stopped at an intersection for lights, I noticed people looking into my car. I checked the back seat, but saw no one there. Nor did I see anything else unusual that would cause people to look. Perhaps they had noticed my erratic driving.

When I reached my destination, I parked the car in the lot outside our office. As I got out of the car and locked the door, I strongly felt a presence also get out of the car. The presence followed me into the office building walking directly behind me, down the hallway, to our office. I ran down the hall to our office to rid myself of this being. As I ran, the presence kept pace with me. Taking deep breaths and trying to get control of myself, I locked the office door behind me and sat down in my chair. I thought I had locked the presence outside of the office. Little did I know I had not!

When I went to turn on the computer, I could not get it to turn on. After investigating the problem and trying several times to turn it on, it finally responded. That was the beginning of all sorts of weird problems with the computer. I was able to get into the programs I needed, but as soon as I would get into a document, I would begin losing my saved material. How that was happening, I did not know. I had to use backup disks to regain what was lost.

After that problem was fixed, I began typing, only to discover that my fingers were on the wrong keys. What I typed was not familiar to me. Books, paper, pencils and weird things began dropping from my desk or from the other desks behind me. I thought someone else was in the office with me. I felt a presence and became even more frightened. I looked through the window down the hall to see if anyone else had entered their offices. I wanted to go be with them, but no one else had come in yet to our section of the building.

I sat, and told the presence to go and leave me alone! It did not leave. It was like it *had* to stay with me. In a way, I was glad no one else had entered their offices, because I was turning into a nervous wreck with this thing. I sat at my computer and tried to do my work. With all the disturbances, I did not accomplish much of anything. It was as if someone did not want me to work that day.

When I looked at the clock it was 11:30 a.m. I knew Michelle would be home for lunch, so I phoned her and told her about the morning's events. I told her about the presence and how I felt it was still with me. She wanted me to leave the office and come home but I told her I felt safer at the office.

I asked if she would do me a favor. I told her to get my binoculars, use the portable phone, and go out on the balcony outside my bedroom. I would then tell her where to look for the spaceships to see if they were still there. Michelle did not see anything in the area, so she decided to climb up on the roof to get a better view.

After scanning the Sandia Mountains, she reported that the spaceships were no longer there. I was very disappointed. I felt dejected and unnerved. Maybe I would just go home. I could not accomplish anything at work because I was feeling out of my mind with nervousness about what had occurred.

I phoned my brother to have someone else to talk to. I informed him of the morning's weird events and told him about seeing the spaceships. I also told him about the presence in the office with me. After speaking with him, I became very drowsy and wanted to fall asleep at my desk. I was quite lethargic.

At 2:00 p.m., I felt a strange sense of relief with regard to the presence that had been shadowing me since my drive to the office. I turned around to see what might be happening. I thought my eyes were playing a joke on me! I saw a being levitate upward and go through the ceiling of our office! (He would also have to go through the upstairs office to get out of the building!) I felt a sudden rush of freedom.

Fred got back from Los Alamos around 4:00 p.m. that day. I told him the whole story. He wanted to go home, get his camera, and drive to the place I had seen the two spaceships. He wanted to take some pictures of the area.

We closed up the office. Fred and I walked to our cars. I turned the key in the ignition of my car and a loud noise filled the inside of the car. It was deafening! It sounded like electronic static but I did not know where it was coming from. I thought something terrible must be wrong with the car. I quickly turned off the ignition. When I started the car a second time, the same noise began again. I turned off the ignition and looked to see if Fred was still in the parking lot. He had already left. Not knowing what was wrong with my car, I was a little hesitant to start it up again. I decided to try one more time.

I opened the car door and stepped outside to listen to the motor. It sounded fine. When I got back into the car, I inadvertently touched the knob on the radio. It was then that I discovered the radio had been turned up as loud as it could possibly go. As I investigated, I found that the channel dial was turned all the way to the left, and was not tuned to any radio station. I had found the source of the loud noise.

I usually kept the dial set on a particular FM radio station I liked to listen to. I knew I had not moved the tuning dial to the far left. How it got there and how the volume had been turned to maximum was a mystery to me. There was something strange about the sound I had heard. After moving the dial to my usual station, I turned it back to where I had just found it, to listen to the noise again. The radio did not make the same noise I had heard previously. I even turned the volume up as loud as it would go. It did not make the same electronic noise. I did not know if the noise I had heard was actually coming from the radio or not.

Fred had a special telescopic lens on his camera. He used it to get good pictures of the area where I had seen the spaceships. Using the camera lens, he looked for downed trees.

I began to question myself about what I had seen. I wondered if the feeling of the presence was reality-based. Had the craziness of that day really happened? I mentally reviewed the day's activities, from the time I got up until the inexplicable experience with the car radio.

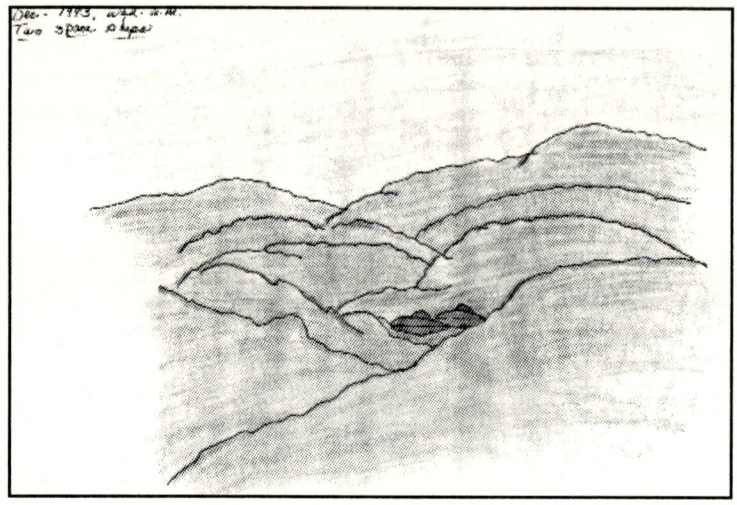

The Two Space Ships

Fred and Michelle questioned me thoroughly for the next two days. Their questions made me feel insecure and rather insane. What I'd definitely seen, along with the presence of the being who briefly showed himself in the car, was just as real to me as the sun coming up in the morning. I was certain I had lived through that experience. I believed what I saw and felt that awful day.

This last experience was just the tip of the iceberg! At that point in my life, a decision had to be made on my part. The horrific dreams and experiences I was having were destroying my life. I could not continue like that. I needed to find some answers. Either I had become insane because of the physical and mental pain of previous hardships, or I was experiencing (and not believing in) alien abductions.

I had become very critical of myself. Alien abduction does not really happen to humans here, on Earth. I was convinced I was going insane. I was certain that the many losses we had lived through were the reason for my terrifying dreams. I needed answers. My belief in myself was shaken. I also had the feeling that Fred no longer believed me. That was very devastating and detrimental to my emotional well-being.

I decided to seek the help of a psychologist or psychiatrist. I wondered if I should find someone who was knowledgeable in the field of alien abductions. Why would a psychologist or psychiatrist believe my particular story of abduction when I had a history of tragedy, pain and loss? I would probably be put into a mental-health hospital. My own personal value system was very strong and I followed it with all my heart. I believed that everything in my life was a gift from God and that no one should ever take away or diminish any gift given by Him.

I chose instead, to go back to the library before seeking professional help. I remembered the titles of some of the books I had read in 1988 while bedridden after my accident. They were books on the phenomena of aliens.

Early the next morning, I was in the library searching the stacks for UFO books. I was embarrassed to ask for directions to the UFO section. I did not want anyone to think I was crazy. I did not even want to check through the library computer for such a topic, thinking someone might walk up behind me and see what I was searching for.

After walking through many stacks, I finally found the section I was looking for. I was lucky enough to find three of the books I had read. I searched for a secluded table so no one would see which books I was reading.

I began to search through each of the books. If my memory was correct, I would find the name of a person located in Albuquerque, who was an abductee. If I found that person's name, I would try to contact them. I spent most of the morning going from page to page in each of the three books. I finally found the name I was looking for in Ruth Montgomery's book. Now the real search would begin!

THE LETTER

I was very happy when I left the library because I had found Mr. Don Paladin's name and address in a book titled Aliens Among Us by Ruth Montgomery. Mr. Paladin lived in Albuquerque. I was ecstatic! I could hardly wait until I reached the office to search the telephone book for his phone number.

His phone number was not in the telephone directory. Nervously, I tried to compose a letter. I found it very difficult to write and had to rewrite the letter several times. I had Fred read the letter. I had tried to compose it in a way that would explain to Mr. Paladin my predicament regarding alien abductions, if in fact, that was what was happening to me.

I needed someone with his knowledge to help my family and me. I explained to him that I felt the members of my family were laughing at me because of this problem. I told him I felt insane because of the seeming reality of it.

I also told him that I thought I might need to search for a psychiatrist, but did not know how to begin. I even told him that I had asked my family to take me to a psychiatrist, but they had not done so. I thanked him for his time and asked that he respond to my letter. The letter I wrote was dated December 16, 1993.

After mailing my letter, I prayed that Mr. Paladin would not ignore it. He must, after all, receive many letters like mine. The following days passed quickly and soon I began checking the mailbox each day hoping and praying that I would receive a response.

Sadly, no telephone call or letter came from Mr. Paladin. I assumed he must be quite busy because it was Christmastime. I resolved to be patient and mentally set a date to contact a psychiatrist if I did not hear back from him. I hoped he would contact me after the holidays. I had no further plans to follow up my initial contact, as Mr. Paladin might have no interest in my predicament.

Before I made contact with a psychiatrist, I would go back to the library and search again for more names out of Ruth

Montgomery's book, and contact those people as well. On December 27, 1993, I received a postcard in the mail. The postcard was from Wendy Paladin. She wrote:

> *Dear Gloria,*
> *You wrote to Don Paladin asking for him to contact you. He died a few years ago. You're welcome to give me a call if you'd care to talk to me.*
>
> *Wendy Paladin*

There was joy in my heart that his wife had responded to my letter, but a deep sadness at news of Mr. Paladin's death. Wendy Paladin had understood what I wrote to her husband.

I felt such great relief! Help was on the way. I called Wendy Paladin, and we spoke for quite awhile. We made plans to meet at a restaurant that was close to both of us.

MEETING WENDY PALADIN

On the evening of January 5, 1994, Michelle and I met with Wendy Paladin at the Purple Plum restaurant at 7:00 p.m. I asked Michelle to come to the meeting with me because of her vibrant, warm and happy personality. She was also funny at times, which I hoped would help ease a potentially stressful encounter. I thought Michelle would be able to share some of our experiences with Wendy without being devastated by the subject.

Michelle had a school meeting that evening. The plan was for her to join us at the restaurant when she finished with her meeting. I gave Wendy a description of myself and what type of clothing I would be wearing. She also described herself and what she would be wearing.

We found each other at the restaurant. We were both nervous and cautious, but warmed up to each other as we spoke about our lives. Wendy appeared to be in her early forties. She was a very private but warm, caring and concerned lady.

She said this was her first time, without her husband, to meet with someone who claimed to be an alien abductee. I had never felt that I was an alien abductee until I heard her say those words. She also agreed with me about the many reservations we both had and the feelings of not knowing what to expect from one another.

We sat in the restaurant for two hours getting to know one another and sharing information. She told me about Don and his involvement with the alien species she called "The Sky People." She said she knew very little about the aliens because her husband had not always told her everything he knew. Wendy herself was not an abductee. She said Don was a Native American and also an artist.

During our meeting, Wendy wanted to know about me and my dreams of being with the alien species. This was the very first time I had been asked by a stranger to talk about the insane content of my terrible dreams.

It was very hard for me to tell the story, especially to a relative stranger I knew nothing about. Her warmth and concern helped put me at ease. I described what the beings looked like and began to briefly tell her about the first "waking" dream experience I'd had in September of 1988. I brought her up to the present time and told her what had led me to contact her husband, Don.

I explained to her that eventually I was going to find a psychiatrist because I felt totally insane and needed help. With compassion, Wendy told me I was not insane and that what I was experiencing was very real. She told me that many people in our world are selected by the Sky People for some unknown reason, to be experimented on and put through a lot of medical abuse.

I told her of the many frightening dreams that had literally scared the hell out of me and instilled such fear that I did not want to go to bed at night. The fear made me toss and turn into the wee hours of the morning before I could get some much needed sleep. I told her that, without knowing why, on some particular evenings, I would experience unknown anxiety, restlessness, nervousness and a knowing that something wrong was going to happen soon.

At first, this had set up a pattern of psychological reactions I did not recognize until after the fact. After a night of holy terror, I would be drained and tired from experiencing the unexplained. I was certain that suffering the aftereffects of such an experience would drive anyone to insanity. I confided to her that I felt I was already there.

I told her that I seemed to have been "taken" many more times than Michelle or Brian. Or that maybe, Brian and Michelle had not been allowed to keep their memories of the experiences. I had hoped that Wendy would be the person who would help me regain my sanity, explain, teach me and answer all the questions I needed answers to.

Some of my questions were: Who are these strange beings? Why did they choose me and two of my children? Where do they come from and is this part of my life for real? Am I to believe it?

Wendy could not answer many of my questions. Before leaving the restaurant that evening, she told me to feel free to telephone her anytime of the day or night if I needed her. She said she would come to my home and try to help me in any way she could. She also invited Michelle and me to her home for our next meeting on January 25, 1994.

That first meeting with Wendy Paladin actually presented me with more questions. Some of the confirmation she gave me provoked an even stronger feeling of not feeling safe in my own home at night.

I did not want to be left alone at home. I found myself going to visit friends or relatives more often, or simply walking through the malls. I used that time to become more involved in our church.

Wendy's warm and loving presentation gave the family and I a lot to think about. We now had a name for the beings. We began calling them The Sky People.

OUR SECOND VISIT WITH WENDY PALADIN

January 25, 1994

Wendy Paladin's home enveloped us in a warm, cozy atmosphere. Her husband Don's artwork decorated every wall in their home. His essence could be felt, almost as if he had never left the earth. Even in death, his soul lived on through Wendy. His artwork showed the unique and strong person he had been. His death was untimely for such a healthy man. It raised the question of whether the Sky People had taken him suddenly for their own reasons. It also brought to mind the question of whether or not he might still be alive. I was betting his wife would like to have an answer to that last question.

Wendy walked us through the rooms that were decorated with Don's paintings. Her home was a museum of art. She explained the story that went with each painting Don had done. She showed us many more catalogued paintings so we could get to know him as he had been when he was alive. In Don's communication with the aliens, The Sky People, he had painted whatever visions or communications he had been given by them.

During our visit, Wendy introduced us to what I remembered as her visual "symbol box." The box held various tangible items she had collected over the years. She used them to help her gain strength in areas of her personality in which she perceived herself to be weak. The box contained items that told something about herself. As she meditated, she would be able to see and hold the objects that represented the feelings she wanted to overcome or grow stronger in.

For example, a weakness could be aggression, selfishness, shyness, or a lack of love. Working with the symbols through meditation would eventually bring forth the needed element to make herself whole and complete as a stronger person. She explained how working with the symbols had helped her overcome various weaknesses in her personality.

She strongly suggested that I start a "symbol box" of my own. She could already tell from my personality, that I was not very aggressive, and that I needed to learn to be more aggressive with The Sky People. She told me she had heard that abductees did have a choice about remaining with and continuing their experiences with The Sky People.

She also said that an abductee could become strong and angry enough to tell The Sky People to leave you and your family alone! I clearly needed to make a decision about whether I wanted the Sky People in or out of our lives. Wendy also wanted me to learn to write my own affirmations to help build up my self-confidence and grow stronger. She directed me to find objects to represent who I was and which weaknesses I needed to work on.

Don had been given some very vital information through his visions. Even while working on his computer, he would be interrupted with unusual hieroglyphics that would appear on the monitor. If I remember correctly, Wendy had said that the Sky People taught him their written language. Don had included written communication from the entities in his paintings.

In a photograph of one of Don's paintings of the Sky People, I saw a symbol that I immediately recognized as the one I had been given by the mean alien. It was the same symbol I had seen when the mean alien put his face right up to mine. It was the symbol the alien had used to tell me to "shut up!" (This symbol is discussed in the section titled "The Face" .)

Don's symbol had only one dot on the right side of it while mine had two dots on the right side. Wendy was hoping I could tell her what the symbol meant. I told her about the dream I'd had of the alien who had put his face close to mine, then visually showed me the symbol I interpreted to mean "shut up!"

I shared with Wendy, some of the horrific dreams Michelle and I had been having. She again told me she did not know a lot about the Sky People and that she really did not know how to help me. Perhaps just being there for us would help.

Wendy said she did not know who the people were who had helped Don, or with whom he had spoken about his experiences. She knew of government contacts, but could not give me their names. She reminded us again that if Michelle or I needed her anytime, day or night, we could call her. We scheduled another time to meet.

"UNIDENTIFIED FLYING OBJECTS: ALIEN SPACE SHIPS? GOVERNMENT COVER-UP? UFO RESEARCH GAINING LEGITIMACY"

This was the headline that ran in the *Trends* section of the *Sunday Albuquerque Journal*. It was accompanied by a half-page simulated picture of a disk spaceship, hovering over a large automobile that had the inside light on, but no people in the car. The make-believe "incident" was portrayed as having happened at night.

Fred and I had just returned home. We were barely through the front door when a wide-eyed Michelle handed us that section of the *Sunday Journal*. She excitedly told us to look at and read the article. What immediately caught my eye were the two red and two green lights located on the bottom of the simulated flying saucer.

I was shaken up because at first glance, I thought it was a real picture of an abduction. The simulated ship seemed to leap right off the page at me. I repeatedly said, "My God, it's like the round, lit object we saw!"

I became incoherent. I cried and was very dazed. I just wanted to be by myself with the article and the picture. After re-reading the article, I had tears running down my face and I became uncontrollably sad.

I remembered what Wendy Paladin had told me. I felt as if I needed to speak with her. When she answered the telephone, she knew, with the first words I managed to get out, that something was terribly wrong. She thought I had been abducted the night before. I calmed myself down and asked her if she had seen the Sunday *Journal Trends* section. She told me she had not.

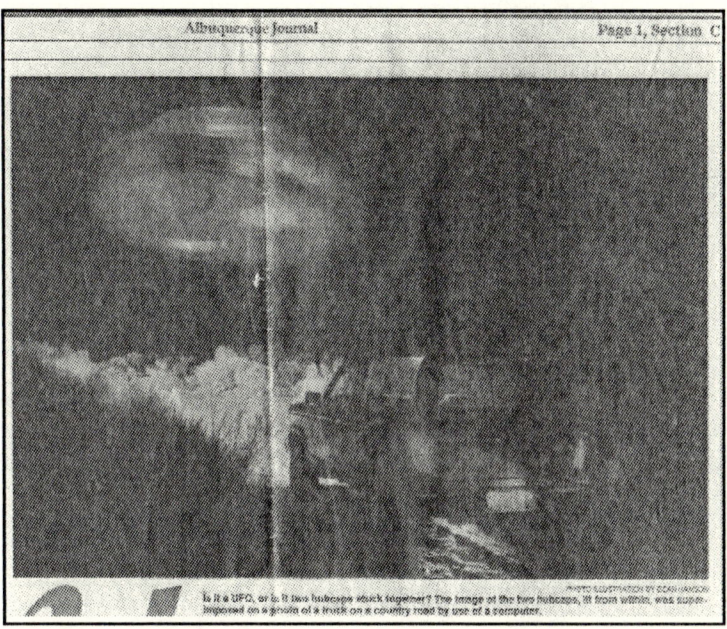

Clipping from the Albuquerque Journal

She went and got the paper and brought it to the phone with her. When she saw the article and the accompanying picture, she too, was deeply affected by it. She talked to me for about an hour, trying to figure out why that particular picture was having such an effect on me. We discussed the probability of an underlying problem.

That was when she suggested I make an appointment with her psychologist. She said she was going to call her psychologist that afternoon and thought she might want to speak with me. Indeed, her psychologist suggested I make an appointment with her that week.

I seriously considered Wendy's suggestion, and after a follow-up call from Wendy, I did make an appointment for the following Monday. I felt certain this would be important to my quest for answers about the terrible dreams.

I reverted back to my original thoughts about how there really were no Sky People in our world who bothered other humans and me. I felt that seeking counseling was a step in the right direction. Soon, I would have some answers. Soon, I would be able to look back on all of this.

The psychologist turned out to be a pleasant person. She made it easy for me to tell my story on the first visit. After listening to me, she said she felt there could be other entities from another universe, here on our Earth. She then proceeded to tell me about a young girl and her mother who lived somewhere in Texas. They had been on a picnic with family members when the young girl wandered off "over a grassy, tree-lined hill." The girl quickly returned for her mother. She said she wanted to show her some new friends. The mother and daughter arrived at the designated spot in time to see a "craft" lifting off and rapidly disappearing into the cloudless sky.

I wondered why a psychologist would tell me this story. What message she was trying to get across to me? Okay, so I would believe everything I had lived through in my dreams. I would acknowledge the fact that other beings inhabited our small universe; and that, yes, they were abducting humans. I made another appointment with the psychologist for the following week.

On the second visit, my sanity became more fragile. Suddenly, the information from the prior week's visit was flip-flopped by the doctor. She told me that my mind had *fabricated* the horrific dreams of abduction by an alien entity!

The reason for this, she said, was the sexual and physical abuse I had endured as a child and young adult. I had also lived through bankruptcy, losing a home, being abused by creditors, nearly losing my son, and the loss of other valued things in my adult life. The dreams were simply a release of my past life problems.

I struggled to understand how my *mind*, in a dream, could create bruising and needle marks on my body!

I did not make another appointment. I was as screwed up as ever.

Easter, 1994

It was the week before Easter, 1994. On the Wednesday night before Easter, Fred was awakened and allowed to see the Greys carry Michelle, our son Brian, and me down the stairs and out the front door. Fred was not allowed to go any further than the front porch. He saw the Greys carry us to some kind of vehicle.

The next morning, Fred asked me if I had gone anywhere during the night. I had no memory of going anywhere and no memory of the abduction. He then told me what he had seen. He had not been able to fight them off or keep them from taking us to wherever they took us. After that, he was made to sleep again. Brian and Michelle did not have any memory of that event either.

MR. MICHAEL LINDEMANN

On January 26, 1994, Mr. Michael Lindemann, whom I knew nothing about, was going to give a lecture at the auditorium of the Indian Pueblo Cultural Center. Mr. Lindemann, who lived in California, was a Futurist and UFO researcher. Wendy Paladin knew of him and invited Michelle and me to go listen to him. She thought the information we would hear would be helpful.

Feeling very excited, we waited in a long line that extended far from the building. When we were second from the ticket booth, we were told that all tickets had been sold. There was no standing room in the auditorium. The three of us were dejected. We were allowed into the reception area to purchase a video of Mr. Lindemann. We took the tape home and viewed it together, along with Fred.

Mr. Lindemann's video was confirming evidence for me. He talked about the government cover-up and contact with intelligent life from elsewhere in the universe. Viewing the video left me wondering what direction my life was taking. Why me? Why my family?

LITTLE DARTH VADER

Spring, 1994

During the latter part of the day, I experienced an overwhelming emotion that I had come to know and recognize. It was a sensation of knowing that something was going to occur, something that would change my life and affect others. I knew that something was imminent.

Over the years, working with those emotions, I discovered that I had psychic abilities. Since 1988, my psychic abilities had become divided and changed into two different elements.

The first element was having a vision. I would "live through" a grim experience of the death of a person or people, right before the event actually happened. These visions were quite accurate because, within the hour, the occurrence would make the news.

If the vision involved the death of a family member or friend, I would receive a phone call shortly after the vision. Those who know of my psychic abilities, have told me I should help locate missing persons. I have described areas where kidnapped and murdered people have been found. I lived and experienced with those people their last moments of life. I saw and felt their demise as if it were my own.

The second element is knowing when the alien species is coming to get me. Though I have no vision of this, I experience the same symptoms of distinctly knowing that something is going to happen. A strong emotion of distress overcomes me. I have unexplainable, uncomfortable feelings that produce fear of not wanting to face the new and impending adventures.

The warm night air, on this particular night, was comforting and soothing to me. Having Fred by my side in bed, holding me close was also comforting.

He was beginning to understand that something was going on in my life, and he was becoming aware of the different emotions I went through before an abduction. Those emotions always coincided with my abductions. Neither of us understood the reality of what, exactly, was occurring in my life. Sleep would come easily for Fred, while I tossed and turned before falling asleep.

I don't know what time I was rudely awakened. I found myself lying on my left side with my left arm extended off the bed. For no apparent reason, there was pain in my left arm. I had the sensation of cold fingers going up and down my arm. It was as if someone was sticking needles or something sharp into my arm. It felt as if something tight was being put around my arm.

Not being fully awake, I looked toward the east wall and saw the black shadow of something. The shadow was right at my bed and it was doing something to my arm! The weird shadow reminded me of a "Vader." It did not look like any of the Sky People I had become familiar with. I had never seen anything like this before.

The being was about three to four feet tall and was dressed in black. It was as if the being was wearing a black cape, resembling what a monk would wear. I saw no face because it appeared to have some kind of black helmet covering its face. The entity's breathing was loud, hard and labored.

I lay frozen in bed as if paralyzed. As my eyes adjusted to the dark, I realized there was bright light shining in from the east window and from our open balcony door. The light illuminated our bedroom. I thought it might be the light of a full moon, but was unsure of its origin. The light made it easier for me to see the black entity.

At first, I thought I was just having a bad dream. But I was not dreaming the pain and the cold fingers I felt on my arm. I began to go through the motions of screaming, not realizing that no sound was coming from my throat. I struggled to move my body. It would not move! I tried harder to call out to Fred, but he did not respond to my cries.

I don't know if my brain was able to comprehend what happened next. I found myself on our balcony, not knowing how I got there. I was standing in front of a small, black vehicle that had only two seats in it. One seat was located directly in front of the other. The back seat was raised up higher than the front seat. There was a panel in front of the forward seat. The panel had a couple of red and yellow lights on it.

Before I knew what was happening, I was sitting in the lower front seat. The entity was sitting close behind me in the rear seat. He told me to push either the red or yellow button on my left. When I did so, a type of steel covering came up over us. It seemed to air lock the vehicle. The sound of moving air inside reminded me of an air conditioner. This was done so I (or we) would not have trouble breathing.

I felt movement and realized we were going upward. I saw the floor of our bedroom balcony, the balcony wall and the outside of the bedroom wall. As we got higher, I saw the roof that connects our side of the townhouse to our neighbor's side. Then I saw our immediate neighborhood and the streets surrounding our neighborhood.

I heard a humming noise coming from the vehicle as we climbed even higher. I looked east toward the Sandia Mountains. We seemed to be above them but not over them. The Sandias were to my right. The front of the vehicle was pointed to the north.

As we gained altitude, our townhouse, the neighborhood, and the streets disappeared. I saw the lighted landscape of Albuquerque and its surrounding suburbs. The night sky was very clear and the lights of Albuquerque sparkled beautifully. The lights and the Sandia Mountains became very small.

92

At that point, I felt those cold fingers touch the bottom of my chin. His fingers had strength as he turned my head upward. The entity wanted me to look up into the vast universe. What he wanted me to see was something I had never seen before in my life. I was looking at billions of the brightest stars! So many clusters of beautiful stars. That beautiful site was the gift the entity gave to me that night.

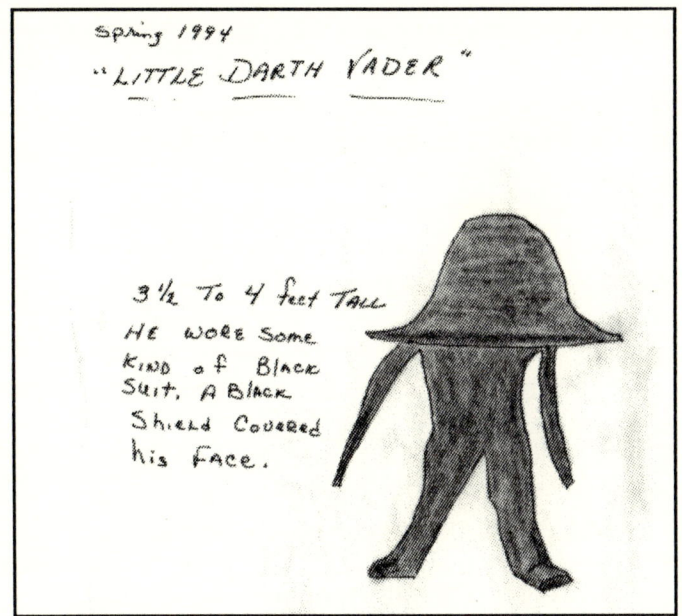

Spring 1994
"LITTLE DARTH VADER"

3½ To 4 feet TALL
HE WORE Some
KIND of BlAck
SUit, A BlAck
Shield Covered
his FAce.

Darth Vader

Where the entity took me after that is unknown to me. After he showed me the stars and planets, I felt his cold fingers touch the sides of my head. I either blacked out or went to sleep.

The sleep was so deep that I woke up the next morning lying in my own bed next to Fred. He was already awake. The first thing out of my mouth was "Why didn't you help me last night?" He asked me, "Where did they take you?" I then told him about the different being and how differently he had been dressed.

Fred is the person who gave the entity the name of "Little Darth Vader." He said I was describing Darth Vader out of the "*Star Wars*" series. Because of that remark, I was uncertain whether or not Fred believed what I had told him about the night's events. He suggested that I document what had happened.

I was beginning to doubt whether or not Fred believed me. That doubt, in turn, sparked feelings of insanity once gain. I felt as if I was losing my mind over what was happening to me. For that reason, I no longer discussed any of my terrifying dreams and experiences with anyone but Fred and Michelle. The things I experienced became my secret.

Many times, I would not even share with Fred and Michelle because of the humiliation I felt. I needed to maintain my own self-worth. I would sit alone and try to re-evaluate myself and attempt to figure out why I was having such real "dream" experiences.

There comes a time when self-doubt enters into the picture. Not only did I have self-doubt about what seemed to be happening to me, but I began to feel as if my own husband doubted me and the stories I told him about my petrifying dreams.

Strong emotions invaded and overcame me after each dream experience. I truly wondered if I was insane. I had not heard of anyone else going through these experiences. The thought of insanity was a constant battle inside me. When your own husband shares his doubts or feels that he doesn't understand what you are going through, your whole support system collapses. Your belief in yourself diminishes. Accepting insanity was a logical explanation for me at the time.

I had always thought that material possessions were a reward from Our Lord. Because of what had been given to us, I had valued those possessions with all my heart. Fred and I lost everything we had worked so hard for. We had endured the embarrassment and humiliation of bankruptcy. As I saw it, that never should have happened to us. It did not seem fair that depraved people, who didn't care about anyone, could destroy others for their own selfish ends. Those people had gone to extremes against the law to gain power over us. They did not care how they accomplished their ends or who they destroyed in the process. Families meant nothing to them. They seemed to fear no one. Not even Satan.

Having been destroyed by *humans* like that, caused me to lose faith in Our Lord, my husband, and people in general. I found the world a difficult place in which to survive. Maybe I valued material things more than my family. I believe Our Lord taught me this when our son was nearly killed. When death approaches your doorstep, no mother or father wants to lose a child. Our Lord answered my cries and prayers for the survival of our son. He also answered the prayers of many others who formed a large circle of love around our family at that time.

In spite of all this, I still could not accept the misfortunes in our lives. I blamed Our Lord. I thought He was the one who took away our dream home. Fred and I had planned to finish raising our children and retire in that home. All Fred's hard work to secure a future for us had suddenly disappeared because he had trusted people that were unscrupulous. He came out of that experience very empty inside and searching within himself for reasons why.

My faith in people who proclaimed they were there to "help" us was quickly destroyed when we found out how devious they truly were. Their question to us could have been, "How much money do you have in your pockets so I can rob you of your future and your well-being?" The tragedy is, they got away with it.

Every day, I shed tears for my children. I wanted to protect them from having to go through such an ordeal. I wanted to save them from the degradation. In the end, my children had more faith and understanding than I did. They proved to me that they had more guts and pride in their lives by accomplishing everything they set out to do. And they did it with honor.

All of those factors along with the dreams I was having, contributed to my feelings of insanity. I had many unanswered questions and I was afraid to seek psychological help. Fred and I had gone for counseling in the past, about the problems that affected our marriage and each one of us personally. I did not feel that I could return to any of those counselors with this "new" problem of mine. I was afraid I would end up in some mental hospital. I feared I would be told that I was indeed, crazy.

I was living a secret life. I was tortured by the fact that I could not answer my own questions. I did not know why I couldn't function for two or more days after having such grim dreams. I did not understand why I secluded myself in my bedroom, sitting in a chair, trying to make sense of a dream that seemed so very real.

Why did my body ache when I had performed no strenuous physical activities? Why did my head hurt so much, and why did I keep finding strange markings on my body? This was the reality of my "dreams."

MR. MICHAEL LINDEMANN RETURNS TO ALBUQUERQUE

April, 1994

Michelle was listening to the radio and called me at work. She had heard Mr. Lindemann speak on the program she had been listening to. Lindemann was going to be at the University's Continuing Education Building that evening to give another lecture.

It was planned that Fred, Michelle and I would attend his lecture. Fred and I went to the lecture together. Michelle had to work that evening. We arrived at the Continuing Education lecture hall around 6:15 p.m. Lindemann was going to speak at 7:00 p.m.

Because Fred and I had arrived early, we were able to get a seat in the lecture hall. We sat in the second row on the left side of the speaker's podium. I had no idea what Lindemann was going to speak about that evening. I had prayed all day that I might be able to talk to him with regard to my family and myself.

Mr. Lindemann was walking around talking to people in the audience. I recognized him from his picture on the video and from the brochure we had been handed when we arrived. He passed by where we were sitting. A couple of times, I wanted to say hello and tell him about my problem, but couldn't bring myself to do it.

I was very nervous and upset. I didn't think he would understand if I told him about my situation. I let him pass by us. Each time that happened, I pleaded with Fred to make the first move in order to speak with him next time he came near our row. Fred would not do that for me. He said I should be the one to approach Mr. Lindemann for my own personal reasons.

I had another chance to speak to him as he moved past us once again. I knew the time was getting close for him to begin his lecture. I knew inside myself that I had to approach him, but just could not get myself together enough to even speak his name. I was literally shaking in my boots as he went by for the third time. I sat there watching as he passed, wanting to call out his name, but unable to do so.

Mr. Lindemann was about three seats past us when I heard myself call out his name. I did not think he could possibly have heard me, but he did! He turned around and looked directly at me! I don't know how he knew it was me calling out his name, but he did.

His eyes pinpointed me as he walked directly toward me. I stood up, thinking I was going to collapse from fright. I was sure he would think I was insane. He stood right in front of me. I introduced Fred and myself. I don't know how I got the words out of my mouth, but I told him I had a problem that I needed help with; a problem I felt he was going to talk about that evening.

The rest of what I said to him is now a blur to me. The look on his face was one of compassion and caring. He told me he would like to speak with me after the lecture, provided he ended at 10:00 p.m. He reached into his pocket and pulled out one of his cards. He wrote a telephone number on the card. If we did not get a chance to talk after the lecture, I was to call him at 9:00 a.m. California time, the following Tuesday.

Throughout his lecture my heart pounded hard as I anticipated the lecture ending early and my having to face him with my story. My head was literally spinning out of control.

I listened to the majority of Mr. Lindemann's lecture on alien abduction and the involvement of the government. By the time the question and answer period ended, it was 11:00 p.m. I was sad that I would not be able to speak with him, but at the same time, relieved about not having to relate my story.

I began to think that maybe it would be wrong to call him on Tuesday. It took me a whole day to regain my confidence about making that phone call. I repeatedly told myself that if I didn't do it right then, I might never get the help I needed.

My biggest fear was about a possible negative outcome. Perhaps Mr. Lindemann would recommend that I see a psychiatrist. A small part of me felt good about the impending phone call, though, because either way, I would finally get some answers to my problem.

I could hardly wait until Tuesday. At least the phone call would be over with and I would be on the way to getting help; even if it was help from a psychiatrist.

Tuesday morning finally came. The time was 8:58 a.m. I wished we had spoken after the lecture that evening. The apprehension I experienced was even worse than the previous week. I hoped that Mr. Lindemann would not answer his phone.

Where and how would I begin to tell him about my problem? I mentally went through my list of "what if he... suppose this... suppose that" as I nervously dialed the number. Oh my God. Lindemann answered the phone.

I told him who I was and that we had spoken briefly last week at the lecture in Albuquerque. He remembered me and said he had been waiting for my telephone call. He apologized for not being able to talk to me after the lecture. He immediately made me feel comfortable as he continued to speak.

He had me tell my stories about each dream / experience. It was not an easy task for me to re-live each story. Through the tears, I related every event. Mr. Lindemann then put his assistant, Ms. Donna Higbee, on the phone. She questioned me also. We spoke for about two hours before Lindemann asked me if I knew of, or had ever spoken with, Mr. Budd Hopkins.

I told him I had read a book written by Hopkins. I knew he was a researcher and investigator, but I had never spoken to him. Mr. Lindemann said he was going to call Budd Hopkins while he had me on the phone. I was to continue our conversation with Donna until he finished talking to Mr. Hopkins.

After a few minutes, Mr. Lindemann got back on the phone and gave me Mr. Hopkins' phone number. He instructed me to call Hopkins as soon as we finished our conversation. Mr. Lindemann asked me to call him back in a day or two just to see how I was doing. He would also want to know what Hopkins had told me.

I took a deep breath before dialing the number. I felt relieved that Mr. Lindemann had told me I was not insane. He had spoken to me with regard to abductions. He confirmed that alien abductions do happen to many people every day, and that my terrible dreams and experiences were very real. Lindemann's information reinforced what I already knew was happening to my family and me.

I was nervous about calling Mr. Hopkins because I did not know where that phone call would lead me. A lady answered the phone and I thought she might be Mrs. Hopkins. Lindemann had told me that Mrs. Hopkins might answer.

As it turned out, the woman who answered was not Mrs. Hopkins but Karen Michael, Mr. Hopkins' assistant. She informed me that he had spoken to Mr. Lindemann about me. Mr. Hopkins had stepped out of the office and would be right back. Ms. Michael stayed on the line with me while we waited. We discussed the reason for my phone call and she asked me if I would call her that evening.

Mr. Hopkins did not return to his office, but a message was left for him that I had called. Later that evening, I received a return call from him. I was excited to have someone who accepted and understood what I had to tell.

The question I pondered was, "Why me and my family?" I wanted to know exactly who the beings were and where they came from. Why had they chosen us? I experienced fear because they seemed to be hurting us! I had many more questions to ask and find answers for. I wanted all my questions to be answered right then!

THE BEGINNING OF A LIFETIME JOURNEY OF LEARNING

The shocking numbness of verification began to settle in. At last, someone believed my story about the unacceptable and unbelievable happenings that had invaded our lives.

I spent five hours on the telephone that D-Day (as I came to call it) with Mr. Lindermann, Mr. Hopkins, and Ms. Michael. I did not yet know if I understood what was happening to us. It was frightening to come to terms with the reality of other entities who looked so different from what we think of as normal. It was frightening to think of someone who came from another planet or another universe. We humans knew nothing about those things except for what was being reported by other humans.

I was told that the entities did not pick on any one type of human. They were not choosy about who they selected. Rich or poor, race or culture did not enter into it. Age was not a factor either when it came to choosing those they experimented upon.

What were they after in our human bodies? Were we just experimental "mice" to them? Were we being used the way our Earth scientists used mice and monkeys for research? I feared and hated the entities. I knew I had a long learning journey ahead of me.

Each night I prayed because I feared nighttime. I hoped my Higher being (meaning my God) would listen to my prayers and answer by not allowing the beings to enter my world and my children's world. For some reason, my God did not answer that prayer. I continued to ask, "Why me?" and "Why us?"

After speaking briefly with Mr. Hopkins, I decided to act on his recommendation that I continue to talk with Ms. Michael. I was to report my "dreams" to her and she would be there to help me and guide me through each horrifying experience. She would then report back to Mr. Hopkins.

She and Mr. Hopkins would locate a hypnotherapist who lived either in Albuquerque, or the state of New Mexico. They both felt that confronting the awful facts about what transpired during the abductions would help me to begin the healing process I so desperately needed.

At the time, I was not aware that the subconscious mind protects against unwanted information that cannot be accepted by the conscious mind. The subconscious acts as a safety valve, storing the memories until one is ready to accept what has happened.

The next day, Ms. Michael gave me the name of Mr. Wade Valdez, a hypnotherapist located in Santa Fe. She wanted me to contact Mr. Valdez, and recommended I call him immediately. I made the call and gave Mr. Valdez the particulars. We made an appointment for the following Sunday. I was to see him in Santa Fe. I did not know much about the process of hypnotherapy.

When Sunday arrived, I was filled with anticipation. I could not even begin to speculate how hidden information would come out of my subconscious mind.

Mr. Valdez had me watch a video that explained the process of hypnosis. We spoke for some time about the dreams I had been having for several years. After filling out the necessary paper work, Mr. Valdez was ready to begin the process of hypnosis with me.

I was overcome with fear and at the last minute, decided I was not ready to accept whatever information might be forthcoming. We met again the following Sunday.

The following week, I had contact with Ms. Michael, Mr. Lindemann, and his assistant, Donna Higbee. Before I knew it, Sunday had arrived, and Fred and I once again drove to Santa Fe for my appointment with Mr. Valdez.

This time, Mr. Valdez did not give me a chance to think about anything as he took me into his office and sat me down in a black leather chair. He asked me to close my eyes. He reminded me that I was in a safe place. I was instructed to begin counting backwards from one hundred to ninety something.

As I sat in that chair, I began to re-live my first encounters with the ugly beings who had come through the illuminated wall in my bedroom. Because I could not totally relax and therefore free my subconscious to release the information I sought, Mr. Valdez had me visualize a movie theater, watching myself on the screen as the main character. He prompted me with questions as the unbelievable story unfolded and my subconscious released the terrifying sequence of events that had happened that first night.

My sense of timing was off. It seemed as if I had only been sitting in the chair for about ten minutes. In reality, it had been much longer than that. The important points that were retrieved through the first hypnosis session were these:

When the five grey beings came through the illuminated wall, two of them carried small black boxes that resembled small suitcases. One being stood at the foot of the bed while two other beings stood at the left side of my wrapped "elephant legs." One being came up to the left side of the bed by my head, and the other stood by the open bedroom door that led down the hallway to Michelle's and Brian's bedrooms.

The two beings by my legs opened the black boxes while the other being unraveled the large bandages my legs were wrapped in. The two beings by the black boxes took an empty tissue-looking container out of a black bag. The container was eventually filled with a substance from my legs. It appeared to be blood or blood mixed with bone marrow.

The being by my head was doing something to my head and left ear. I could not move my body but I was able to move my head from side to side, trying to stop the being from doing whatever he was trying to do to my head.

I kept trying to look at the being by the bedroom door. I was yelling and telling him that he'd better not go down the hall to Brian's and Michelle's bedrooms. He'd better not dare touch them! He'd better leave them alone! I kept repeating that over and over to him. I thought I was producing a normal vocal sound, hoping someone would hear my screams.

There was a very bright light shining toward the hall that illuminated the being. He did eventually leave my bedroom and went into Michelle's and Brian's bedrooms.

When I looked at the other four beings at the end of the bed by my legs, I saw two of them on the left side of my leg, lift up the clear tissue looking bag. The bag resembled tissue from the inside of a human body. The container held a substance that was red, peach-orange in color. The beings carefully put the container into one of the black bags. As they re-wrapped my legs, I noticed that my legs felt very numb.

When I woke up it was morning.

The scenario was quite traumatic for me and I was left with a lot of emotions to deal with. Mr. Valdez never suggested I go back into that experience through hypnosis to gain more information for myself. However, he questioned me repeatedly on "The White Light" experience.

Mr. Valdez and Ms. Michael suggested that I draw my experiences from the hypnosis sessions and my dreams. "Draw?" I asked myself, "I can't even draw stick people!"

I saw Mr. Valdez a second time and again underwent hypnosis on "The White Light" experience. Not much new information was gained from that session. We discussed the experience, trying to determine the size of the ships I had seen. We went over the experience repeatedly.

On the third, and what was to be the last hypnosis session with Mr. Valdez, I arrived at his home and we spoke about the last two sessions. Mr. Valdez suggested that I see a psychiatrist to take a psychological test called the MMPI test. He knew of a psychiatrist who would administer the test.

During the following week, an appointment was set up with Dr. Carolyn Miller for evaluation before the test. The week after that, Dr. Miller administered the test. The week after the test results were sent to Dr. Miller, another appointment was scheduled with Dr. Miller, Mr. Valdez, Fred, and myself.

The test results showed that I was a normal person. It also showed that I had a problem with anger management. I supposedly, was going to need more counseling than had been earlier assumed.

After the third session with Dr. Miller, my intuition told me that something was not right. I had relied upon my intuition in the past, and it had always been quite accurate.

I'd had counseling from both psychologists and marriage counselors in the past; but the counseling from Dr. Miller felt different somehow, from the way my other sessions had been conducted. Not only were the sessions not helpful to me, but I also felt that a money game might be going on between two of the people involved in my treatment.

I began to think about the sessions, and sought the opinions of psychiatrists and psychologists I had worked for. Ms. Michael and one of my psychologist friends brought up an interesting question: "Who would not have anger as a result of having their life invaded by alien beings that caused such terrifying experiences?"

After carefully thinking through what my friends had told me, I decided to end the sessions with Dr. Miller. I was tired of being used. Mr. Valdez implied that he could no longer work with me since I was not willing to take care of my anger management problem with Dr. Miller. Other professionals had told me they did not see an anger management problem in me.

I found the separation from Mr. Valdez very hurtful because I had trusted him and had opened up to him about my abductions by the alien entities. That was something I had kept secret from everyone except Fred and my children.

Another issue that had been very painful for me was the discussion of my past physical and sexual abuse as a child. I felt that Mr. Valdez and Dr. Miller had not believed me when I told them I was being abducted by alien beings. The experience with Dr. Miller and Mr. Valdez had shattered my belief and trust in them. It took me some time to recover from that.

SOMEONE PLAYING WITH OUR CATS

April, 1994

This event happened approximately the end of April, 1994. Fred was teaching that particular evening at Albuquerque Technical Vocational Institute. Michelle was working at Chuck-E-Cheese Restaurant.

At 8:00 p.m., I decided to go upstairs and take a shower. I checked all the downstairs doors and made sure they were locked. Our bathroom had two separate doors. I closed the inside door where the bathtub was. I was alone in the house that night.

While I was showering, I heard footsteps in the outer part of the bathroom. It sounded as if someone was running into the bathroom. I thought either Michelle or Fred had come home early, but did not hear them calling out my name to let me know they were home.

Someone ran into the closed bathroom door. The door shook. I called out Fred's and Michelle's names but got no

105

response. By then, I was afraid to open the door to see who was in the outer part of the bathroom. I stood there in the tub with the shower running, and listened.

The next noise I heard was something brushing up against the bathroom door. It was as if a person had brushed up against the door with his body. I felt a presence. I was upset that Fred or Michelle might be trying to scare me. I kept calling out their names and asking if they were home, and to please stop trying to scare me. There was no response.

I quietly opened the shower door just enough to let myself out. I left the water running to mask any noise of movement I might make. I wrapped a towel around myself. I tried to lock the bathroom door but was unable to do so. Then I heard the footsteps again and my heart pounded. The steps seemed to be going away from the bathroom door and into the bedroom area.

I very quietly opened the inner bathroom door and hollered as loud as I could: "Who is there? Who is it!?" As I stepped through the door, I almost tripped over one of our Persian cats! It was Puffy!

Puffy's fur was sticking straight out from her body and her back was arched. Her eyes were opened wider than I'd ever seen before. She stood there, paralyzed, frozen in place. Dutchess, our other Persian cat was under the kneehole between the two sinks. She too, was terrified and seemed to be frozen in place. Her large orange eyes warned me to beware.

I instantly slammed the outer bathroom door shut and locked it. I dressed as quickly as I could. I heard footsteps again in the bedroom, then they seemed to just disappear. I was going to open the bathroom window and call for help, but thought I would be brave instead. I was still under the impression that Fred or Michelle was trying to play a mean trick on me. I cautiously unlocked the bathroom door and picked up something to defend myself with just in case it was *not* Fred or Michelle.

I began to search the house, checking to make sure all the doors were locked. I checked all the closets and bedrooms.

No one was in the house! Had it been my imagination? I went back upstairs and checked the outside balcony. No one was there. I went back into the outer bathroom only to find the cats in the same position. I picked up Puffy first. She was shaking violently. When I picked up Dutch I found that she too, was shaking. I held them close to me and could not even imagine what had scared them so badly.

The cats stayed very close and followed me around the house for the rest of the evening until Fred got home. I wondered if one of the Greys had come into the house while I was in the shower.

That thought was confirmed a couple weeks later when I was abducted. A hybrid daughter (whom I have not spoken about yet in this story) told me that she came one night when I was in a closed room. It was not the same room she was in.

She found our "cots" (cats) and tried to play with them, just as she used to play with our Carin Terrier, Queenie, our "dat" (dog). She told me she came and played with Queenie a lot until the dat died. That was when I found out that one of my hybrid daughters had a voice like mine!

A HEALING?

For two years I had gone to the Arthritis Foundation for the swim exercise prescribed for my post polio-syndrome. One day, all that came to a grinding halt. The Foundation had hired new swim therapists. Since I was doing a lot better, a new therapist started new, more strenuous exercises.

Either I was at a point where the post-polio syndrome was getting worse or the exercises were too difficult for my body. After two weeks of the new regimen, I was in severe pain. The doctor recommended that I not go back for at least two weeks, or until the pain went away.

When the pain subsided, I returned to swim therapy. After a week, the pain was back. Again, I took a week off from therapy. The pain seemed to be worse. The doctor put me to bed for a week. I was given shots to make me sleep. This was done to give me relief from the pain.

After three weeks, I felt better, so I returned to swim therapy. I could not make it through the end of the week, even with the simple water exercises the therapists gave me. I decided, after another bout of pain and more medication, to stop going to the Foundation.

Further medical tests determined that post-polio syndrome had deteriorated my body to the point where I would finally end up in a wheel chair. I said "no" to that diagnosis. I wanted to try walking.

Fred began to walk with me every day. The first day I made it as far as our short cul-de-sac. Fred practically had to carry me home. Each week I marked my progress, even if it was just a few footsteps further away from our driveway.

Then a dear friend of mine, Juanita, began to take me on short walks every morning. My right leg seemed to have quit atrophying. Those walks took every bit of energy I had for the day. When we finished walking, the pain would return.

May, 1994

Along with my daily walks, I had to help plan my oldest daughter's wedding. I cut back to every other day on my walking, leaving the days between, pain free. I searched for a place to have a garden wedding. I also helped out with all the other details involved in planning a large, garden wedding. The wedding date was set for June 11, 1994.

During that time, I had much activity with the Sky People. Because I was busy with my daughter's wedding plans, I did not have time to document the experiences. The wedding date was drawing closer and I had purchased a beautiful aqua colored dress to wear. My problem was that I just could not see myself walking down the aisle in the lacy-type white tennis shoes I had found to wear with my dress.

I had purchased the tennis shoes to accommodate the leg brace I was still wearing. I was disappointed about the shoes, but at least they were "prettier" than the ugly ones I had been wearing all along. All I really wanted was to wear normal looking shoes to my daughter's wedding. I thought about how ridiculous it was to get so emotional over a pair of shoes.

The latter part of May arrived, and the wedding festivities began. I was also having experiences with the Sky People. I was able to document what occurred, but not the dates of the occurrences. As it turned out, I was filled with gratitude and joy because of what finally happened.

It was normal for me to feel extreme exhaustion every evening, because of all the wedding plans, anxieties and problems that go along with it. I had retired early since the following day was going to be a much fuller day than I was used to. I decided I needed the extra rest.

That night, my "Friends" (another name my family had given to the beings) came and took Michelle and me. I remember waking up, lying on a familiar table with bright lights around me. For some reason, it seemed as if the table was in a small hallway. My friendly Grey was there with me. He knew about my daughter's wedding. I told him I did not want to wear the brace or my tennis shoes to the wedding. I told him that I wanted to walk down the aisle in normal shoes.

I did not know what the Greys had planned for me that night. I kept moving my head around, looking for Michelle, but could not see her. I knew something harmful was going to happen to her. I became upset because I could not locate her. The other Greys began to surround the table I was lying on. Everything went black.

The next memory I had, was waking up in my own bed. There was a numbness and a crawling sensation in each muscle and nerve in my right leg. This was the leg I wore my brace on. I also felt a "jumping" sensation in that leg. My right leg was very hot.

I realized there was a bright light in my bedroom, even though it was still dark outside. At the foot of the bed stood my friendly Grey. I began to holler in an attempt to wake up Fred.

Somehow, the Grey turned on Fred's lamp on the nightstand and then just left!

When I was finally able to wake Fred, I told him about my right leg. I told him to look at what it was doing. The crawling and jumping sensations continued from the tips of my toes to my hip. Then I remembered about Michelle. I didn't remember them bringing her home with me! I screamed for Fred to go check and see if Michelle was in her bed. He could not move fast enough for me, nor could he understand what I was trying to tell him. It was as if he was in a trance from the look on his face. It took him a few minutes to come fully awake. He slowly got out of bed and went to check on Michelle. When he returned to our room, he reported that she was in bed.

I laid there in bed, unable to move. My body and leg kept jumping. I could still feel the weird crawling sensation and the fiery heat. I asked Fred to keep the leg from jumping and to rub it for me. Rubbing the leg only made it hotter. Fred was able to get my leg to be still, and both of us fell into a deep sleep.

The next morning, I woke up feeling dizzy. I couldn't seem to wake up. I pushed myself up in bed and turned to the side to put my brace on so I could go to the bathroom. As I hung my right leg over the edge of the bed, I felt no pain whatsoever. The leg felt unexplainably weird. I stood up on both legs and there was no pain in my right leg! I took a couple of steps and still, there was no pain! I walked all the way to the bathroom without my brace. No pain! I was able to walk!

By then, Fred was already downstairs in the kitchen making coffee. I went back to the bed, picked up my brace, and carried it down to the kitchen with no pain! I remembered the abduction of the night before. I remembered speaking to my friendly Grey about my wish. Michelle did not remember being taken during the night, but felt strange in the morning.

A few days later, I was lying on a different table and the Greys were doing something to my leg to make it vibrate fast and hard. I do not remember what else they did to my leg, but

I know now that they intended to heal me. I thank them dearly for this, with tears in my eyes.

A miracle had taken place in time for my daughter's wedding. I wore the prettiest "normal" looking shoes for the ceremony. I surprised everyone and had to make up a story about how my leg was suddenly healed.

From that time on, there were only a few occasions when I had to revert back to wearing the brace. That was something I could not even explain to my doctors. They were astonished when I walked into their office carrying my leg brace!

The July 30th experience was documented by Fred Hawker

July 30, 1994

"Gloria and I were relaxing on our upstairs bedroom balcony. The time was between 10:30 and 11:00 p.m. The sky was clear, and we were sitting on lounge chairs watching the beautiful cloud formations go by.

We both noticed a very bright white spot of light in the sky, east, toward the mountains and slightly south. The light appeared for only one or two seconds at most. It appeared to have a strobe effect, but was not repeated. We decided it was not lightening because of its circular shape and the fact that it did not flash elsewhere in the clouds."

August 14, 1994

This dream occurred in the evening after I had been asleep for some time. I awoke twice during the night because our bed was vibrating very hard. Or had it been vibrating? I was lying on my back. My legs were drawn together and extended straight out from my body. I was looking at the white socks I had put on my feet before going to bed. It was as if my body was floating and vibrating over our bed.

The second time this occurred, I awoke again and asked Fred to please quit moving the bed! He was sound asleep and could not be wakened. During both episodes, there was light coming from an unknown source within the bedroom.

THE MOUNTAIN FOREST

August 15, 1994

I woke up lying on a cold table. The small Greys came and helped me sit up. The Greys were about three feet tall. At times, their skin looked a little grayish, but at other times, their skin color appeared to be the same pink as mine. They had large, black, glassy eyes. There seemed to be an air of excitement about something. Some of them were running around frantically. I sensed urgency and tension. I became more frightened.

The Greys stood me up and we walked toward a sliding door that opened in front of us. I had two beings on either side of my body. I was so frightened, it was difficult for me to walk. I did not know where they were taking me. Suddenly, I felt a breeze and saw black as we walked through the door.

I realized we were outside the ship. It was nighttime, and I saw a large, full moon to my left. Suddenly, the area was lit up with bright lights. The lights were coming from somewhere behind me as we walked down a ramp of some sort. The beings would not let me turn my head to look back toward the source of the lights.

We stopped half way down the ramp. I was shaking and very nervous. There were other little Sky People running quickly past us. They were running to the right of where we had stopped on the ramp. I looked at the area the Sky People were running toward. I saw many tall pine trees and some juniper trees. I also saw large and small boulders. I recognized the terrain as mountainous. I saw the beings running sporadically, scattering into the forest, and I too, wanted to run. In my mind I heard the command, "Search and Find."

112

I ran off the ramp. I felt sharp rocks and pine needles sticking into my bare feet. I knew that I had to run, go find, and look; only I did not know what I was supposed to find or why I was running. I felt very uncomfortable, but I knew I had to run with them. I only ran about five or six feet before a sudden restraint stopped me. It was like running into an invisible wall. The two beings who had been escorting me, came to either side of me and held me. At the time, I was unsure as to whether or not I had even been inside a ship.

I tried to run again, but the two beings at my side held on to me even tighter. I tried to move my body, but could not move. I wanted and needed to go wherever they were running to.

The Greys' Searching

As the beings scattered into the forest, I was held back by the two Sky People. They communicated to me that they had to go search and find. When I tried to turn my body to see where we had just come from, I found I could not move - not even my head. I moved my eyes to the far right, then to the far left in an attempt to see something.

113

Out of the corner of my eye, I caught a glimpse of the edge of a smooth, silver-colored disk shape. The bright light that illuminated the area appeared to be coming from behind me. I looked down to see what I was wearing and noticed that I had my long, purple summer nightgown on. The mountain air was not all that cold outside because I was not shivering from the cold that much.

When I awakened the next morning with that memory, for some reason, I was worried about the bears in that area. I remembered that my son, Brian was with the Boy Scouts camping out that night. I also wondered if the Sky People had been looking for my son. Had we been in the same mountains where the Scouts were camping? Did the Sky People go after my son?

Brian was in the Order of the Arrow and was an Eagle Scout. I felt a little safe in knowing that he had been out camping with other scouts and their leaders. So it was possible that the beings had not bothered him last night.

A week after the dream, several bears came down from the Sandia Mountains looking for food. Since we lived very close to the mountains, the bears came into our neighborhood looking for food. I knew, for some reason, before the bears came down, that they would be visiting us. I was not all that surprised when they did, but I am not so sure the bears were actually looking for food, as we had been told by the media.

August 16, 1994

Since having the dream of August 15th, I had been smelling a strong odor of menstrual blood. As I previously said, I no longer menstruated because of the hysterectomy I'd had in 1984, so I determined that it could not be coming from me. No one else in our household smelled the odor. The odor remained with me until the following Friday.

During that time, I pleaded with Fred to help me change the bedroom furniture around. I wanted our bed away from the window, the balcony door, and the east wall. I thought if

114

we did this, I would finally be able to get some much needed rest. We were unable to move the furniture since some of the pieces were too large for their new location in the bedroom.

That evening, after the lights were turned off, I lay in bed staring at the window and the balcony door. I was feeling the strange anxiety I had come to associate with abduction. I knew "they" were coming that night.

I began to pray to Our Lord. I did that whenever the feelings of anxiety came. I asked for protection from "them." I asked the Lord to not let them bother me or my children any more. I asked Him to intercede and answer my prayers. I prayed myself to sleep.

I was awakened by the vibrating bed. I tried to ignore it and tried to close my eyes. I thought I was lying flat on our bed. I opened my eyes when I felt a presence nearby. I was ready to scream at them to go away and leave us alone. I saw shadows moving around the bed. I said to myself "Quit being paranoid, Gloria."

I was so tired, I don't even remember falling asleep.

THE ROSWELL TRIP

August 26, 1994

Fred had an extra day off work and we decided to take a short trip to El Paso, Texas, to visit a sick relative. We had not had any kind of vacation for a very long time. It would be good to get away from the beings and the Sky People, or the Greys, as I had come to call them. I was looking forward to at least four days during which they would not be able to find me.

Michelle also took time off work to go with us. She wanted to take a different route that would go through Roswell, New Mexico. She suggested we visit the UFO Museum there. I was in total agreement, as I thought the museum would have some artifacts from the movies and some "nonsense" stuff. It would be our first visit to the UFO museum.

We left late in the afternoon and arrived in Roswell late that evening. We took our time, making other stops along the way and enjoying the drive. The next morning after breakfast, we toured the small UFO Museum. We heard that there was also another UFO museum in Roswell. We thought we would go look for it as well.

As we toured each room of the small museum, I was surprised to find out that not only New Mexico had a history of UFOs. The rooms were divided into different sections pertaining to UFO history. I found the first room very interesting as I read newspaper articles and letters from around the world talking about UFO sightings and abduction experiences. I also read articles from the *Albuquerque Journal* and the *Albuquerque Tribune* about the "Crashed Saucer in Roswell, New Mexico." Another room housed documentary films about the 1947 Roswell crash and we viewed those, as well.

I was astounded to find a large display of UFO photographs that had been taken by people from all over the world. A couple of those photographs could have been the UFO we had first seen (documented here as "The Large White Light"). The lights circling the middle of the two disks appeared to be the same as those we had seen that Labor Day weekend in 1988. The two snapshots we looked at even showed a large white light on the bottom of the two crafts! They also resembled the two ships I had seen in broad daylight in the canyon at the base of the Sandia Mountains. I stood there in awe, just staring at the two pictures until Fred came and broke my concentration.

We walked into another part of the museum and found a replica of the 1947 Roswell crash site. The replica had a huge impact on me. I saw beings standing beside their ship. Along either side were mannequins dressed as MP's. I was shocked to see the mock-up ET's because those were the beings that had abducted me! There they were, standing right in front of me!

I knew they were only sculpted metal, yet they seemed alive to me. They were the same size, height and thinness of

116

body. I stood there in shock. I nearly fell over from fright. I knew they were not alive, but I kept feeling like they were going to come and take me! I stood there longer than Michelle did, staring into their large, black, glassy eyes. I became mesmerized by the close proximity of those beings.

The thoughts that raced through my mind made my head spin. After awhile, Michelle came and pulled me away from the exhibit and we went back into the room containing snapshots of UFOs. We overheard two men speaking. We thought one of the men was the manager.

We later found out that the other man was a movie producer. We were introduced to the movie producer whose name was Mr. Paul David. He was a researcher-producer from Los Angeles, California. He also had a few actors with him at the museum as well. Mr. David asked us if he could photograph us looking at some of the pictures there at the museum. We both agreed. Michelle and I stood by the large picture Mr. David had selected. Then he asked us to stand by some other pictures as he photographed us again.

We overheard the conversation between the manager and Mr. David regarding the release of a documentary on UFOs for the following year. Michelle and I felt special about having had our pictures taken by the producer. I was rather embarrassed by the attention and quickly left the room to go find Fred.

I entered another room partitioned off with white screens and boards. I heard loud, heavy, erratic breathing. Hearing the breathing disturbed me because it reminded me of my experience with the "Darth Vadar" being. I felt chilled. I needed to find out who or what was breathing that way. Fearfully, I took small steps and followed the sound of the breathing.

As I approached an opening between the dividers, I saw a very large, heavy-set man, sitting on a chair, putting together another display. He was the source of the heavy breathing! I was so relieved, I practically had to pick myself up off the floor.

After my heart quit pounding, I heard the man say he worked with a Mufon Group and was getting ready for a conference.

The UFO Museum proved to be too much for me. It wasn't until we were back in the van that I realized how hard my heart was pounding. I felt dizzy and wanted to vomit. The tears rolled slowly down my face as the emotions caught up with me. I was not ready to explore the other UFO museum that day. We drove by it, however and discovered that it was closed.

August 28, 1994

We spent two days in El Paso visiting my close cousin, Helen, and her husband, John and their family. We visited with a favorite uncle who was dying of cancer and not expected to live much longer.

I pretty much forgot about my experience at the Roswell UFO Museum. I was feeling very safe and happy, knowing the Greys could not find me, since I was not at home. Little did I know that their reach extended far beyond my home territory!

We went back to the motel that night of the 28th. I began to feel insecure, nervous, and anxious. I recognized the emotions but continually told myself that the Greys could not possibly find me since they did not know where I had gone. The room was deathly quiet as Michelle and Fred fell asleep. I began to toss and turn. I could not get to sleep.

I finally did fall asleep but was soon awakened. I was walking down a curved hallway with the beings. We entered a room that held a large, silver tank that stood about three or four feet high. The Grey that brought me into the brightly lit room walked me over to the round tank. The tank felt warm to the touch. On the opposite side of the tank was a slanted slide that went into whatever solution was in the tank. The slide was part of the tank.

The Grey would not let me put my hand into the solution. I wanted to know what kind of solution they were going to put me into. I was so afraid of what they were going

118

to do to me, I began to shake. I planned to hit and fight off each one of them because I was determined they were not going to put me in their tank!

While we stood there, five other Greys came into the room through another door. One Grey was carrying something that I thought he was bringing to me. It did not connect in my head what they were carrying until they got very close to the tank. My God! They were carrying what appeared to be a "little me"!

It was a little girl who looked like me when I was her age! With her light brown hair, her face looked like mine had at the age of three or four years old! They told me that she was defective. She was wearing a uniform that had blue, white, and black stripes on it. It had a checkered appearance.

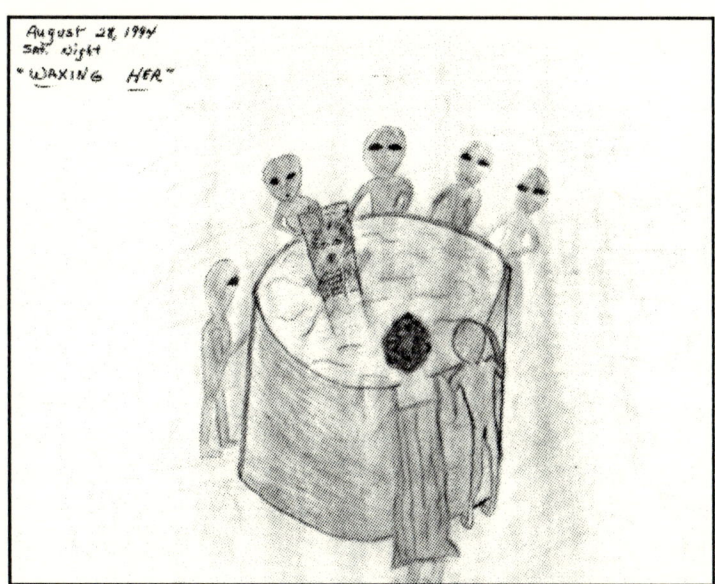

Waxing the Little Hybrid

They laid the quiet little half-breed on the slide. I did not understand the motives of entities who bred humans with themselves to produce offspring like that little girl.

As the other four Greys circled the tub, they told me that she was my girl child. One of the Greys put her on the slide and she screamed loudly as he gently held her in the solution. I felt myself screaming along with her. As I looked at her, she closed her large eyes and raised both small arms up.

She had her mouth open and I stood there watching her tongue quiver in her mouth as she cried. Then I cried with her as they pushed her deeper into the solution. I asked them to stop what they were doing to the little one. The Grey on my right, who had brought me into the room, told me they were "waxing her" because she was defective. They told me that something in her body would dissolve. At the time, I thought they had told me they were going to dissolve her body!

The next morning, I awoke and remembered the event. I was devastated. I just wanted to cry and cry. I did not remember the outcome of what had happened to my little girl child. I did not know if she had survived or not.

The day was ruined for me, but I knew that somehow, I had to keep a smile on my face and look happy. I could not tell anyone but Fred and Michelle about the dream of my girl child who looked like me when I was three or four years old. My heart ached for her and for knowledge of her whereabouts.

September, 1994

The morning after, as Fred was getting out of bed, he found a strange looking substance on his side of the bed. It had a soft, sticky consistency and was a little "puffy." The color was soft peach to light pink with some white interwoven in it. It was perfectly circular, doughnut shaped. We had no idea what it was or where it had come from.

Today, it is no longer soft. Several people have handled it and it broke in half. I showed the substance to Budd Hopkins. He did not know what it could be.

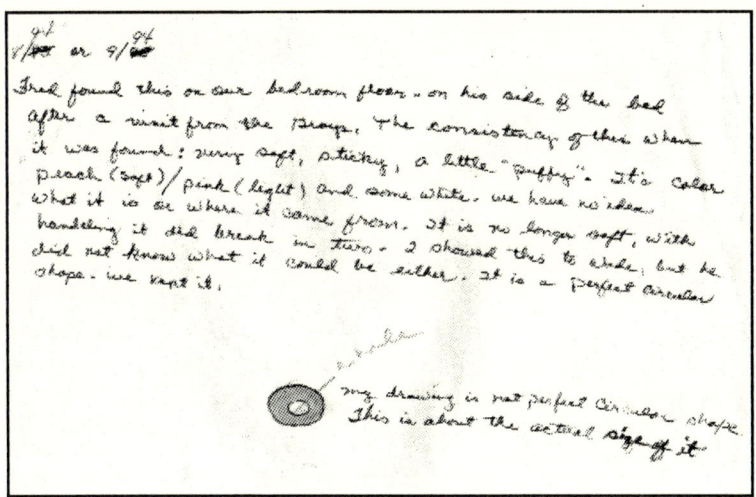

The Orange Doughnut

THE LABORATORY

October, 1994

This experience is still very difficult for me to comprehend and even harder for me to accept, but I have heard many other people's accounts of the same experience so I know my story is valid and has some truth to it. As of this writing, I still do not like to think of this particular abduction, where I was taken, what transpired there, and what I saw.

From reviewing my notes, I know that the following day was horrible for me, and I spoke to Karen Michael about it. However, in its entirety, it is inconceivable to me that it could have happened at all.

As usual, I woke up lying on a table in the room I had become so familiar with. The Grey told me to sit up and I was helped down from the table. He told me to follow him. We went through a door, out into a circular hallway, and began to walk. The hallway was brightly lit and I saw familiar cream colored walls. As we walked in the circular hallway (which I later noted was approximately seven feet from the entrance to the room where the Grey was taking me), two small Hispanic boys came running out of the room we would later enter. The boys seemed to be about four and five years old.

I can still see them in my mind to this day, as they ran by themselves down the circular hallway. They appeared to be more frightened than I was and they were staying very close to each other. They had a scared look on their pudgy baby faces.

The boys had short, black hair and light olive skin. Their eyes were dark brown. One boy was dressed in a red-and-blue-striped, short-sleeved, cotton tee shirt with a white collar. He wore dark pants. The other boy had on a short, blue-and-white-striped tee shirt and dark pants.

The Small Boys

As the boys ran past us, I stopped to turn and look at them. We seemed to be invisible to the small young boys because they did not pay any attention to me or the Grey I was with. One little boy kept telling the other that he was going to tell his mom what the other one had (apparently) done. He repeated it twice to the younger boy and seemed to be quite upset over whatever incident had occurred, they were out of sight.

My Grey told me to continue walking with him. I did. We came to a darkened room and stood in the doorway. I was then told to follow him to the right side of the room. The room was dark except for the right side. Along the wall were large tanks. I remember thinking that they looked like large fish tanks. As I was brought closer to each of the tanks, I saw that they were filled with some kind of solution. There were soft lights on the tops of the tanks.

I turned toward another area of light that seemed to originate in the center of the room. There I saw a young man on a table. He was covered with a blanket. I was told to turn around and look at the tanks. I felt as if I was in a large room and could not understand why it was kept so dark.

As we got closer to the tanks, the Grey began to show me what was in each tank. The sight was unbelievable and sickening. The first tank held human legs. The second, appeared to have human babies floating in it. The babies could also have been hybrid babies. They were in different stages of development. The babies were left in the tanks to mature to a certain age, then removed. The third tank held various human and entity hands and arms.

When I later drew pictures the "fish tanks," I could not finish drawing what I had seen in the last two tanks because of what they contained. Through hypnosis, my subconscious revealed what the last two tanks had held: more body parts and various human and entity heads, floating in the solution. I also saw human organs in the tanks, but was not certain if there were alien organs as well.

I was told that the body parts were used for medical experiments. They were re-grown *onto* humans, entities, and other aliens. Individuals that should have been dead could now be made whole again and able to live.

At the end of the row of tanks, on the back wall, a dim light illuminated various types of medical equipment. I was held back when I began to walk toward that area and the light was turned off.

I was then taken to a table where a human male was sitting up. A much stronger light was turned on, shining directly on the man. I noticed that he had black hair, fair skin, dark eyes and a medium build. He appeared to be of Hispanic or Mexican origin and he was attractive. He was covered with a familiar cream colored blanket similar to the ones I had been covered with before.

Another Grey was standing by the table. I was told that he was the doctor. He pulled off the blanket that covered the man from the neck down. I was shocked to see that the man had no arms or legs. I was told that the man, who was also an abductee, had been involved in an accident on earth. The Greys had been able to rescue him and help him. (I initially thought the entities had been using the man for one of their experiments).

The man had been close to death because of his injuries. The Greys had saved him. Evidently, the man had been presumed dead on Earth. He had been on the ship for a long time, though I was not told how many months or years he had been there. That is what the doctor told me.

The man appeared to be 35 to 40 years old. He had not spoken to me, or perhaps, he was not allowed to speak to me. Apparently, his kidney, liver, spleen, and other organs had been damaged in the accident. The doctor proceeded to show me an area on the left side of the man's body.

I saw what appeared to be several small skin colored "plates" protruding from large slits in the man's body. These were the sites of organ restorations that had been performed on him. The "plates" were about 1 ½ to 2 inches apart, the plates protruded 5 to 6 inches out from the man's body. The plates held many layers of new skin that would be attached and grown as new skin on the man.

The doctor picked up many paper-thin layers of the newly grown skin and let them drop onto the plates. The sight of this greatly disturbed me. To protect my mind, I thought of it as an open book with the pages being thumbed.

The Laboratory

Next I was shown, between the separation of plates, a thin, clear tissue that protected the man's new ribs and internal organs. The doctor showed me his liver and some of the other organs that were being held in by the thin, clear tissue. I am not sure if I was seeing muscle or nerve tissue. I felt sick to my stomach.

I was then able to ask the man if he was in pain. He answered by saying he was not in pain and that his name was Paul. I felt so dizzy and my stomach hurt so badly that I turned around and vomited. This was my reaction to seeing that poor person being used as a medical experiment of the entities and thinking of him having to endure his condition. The room held too much awful information for me to process or absorb and I passed out.

To my dismay, I woke up lying on a table in the darkened room with the "fish tanks." I felt movement at my side and realized I was now lying next to the man. The doctor Grey was standing a few feet away from us. All I could think and imagine was that now I was going to be experimented on in some fashion.

The man turned his head toward my ear and began whispering something to me. I could not quite grasp what he was saying at first. He repeated his message. His name was Paul (Pablo) Pacheco. He told me he was married and that his wife's name was Rosa or Rosita. I was quite certain he told me he lived in Mexico.

He said he wanted to go home and be with his family. Could I find his wife and let her know that he was alive and that maybe one day might be able to return home to them? I was to tell her where I had seen him. (His dialect confirmed that he was Hispanic or from Mexico).

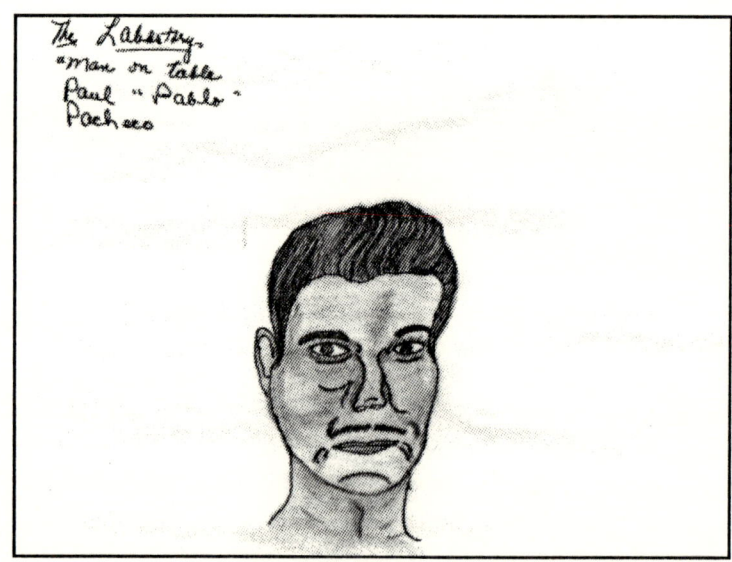

Drawing of Paul Pacheco

I was so frightened I thought my heart was going to pound out of my body. My head spun and I prayed I had gotten the correct information from Paul.

I re-lived this experience in its entirety, through hypnosis. There is a good possibility that the two small Hispanic boys who were running down the circular hallway were Paul's children. To this day, the experience still effect me.

I have searched for the whereabouts of Paul and his wife and children. I hope that one day I find them. I felt as if I had witnessed or participated in some kind of experiment in that laboratory.

On the Thursday evening following the laboratory experience, I was watching a television documentary that aired on "Prime Time." The segment that disturbed me was reminiscent of the laboratory I had been in on the entities' ship. The segment showed Japanese doctors dissecting a Japanese man. The man had his arms and legs cut off. His chest was cut open from the neck to the groin area.

If I am not mistaken, the commentary said that the man was still alive while this was done to him. I believe I understood the commentator to say that Japanese doctors do this to their criminals and that the people of Japan are protesting the procedure. I was very devastated by that segment.

OUT OF BODY?

November, 1994

Before retiring for the evening, I began experiencing symptoms of "something is going to happen." This had been going on for several hours. I tossed and turned, unable to fall asleep, overcome by the strong feelings. Finally, I did sleep, only to awake in an awkward position.

I looked around and down below me. I appeared to be in an operating room. There were six Greys around a silver table below me. On the table lay a woman. I don't remember if they had her covered with a sheet or uncovered and nude. I also don't remember what the Greys were doing to her. They were working on areas of her body. I was observing this from high above, so I had a very good view of what was transpiring down below me.

I remember thinking, "Why did the Greys bring me here to observe a medical procedure?" I did not understand at the time, that I was floating above the scene. I thought I was sitting in some kind of chair or on a bench located above the operating room.

I kept wondering why I had been brought there and who the woman was, and did I know her. I was very curious about her identity and wanted to get a closer view of her. Suddenly, I was projected forward and down toward her. As I drew closer, I realized that the woman looked like me! I was within inches of the woman when I realized the woman was me! How could that be

Through a process I did not understand, I made the transition back into my own body. Something suddenly grabbed me and pulled me into my body. I experienced a sensation of turning around and lying on my back. My eyes were closed - just as the woman's eyes had been closed.

A VISION ABOUT PRISCILLA

November 13, 1994

I awoke on a familiar ship. I was immediately taken to another room I had never been in before. The room was circular and very well lit. I was not familiar with holograms at the time, and did not acquire that knowledge until several years later.

I assumed that I had an assigned Grey. I recognized him because he seemed to be different from the other Greys. My Grey seemed to be more compassionate than the others and would speak to me respectfully. The other Greys spoke telepathically in a demanding or strict manner. My Grey was always at my side during the medical tests or any other test I was put through. When I was directed to go to another room, my Grey was always at my side, to make me feel more comfortable, I guess.

My Grey was walking with me down a hall and we made a left turn into the circular room. The ceiling seemed very high. When we were a few feet into the room, the Grey told me to turn to my left and face the wall. There was nothing unusual about the blank, smooth, cream-colored wall. I was about five feet away from it with the friendly Grey (as I had come to call him) standing beside me.

The lights dimmed a bit and high above me, a silver panel slid open. In the opening was the head of a Grey. He looked at me very sternly and began to speak to me. I heard him giving me some instructions and information.

I listened intently as he told me I was going to meet someone I had known, another human, a young woman. The woman had been with them for some time and was now working with them. It was her wish that I locate her parents and tell them where she was and that she was alive. She could not go back down to Earth because of some kind of problem there regarding our government.

I did not fully remember the story of the young woman who had chosen to stay with the entities and live out her life working with them.

By the same door through which we had come, the young woman and another Grey entered the room. She was beautiful, with fair skin, black hair, and a small build. She was about my height, five feet, two inches tall, and appeared to be in her late twenties or early thirties. The Grey told me her name was Priscilla. I think her last name was Chavez.

The Grey told me that Pricilla lived in the same area of the earth as I do. Immediately after her entrance into the room, I was shown a hologram of her parents. I was also given their first names, though to this day, I cannot remember their names. I was able to see them quite clearly, but also able to look right through them. The hologram was to the left of where I stood.

I was then told about the government men who were searching for Priscilla. I was shown holograms of three government men to the right of where I was standing. I was also told that I would have an encounter with the government men. Two of the men were of medium build. The third was a large, heavy-set man with black hair and dark skin. The other two were fair skinned. The Grey told me to avoid these men and give them no information about Priscilla. I was to say that I had never seen her, nor did I know her.

When it was time for Priscilla to go, she walked close to me. Without saying a word, she handed me something. I was told that her parents would recognize it as being hers. After she gave me the item, she closed my hand tightly over it. As she turned to leave the room, she swung her head of beautiful shiny black hair.

I remember being awake in my darkened bedroom, standing between the window and the balcony door, facing the west wall. I did not know why my right hand was in such pain until the memory came back. I was clutching the item Priscilla had given me so tightly that my long nails were digging deeply into the palm of my hand. I knew I had to hide the item somewhere and that I had to do it right then.

On Fred's nightstand, there was a clear blue glass bowl filled with potpourri. I thought this would be a good hiding place until morning. Then I would find a safer place for it. I looked at the item before placing it in the bowl. It appeared to be a beautiful cameo that was missing its chain. I reached down deep into the bowl and buried it in the potpourri, making sure it was covered.

I went back to bed but felt that a presence was still with me. The back of the lower part of my head was extremely painful. It was a pinpoint, sharp pain that went deep into my head. I felt nauseous and I thought I had just awakened. But something was different with me and I felt that I had not been in bed at all. I had a sensation of floating.

I woke Fred up and asked him if I had been in bed all night. I don't know what kind of response I was expecting from someone who had been asleep the whole time. I then told him that I felt as if I had not been in bed all night. Then, it was as if someone put me into a deep sleep.

Waking up a few hours later, I was barely able to get out of bed. I felt as if I had been hit hard by a freight train. I was dizzy and weak. I had totally forgotten about the abduction of the night before. I had intense pain on the lower left part of my head. It throbbed so badly that the pain seemed localized in just that one spot on my head. The pain was deep in my head.

Later that morning, I remembered the abduction of the night before. I remembered the experience but the names were not clear to me. I remembered the young woman with the beautiful black shiny hair, yet I could not remember if her name was Patricia or Priscilla. I remembered everyone's face except hers. I also remembered that I was supposed to give her parents a message. To this day, I still recall what the government men looked like.

I remember thinking to myself, "Yeah, right! Who is going to believe this story, and where do I begin looking for the woman's parents? What if the experience was not real?" I had many questions. The story itself seemed unbelievable to me. Then suddenly, I remembered hiding something the woman had given me. That would prove my story. I looked at my hand. The nail imprints from the night before were still there. The palm of my hand was still red, as if I had held onto something very tightly.

I rushed to the bedroom and dug in the bowl of potpourri. I knew I had put her cameo into that bowl. I dug through the potpourri, moving it around and found…nothing. I took the bowl into the bathroom and emptied it out on the counter. There was nothing in the bowl but potpourri. I began checking every bowl, dish, and box in the house. I never did find that beautiful cameo.

Over the years, I have located two ladies that looked like the mother of Patricia/Priscilla. One lady goes to our church. The other was in the grocery store where I shop. How could I approach those mothers to find out if they had a missing daughter? And how was I going to tell them that I had seen their daughter? I don't think they would be able to comprehend the story I had to tell them, and to deal with the emotions they would experience, knowing the true whereabouts of their daughter.

I had thought the episode of the hologram of government men was a test or a lie from the entities until February 27, 1997.

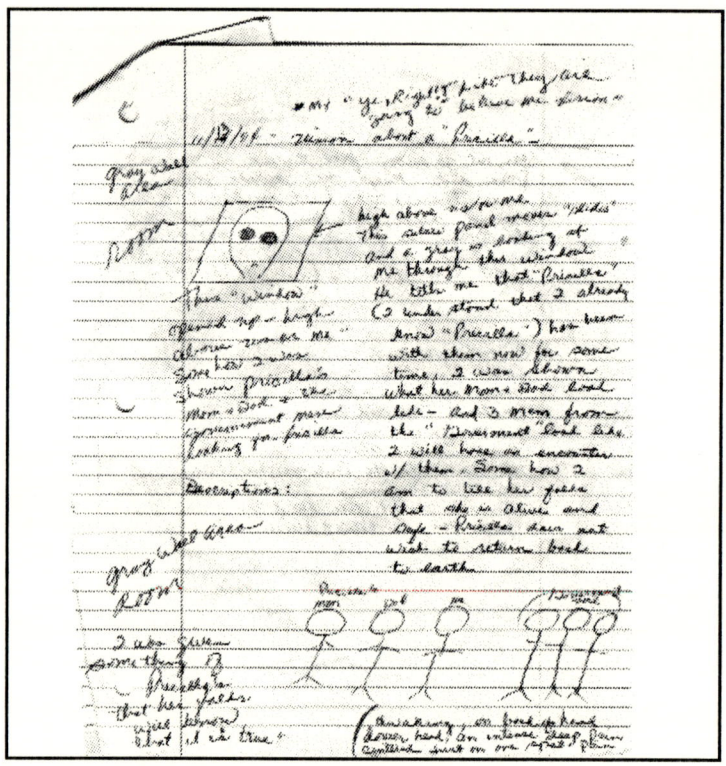

A Diagram of this Experience of Priscilla

I was flying to New York. On the flight from Albuquerque, New Mexico to Houston, Texas, a man who looked very familiar was seated next to me. He was a large man with dark skin, black hair and very dark eyes. He was dressed in a dark brown suit, similar to the one he wore in the hologram. I was sure I had met him somewhere before, but could not figure out when or where.

We began a conversation. He told me he worked for the government at the Pentagon in Washington, DC. He lived in Virginia. He had been visiting Sandia Base and Los Alamos National Laboratories.

Was this just a coincidence, or was this the government man in the hologram that I was supposed to encounter at some point in time? The man looked very much like the one I had seen in the hologram.

THE FRIENDLY GREY

Fall, 1994

I was curious whether or not the Greys had names for themselves. I had begun to recognize a particular Grey who seemed to be with me a good deal of the time. I finally asked him what his name was and he told me.

I later recalled his name as "Raytheon," although that is not exactly the name he gave me. However, Raytheon is similar, and has stuck in my memory as the name of my friendly Grey.

THE FAMILY

November 18, 1994

I awakened in the small familiar room. Raytheon, my friendly Grey, was present, standing by the table I was lying on. Raytheon told me to get up because he had to take me someplace. We went out the door to a short hallway and into a very large, round room. There were many people sitting on a circular bench that seemed to be attached to the wall. Most of the people appeared to be dressed in nighttime attire. To the far right of the circular room were some tables. There were people standing around two or three small tables.

The Mother and Daughter I spoke with

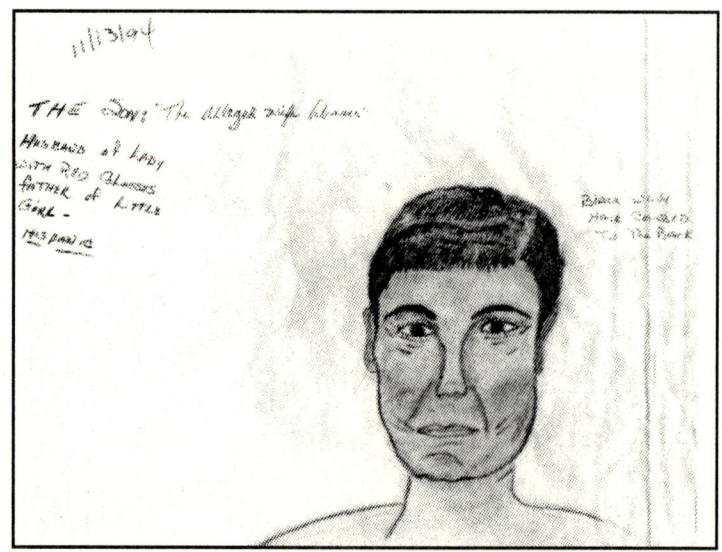

The Husband

The Grandparents

Raytheon led me toward a lady who was holding a small girl in her arms. The little girl was approximately six years old and was more irritable than her mother. She was fearful, restless and over-tired and wanted to go home. Raytheon introduced me to the mother and the little girl. He told me that the man and the two younger boys standing against the wall were her abusive husband and their two sons. The husband had been verbally and physically abusive to his wife. The grandmother and grandfather of the children were also standing next to the boys' father. I was told their names but the memory of their names has not stayed with me.

The little girl began to fidget and complain that she was hungry. Raytheon saw this and asked the mother if he could bring her something to eat. The mother said yes. Raytheon returned a few minutes later with a cup-like spoon and a small, narrow round bowl. The bowl contained a substance that looked like over-cooked oatmeal. It was light brown, but a little darker than oatmeal.

The mother sat the little girl down at a table and told her to eat. The little girl dug the cup-like spoon into the bowl. The substance seemed to be extremely sticky as she pulled it toward her mouth. Evidently, it did not taste very good because the little girl complained about it and did not want to eat it.

I spoke with the mother. She told me that she and her family were frightened and did not want to be there. We asked each other's names, but again, immediately after arriving home, I did not remember hers or any of the family's names. I only remembered what they looked like.

Twice, I thought I had found that family in Albuquerque. I had seen a small girl on TV in 1997 on a local news program, but was unable to obtain her name. On another family outing, I walked into a metaphysical bookstore where the mother worked. We both recognized each other and I thought that I had found the family. I met with the mother twice and we shared pictures. Her daughter could have been the small girl but I felt that her age was not correct at the time. The mother said the pictures I had drawn resembled all of her family, including the grandmother and grandfather.

It is still questionable as to whether or not this was the family I had met on the ship. I felt more certain about the girl I had seen on TV.

She could have been the small girl from the ship, though she would have been about 1 ½ years older at the time of the news broadcast.

HER NAME IS WINSHA

November 24, 1994

I was lying in bed, restlessly tossing and turning, unable to get to sleep. I had become quite weary and would have welcomed some much- needed, restful sleep. As I gazed out the east bedroom window, looking at the night sky and stars, my attention was suddenly drawn to a sharp flash of white light in the southeastern sky.

I quickly jumped out of bed and went to the window to look southeast of the Sandia Mountains. I saw something that produced a colored, pulsating light. In order to get a better look at the object, I got out my binoculars so I could make a comparison between the stars, the planets, and the object.

What I was looking at was definitely not a star or planet but appeared to be a round object. The pulsating, colored lights coming from it were very different from any of the stars or planets. I opened the balcony door to get a better look. At that point, I began to feel more nervous and I became shaky.

I didn't like the way I was feeling, so I stepped back inside the bedroom. I made certain the door was shut tightly and locked. Fred stirred in his sleep and was almost awake when I returned to bed. I grabbed hold of his body and covered my head with a pillow. I had a feeling of uncertainty and tried to doze off. I had my eyes tightly closed.

I then heard a woman's voice, and at the same time, a fluttering noise coming from the east bedroom wall. The noise was familiar to me. I had come to associate that fluttering with the arrival of "them." The beings were in my bedroom!

I again heard the woman's voice saying, "Gloria... Gloria, is this you?" I was stricken with fear. I did not hear the rest of her sentence. Suddenly, Fred's whole body jumped hard on the bed. I tried nudging him and called out for him to wake up, but he would not wake up. Fred had a bad cold and had taken medication to help him get over the cold.

I cautiously slipped the pillow off my head to see what was going on. I didn't notice anything unusual, but I felt the presence of someone standing there in our bedroom. Even though I could not see the entity, I heard movement, as if someone was walking. I lay in bed, looking around the room.

Suddenly, it felt as if someone was standing on the end of the bed. The mattress was indented (just as it had been the week before) as if someone was standing or sitting on the mattress! I began to take deep breaths to slow my frantic breathing. It felt as if the entity was walking toward me on the mattress! I fell asleep.

I awoke on board the ship. I was walking with Raytheon down a hallway into a room. I felt very drugged as we walked toward a silver- colored half wall. From my vantage point, I noticed a large round metal tube protruding out of the floor on the other side of the wall. I heard a sound like air pushing something out of the tube. In the tube, there appeared a large glass case with a small person inside.

Winsha

I recognized the person immediately! It was the little girl child I had met - my little hybrid daughter! Raytheon had told me she was conceived several years ago when they had taken eggs from my body. I was able to see her very close up. She had a blank look on her face. The face looked soft and delicate, so sweet, but not happy. She had tiny, thin lips (just as I'd had as a child). She looked half human and half alien with her pear-shaped face and large, almond-shaped eyes.

138

I was ecstatic! I kept repeating to myself, "She is alive! She is alive!" The last time I had seen her, the beings were putting her into the large tank of solution. Since then, I had believed they let her die in there.

As I looked at my daughter, I realized there was something unusual about her eyes. As she stared out at me, I cried out to myself, "She has irises! Blue irises!" She had the same thin, light brown, straight hair that I'd had as a child.

Inside the glass tube, her head was held by a silver metal band. I also noticed the same silver metal bands across her chest, lower abdomen and hips. Raytheon told me she was in pain. The beings took her out of the transport device and took her to the large silver tank with warm liquid in it. After her treatment, I was allowed to hold her. Then I was taken away.

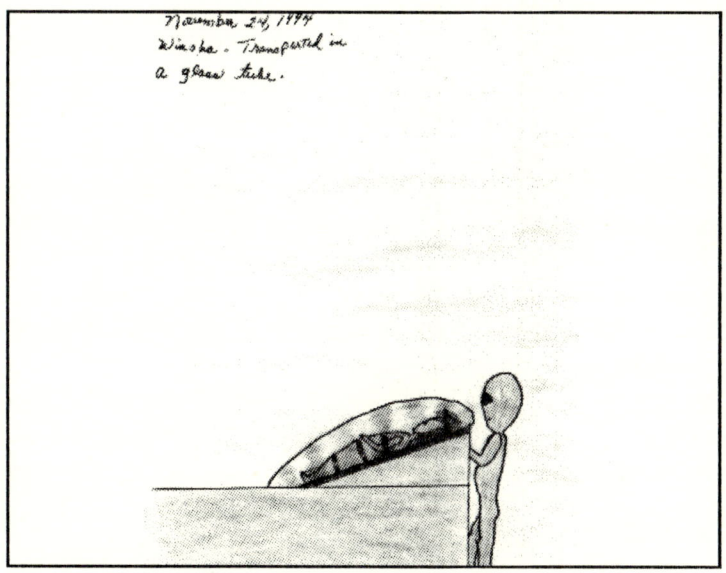

Winsha Transported in Glass Tube

Evidently, when they took me away from Winsha (my hybrid daughter), they performed medical work on me. I had no memory of them doing such, but the next morning, I had a spot on my lower spine that was very painful. It was as if I had been stuck with large needles. The pain radiated in a circle on my lower spine. I again felt as if I'd been hit by a brick wall. My thighs had been pulled so far apart, I felt like a split pea. I was very confused and disoriented.

December 15, 1994

I had little knowledge at the time, of how the beings brought me into our bedroom when an abduction occurred. I thought the Greys actually opened the balcony door to remove me from the bedroom, then returned me to my bed in the same fashion.

How wrong I was! I found out, in the early morning hours of December 15th, exactly *how* this is accomplished. To this day, I still do not understand the process they use, though I have experienced it many times.

I woke up outside that chilly morning, looking straight up into the dark sky. I was lying flat with no device under my body for support. I was floating in the air! I could not figure out how I had gotten into that predicament, lying straight and stiff, unable to move my body, and floating in the air with nothing to support me. I kept waiting to hit the wood floor of our balcony, but I never fell to the floor.

I thought I was alone out there until I felt strangely familiar cold hands touch my head, then my shoulders. I was fully awake, but felt as if I was dreaming. I thought I could not possibly be having a real experience like that. Then it happened. I was allowed to see my feet go *through* my closed bedroom window. Then my body just seemed to float *through* the closed window!

For a moment, the Grey put me to sleep, but immediately woke me up again. Why hadn't the glass broken when my feet went through the closed window? Half my body was still outside! The Grey who was standing behind me, gently pushed me as I floated through to the inside of my bedroom. He was right behind me all the time! As we entered my bedroom, light from an unknown source filled the room. I

December 15, 1994
"Going Through The
Bedroom Window"

Gloria going through the Closed Window

was floated to my disheveled bed as blankets and sheets were pulled down to the end of the bed.

Fred was asleep on his right side with his left leg crossed over his right leg. I was put into the bed by floating downward onto it. I had seen this procedure done to me once before. I do not know if I requested they show me this or if they thought I needed to know this.

Since that experience, I have walked through my bedroom wall without injury after being brought home from an abduction. I often wondered, over the years, why my body always felt as if it had hit a wall, the day after an abduction. Now I knew! The physical effect lasted about a day and a half.

Foolishly, I thought I could go through walls and windows on my own. I tried it on several different occasions and discovered that I cannot do this without the help of the beings.

I finally did find out how they go through walls. Around their waist is a magical little black box. A person has to be within range of a few inches for the process to work, otherwise, you cannot float through your windows or walk through walls. The being must be along side of you!

MY SHADOW

February 20, 1995

If my memory is correct, January of 1995 had been somewhat free of the nighttime visitors. I would hear extra noises in the house, especially during the day or when I was home alone. My investigations never produced anyone else in the house but myself.

For example, I would hear doorknobs turning or footsteps, as if someone had come in through the front door. The inside doors would slam or open and close (usually, the upstairs bedroom door). I would hear the stairs creak as if someone was walking down the stairs. I would run to look, but see no one.

I would hear footsteps on the linoleum floor in the kitchen, knocks on the windows and walls. I would hear drawers open and close and papers being moved around as well as the clinking of utensils. I would hear my name called out, both at home when I was alone, and while driving in the car. All this was just the beginning of the paranormal events I would eventually have to get used to living with.

On Monday morning, February 20th, I was cleaning the house. No one else was home but me. Around mid-morning, I sensed a presence in the house with me. I guess it had decided to come see what I do on Mondays. Maybe it thought Monday was an exciting day for me since I cleaned house that day!

Every room I went into, every step I took, was marked by the presence behind me. That particular Monday, I was going to give the place a thorough cleaning and did not expect to finish until around 8:00 p.m. I was downstairs in the early afternoon, vacuuming the living room furniture. My back was toward the front room window. I had the feeling that someone had walked up to the window and was watching me clean the room.

I quickly turned around to look and the presence was even stronger. I looked toward the north window and saw no one. Then I turned my body to look at the east window. What I saw seemed to be moving in slow motion. "It" was just standing there, not moving, with its hands outstretched! It was large and different looking, and its eyes stared directly into mine, a stare that would not let go. He was a lot taller than any of the Greys I had seen before. His skin appeared to be a different color than the Greys'. He was brown.

I stood there, unable to move. I thought he was a Grey who had done something to cover his body and make it look brown, as if he was a shadow. The brown shadow then turned to his left and ran or floated through the east wall of the room! Right through the wall, in broad daylight!

I had originally described him as having a large head and very long arms, his height taller than the Greys. But there

My Shadow

was something very different about his eyes that I could not describe. They seemed to be yellow or orange, with dark slits in them. My God, maybe he had been a human snake that had come up out of the ground! I did not understand what I had seen. I was in great shock.

I don't know what transpired during the next few hours that Monday afternoon. Suddenly, it was 4:00 p.m. and the entire house had been cleaned! The kitchen floor had been washed, windows cleaned, everything in its proper place.

I had expected to finish cleaning at 8:00 that evening. The last thing I remembered was having just started to clean the living room. Yet, four hours ahead of schedule, the entire house was now cleaned! I don't know what happened that day.

THE OFFICE

February 21, 1995

The previous day was still questionable in my mind. I did not understand how I had cleaned so quickly. I could not account for the missing hours. How had my house gotten clean without expending any energy on my part? I asked myself who exactly, was the "brown dude" and where had he come from? Had he been sent to help me clean house yesterday?

Another abductee friend told me that the being I had seen was a "Mahogany," and that she had seen them too. Evidently, they are a different type of alien. I remember thinking, "Now I have to learn that there are entities other than the Greys!"

Bright and early that morning, I made my way to the office. At my desk, I worked eagerly and got a lot accomplished by 11:00 a.m. Fred left the office to go check on our employees at Honeywell, a large corporation we had a contract with.

There was a small oak bookcase to the left of my desk. I turned my swivel chair to the left and began to take care of some paperwork I had recently put there. I felt a presence in the room, and a strong feeling that someone was watching me. I chalked it up to being edgy after the previous day's incident.

Out of the corner of my eye, I caught a glimpse of something. I swiveled my chair around to face the large file cabinets that separated the computer work area from the front office. I found myself staring at the same brown entity I had encountered at home the day before!

He saw me looking at him, and once again, our eyes locked. He turned and ran behind the file cabinets. I quickly got up from the chair and ran in the direction he'd gone. When I got there, he'd simply vanished! I didn't know where he was. I thought he must have gone through the wall again.

I became very frightened. My heart pounded in my chest. Then I saw just it's eyes. Except for the strange, large eyes (yellow-orange with dark slits in them), the entity was faceless. Yesterday, I had thought it was gone for good, yet, here it was again! Who was he and what did "it" want?

Nothing was amiss in the office and I did not see him any more that day. I welcomed our customers and tried to

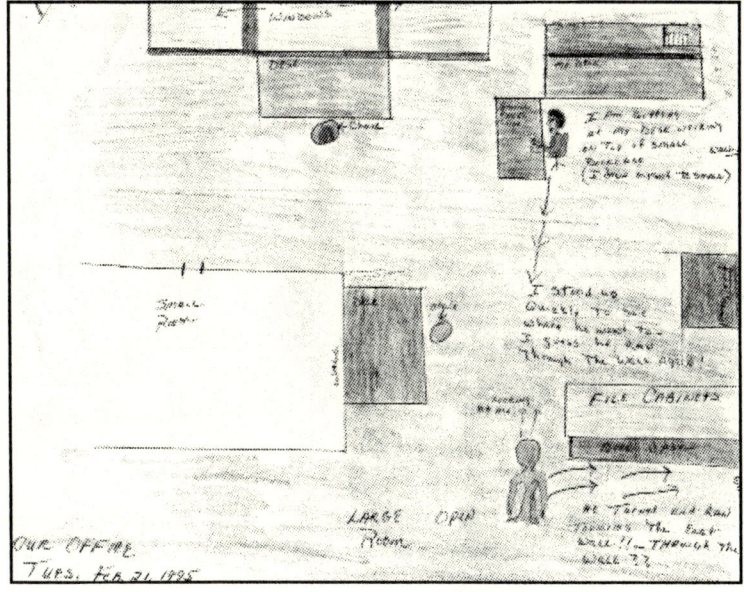

My Shadow at The Office

detain them so I would not have to be alone. Fred returned later that afternoon.

EAR PAIN AND IMPLANTS

February 27, 1995

An unexplained noise woke me during the night. I could not identify the sound. It was a funny "humming" noise that lasted ten to twenty seconds. I was laying on my left side. The sound seemed to be coming from around or behind my head. There was a very sharp pain in my right ear. Fully awake at that point, I heard the sound again.

When I had first awakened, it felt as if something was being done to my ear. The ear felt as if it was on fire. The pain extended down to the lower right side of my face. This did not feel like an earache.

I attempted to locate the source of the sound. I noticed that there was no one at my side of the bed. I moved my body toward Fred. He was laying on his left side so I pushed my body up against his backside in an attempt to get away from whoever was working on my ear and face. I held my hand over my ear.

There is a place on my spine, in my lower back, where I have extra bone growth that causes me pain. That night, I felt a finger poke at that area more than once. It was a narrow finger with no noticeable fingernail.

I spoke out loudly to wake up Fred. I told him what was happening, and about the awful pain in my ear. He mumbled something that I could not understand.

I rolled over quickly to see who kept poking at my back, and was surprised to discover that no one was there! I turned onto my left side and moved even closer to Fred, nearly pushing him out of the bed. I don't think I slept the rest of the night because of the constant, sharp pain in my ear. At times, the right side of my face felt as if it would burst open.

146

When sunrise came at 6:00 a.m., Fred finally woke up. I asked him why he had not stayed awake when I'd tried three times to talk to him during the night. He said he did not remember me waking him up to tell him about the pain in my ear or the finger poking at my back. I told him I had almost pushed him off the bed by clinging to his body so tightly. He did not remember anything!

Fred asked me why I hadn't gotten up to take medicine for my ear pain. I told him I was too frightened to get out of bed, even with the light on. I was too afraid of what might happen to me.

The intense ear pain stayed with me all day. Several times during the day, my ear and face felt as if they would explode. When Fred got home from work that evening, he suggested I call Karen. At the time, I thought maybe there was a problem with my ear and face, other than some entity messing around. Moving my jaw made it hurt worse. I could not speak without experiencing sharp pain, even if I opened my mouth very little.

I promised Fred that I would call Karen when I felt better. I was on pain medication but it was not helping at all. I also began shaking uncontrollably during the day.

When nighttime came, I doubled up on the medication. I planned to go to the doctor the next day if things were not better. Somehow, I got through the night and was actually able to sleep.

To my surprise, I woke up feeling refreshed the next morning. The pain had dissipated. The shaking was also gone, but I soon discovered large sores on my tongue that hurt just as badly as the pain in my ears had. I could not talk or eat. I also had a severe nosebleed. It was a long time before the blood quit flowing. My nose bled off and on all day.

This experience brought back a more recent memory of being on the entities' ship. I had a similar experience, but this time, I was half awake as I watched them put something into my ear. I remembered having the same terrible pain, body shakes and nosebleeds. I remember trying to get away from them by moving my body or turning my head back and forth. Had I been abducted on the 27th without being aware of it?

My conversation with Karen confirmed the possibility that the Greys had placed an implant in my ear and nose. I believe it happened when the Grey put his face into my face. That was when I think they put something into my left ear. From that time on, I continually felt a crawling sensation in my ear. Also, the ear began to hurt a lot after that.

Many times when I was taken by the entities, I would awaken with a sore throat and no voice. It would feel as if I had been screaming a lot. I compared it to the way I felt after hollering and screaming at one of the kids' soccer or football games.

All the next day, my throat would be scratchy and my voice would be hoarse. I had assumed my throat and voice were this way from the games I attended with my children. The thing that puzzled me was the two-year period my son did not play sports after his accident. I would still wake-up hoarse, with a scratchy, sore throat. This suggested to me that I must have screamed and hollered while being abducted.

A WHITE IMPLANT?

February, 1995

I woke up later than usual that morning. I remember being rushed to eat breakfast and get dressed for work. I had an important meeting scheduled in about 1 ½ hours, and I needed to finish preparing for it. The meeting was all I could think about.

I'd had a toothache since the day before, in the upper left side of my mouth. At least, I thought it was a toothache. It actually felt as if there were food particles stuck between my teeth. At work I had used sewing thread, paper, my fingernail, anything I could find, to try to dig out the stuck food. As a result, the gum had become inflamed and the food particles were still in there.

When I brushed my teeth that morning, I used the toothbrush bristles to try to dislodge the food particles. That did not work, so I flossed my teeth, hoping to dislodge whatever was stuck back there. Flossing did not help either.

I finally gave up and went downstairs, purse in hand, ready to leave for the office. As I rubbed my tongue over the tooth and the inflamed gum, I felt something protruding from between the teeth. I began to dig at the object with my fingernails, but could not retrieve it.

Using my nails as tweezers, I grabbed hold of the food particle and tugged, wondering what in the world could be stuck so tightly between my teeth. As I pulled, I felt intense pain. The object slowly came out. .I felt an "exploding" sensation and thought for sure the left side of my teeth had been ripped apart in my mouth. I was certain my face had blown-up as well.

I stood there, waiting for the taste of blood and the sensation of loose teeth in my mouth. I waited for blood and skin to drop from my face. Nothing like that happened. I was still holding onto what I had pulled out of my mouth.

I was astonished to see what I held between my fingers! It was a white object about half an inch long. It was small and round. I stood there in pain, shocked at what I saw. I did not realize what I had just pulled out of my mouth had actually caused the "exploding" sensation. My first thought was that a filling had come out, but I have never had any white fillings. I have only a few fillings in my teeth, and they are all gray.

I pushed down on the object with my thumb and forefinger. The object was flexible. I pushed on it a couple of times to see if it would break, but it did not. The object suddenly became stiff, then instantly very rigid.

I thought I should go to the dentist and just skip the meeting. In the end, I chose the meeting over the dentist since it was so close to meeting time. I decided I would call the dentist after the meeting was over.

The telephone rang. I started not to answer it because I was now running very late, but picked it up anyway. Not wanting to lose the white object, I grabbed a blue napkin and laid the white object on it.

The phone call was lengthy and important. As I hung up the phone, I realized that I was going to be late. The pain in my mouth was intense. The white object, forgotten. I suddenly had a very bad toothache. I saw the crumbled blue napkin on the kitchen counter and, without thinking, tossed it into the trash compactor. I grabbed my purse, ran out to the car, and left for the office.

Once the meeting was over, I felt a lot calmer but my mouth was still painful. Abruptly, I remembered what had come out of my mouth that morning. I also remembered wrapping the object in a blue napkin, then later, throwing it into the trash compactor. I wanted to go home immediately and retrieve it, but could not leave the office. I prayed that Fred or Michelle would not go home for lunch and turn on the trash compactor.

That evening, I drove home from work faster than usual. When I got home, I ran directly to the kitchen and looked in the trash compactor. The blue napkin was not there. I got a large plastic bag and emptied the garbage piece by piece, examining each crumpled paper and piece of trash. The blue napkin simply was not there! I looked all around the inside of the compactor. No blue napkin. I checked all the places I thought I might have put the napkin, but could not find the white object or the blue napkin.

When Fred and Michelle came home, I questioned them about the trash compactor. Neither of them had been home during the day. I told Fred what had happened and what had come out of my mouth. He too, went through the trash and the entire kitchen, as I had done. We could not locate the object or the blue napkin. We swept the kitchen floor with our hands, in hopes of finding the white object. It was never found.

The pain had lessened somewhat during the day. By the next morning, it was not very bad at all; but the gum was swollen and quite red. I examined the gum where the object had come out and saw dried blood. There also seemed to be a hole in my gum.

I wondered if the Greys or the other entity (who looked like a snake) had taken me and done this to me. How could I explain the whole scenario to my dentist? I decided there was no way I could explain my mouth problem or the abductions to my dentist!

My mouth hurt constantly every day for two and a half weeks after the object came out from between my teeth. I could see a definite hole in my gum where the object had been. The area soon healed over, and only a small, painful, round red circle was left.

Once the initial pain cleared up, I only experienced pain when I ate chili, spicy food, or stove-hot meals. The pain was concentrated in the red circle and would go deep into the gum and mouth. The pain stayed with me for six to eight weeks afterward. Eventually, I thought I had better have the dentist look at the area. I was due to have my teeth cleaned, so I had a valid reason to go in.

I asked the dentist to check for a lost filling from that particular tooth. He said no fillings had come out and that I had no fillings in or near that molar. He questioned me about what I had found and the reaction I'd had to the object that had come out of my mouth. He saw what appeared to be a hole in the gum. He took x-rays of the area and said that he was stumped. The gum was still very inflamed.

I described what the object had looked like. I also told him that it had been flexible, but became rigid after playing with it. My dentist did not know what had come out of my mouth, and the x-rays were not helpful. They showed that my mouth seemed to be healing from a hole or other dental work that had been done on me.

I told him that I had not been to another dentist and had no reason to go to another dentist. He also had his assistant examine my mouth as well. When I left his office, he was very curious and mystified about the whole situation. He told me to contact him as soon as possible if this ever happened to me again.

MEETING THE ROWLISONS

Spring, 1995

Sometime around March of 1995, Karen asked if I knew of a support group or Mufon group in Albuquerque. I did not know what Mufon was about at the time, but Michelle remembered picking up a newsletter about Mufon when we were at the UFO Museum in Roswell. She brought me the newsletter. It was a roster of people in Albuquerque who were leaders of the Mufon group.

I contacted the first name on the newsletter but no one answered the phone. The Rowlisons name was next. I spoke with Mary Rowlison. I found it very difficult to tell my story of alien abduction over the phone. We set up an appointment for an interview the following Sunday.

The Rowlisons came to my home to interview me and get to know me. They asked if I had been documenting all my experiences. I shared what documentation I had with them on that first visit. They apparently believed my story.

They said they knew of other abductees and would eventually introduce me to many whom they knew. The Rowlisons said they would keep me safe under their wings.

I was in contact with Mary Rowlison at least twice a week, if not more, during the friendship that eventually went sour. An agreement was made between Mary, Ray and myself, that I would turn over current copies of my documentation to them --- for safety reasons. They knew of abductee's documentations that had disappeared. This way, they would be helping me by always having an extra copy.

As time went by, I began to think that I shared a close relationship with the Rowlisons. I soon found out how deceiving the relationship was. Communication was shared with Mrs. Rowlison and she gave me advice.

At the Rowlison's holiday parties, I met a couple of other abductees. However, only two out of the three I met would share their own experiences. I met a married couple who were close friends of the Rowlisons. I was uncertain at the time whether or not the couple were indeed, abductees. They would not share their experiences. Instead, they showed a video of a night-sighting of a craft.

The other woman I met, who seemed to be about my age, shared very little with me. However, as our friendship grew, the trust and honesty between us helped us to be more open with each other. It took my new friend awhile to make contact with me. That finally happened toward the end of my relationship with the Rowlisons.

The reason for the lack of contact was given by Mary. We were to remain separated from one another "for our own good." These were the instructions I was given by Mary Rowlison. The three of us saw each other at gatherings at Rowlison's home. I was also invited to local restaurants with the Rowlisons and a few of their special UFO friends. My lady friend was excluded but the other married couple would be there. These were the only communications I was allowed to have with any UFO-related people.

The Rowlisons mentioned many important people in the UFO field as being good friends of theirs. They also claimed to visit those people. I was told I would soon meet them, but I never did come into contact with researchers or investigators during the course of my relationship with the Rowlisons.

I had hoped to meet many other abductees through my friendship with the Rowlisons. I had hoped to hear confirming stories so I could grow, and feel sane, knowing someone else had experienced similar "dreams" and events.

The Rowlisons' small entourage of UFO friends began to meet monthly at restaurants to visit and talk about new findings and new books by well-known authors. Fred and I were made to feel comfortable in the beginning, but many months later, I realized that Mrs. Rowlison actually had a personal, selfish tie around me.

June 5, 1995

On June 5th, I had feelings of apprehension and anxiety. I also had a feeling of knowing that something was about to happen, or had already happened. If something had happened the night of the 4th, I was unaware of it. I was in a dazed state of mind, and unaware of most of my surroundings.

I called Karen on Tuesday, June 6th. She told me that the nights of the 4th and 5th had been quite busy for abductees. She had received many reports from other abductees she was helping at the time.

Karen also had a "dream" of her own that night. She had a shared dream with her sister. The Greys had taken them to a familiar area where they'd been taken before. The place was on top of a very tall building in Manhattan. She said that she and her sister had not been taken aboard the spaceship, though they did see a ship above them. She said she believed the meeting was "high profile" with some very important government people.

Karen told me that I had probably been taken on the 4th as well. Sometimes when they take you, they do not allow you to see what is going on. The Greys do not want you to know what is happening to you, but you still experience the aftereffects the next day.

A TEST

June 11, 1995

Some time during the night I had a "dream." When I woke up, I thought I was in my own bed, but then recognized the inside of the Greys' ship. I saw my two Greys standing nearby: Raytheon and the mean Grey. I felt something solid against my back. I was lying on my left side on the familiar table.

I turned my head to check out my surroundings and to discover what it was I was lying up against. When I turned my

154

head, I saw a person with short hair. I thought the person was a male. He was laying next to me with his back to my back. I quickly got up and someone helped me step down from the table.

I asked, "Who is this male person?" One of the Greys said, "It is your husband, Fred." I did not believe the Grey. I walked around the table and saw that it was Fred, lying there asleep. I tried to wake him by shaking his body and calling out his name, but he would not wake up. One of the Greys immediately came and took me away from the table.

The room we were in was dimly lit. I saw some other humans, but was not allowed to approach them. I do not remember most of the conversation I had with the Greys. I vaguely remember being told I was going to be put through a test, working with some human beings who were having difficulties with their lives. I was told there was a husband who abused his wife physically and verbally. I was told by one of the Greys that if I succeeded in the test, I would be able to help (the Greys) with this type of situation.

I was instructed to speak to the abusive man who was also in the same room. One of the Greys brought people to me that I recognized from a previous visit. There was a young lady who wears glasses with red frames (though she did not have her glasses on). She was holding a very sleepy, blond-haired little girl (the same girl that was with her before). I had drawn their pictures from a previous visit. Her husband was there again also and from the expression on his face, he was not very happy about it.

There was an older lady with her husband, and I recognized them as people I had met before. I was told that the older couple were the parents of the abusive husband.

A Grey was walking toward me with the alleged abusive husband. He had the husband stand next to me. His wife, who was carrying the little girl, followed her husband, but was stopped a few feet away. The older couple followed and were also stopped.

155

As the wife and the husband's parents approached us, the Greys somehow made them stop walking. They had been walking quite fast to where the young husband and I were standing.

At that point, there was a lot of commotion. The wife was yelling obscenities at me. I don't exactly remember what they were saying, as their screaming voices became confusing. The older woman came up very close to me. I thought she was going to slap me. She was very upset.

The wife had a worried and tearful look on her face. She also kept trying to yell something at me. Evidently, the Greys had told them something about me that upset and scared them. I was not told what had been said to them by the Greys.

Suddenly, a peacefulness came over everyone and the room became deathly quiet. Then, one of the Greys (telepathically) told me to proceed with what I had been instructed to do. I had not been given any instructions by the Greys! I gathered that the disruptive situation I had just witnessed, was a demonstration of the way this family lived their lives.

I stood there, not knowing what I was supposed to do or say. At that moment, I looked over at the table where Fred was still sleeping. I wondered how he could possibly sleep through all the yelling and screaming that had been going on. Then, that part of the room went dark. I heard movement, as if they were taking Fred out of the room to someplace else.

I stood by the young husband thinking about what the Greys wanted me to do. After looking into his sad face and glancing at his wife, something told me they must be having marital problems. He wanted out of the situation. His folks' involvement was too much for him to bear. He did not care about them and just wanted to go on without them.

I don't know how I received that information, but I did. I did not know that family, the husband and wife, or his parents. Somehow, I was being fed information, not knowing if it was the truth or not. I did not realize this was the test the Greys had set up for me.

After being fed the information, I got the idea that I was supposed to speak to the young man and try to change his mind about his family and go forth with them.

Instantly, I started yelling at him. I remember being aggressive, loud, and not giving the alleged abusive husband a chance to speak. I felt as if I had an uncontrollable authority over him. I knew this was the only way he could communicate with others.

I felt that some of the thinking process was not actually coming from me, but rather *through* me and controlled by someone (or something) else. I wondered if the man would react violently to me, or begin slapping me because of what I was saying to him. It seemed that I was to change his attitude and get him to accept what and who he was, for his own good and the good of the family.

I didn't really understand the whats and whys of the scenario, but evidently, the answers to whatever questions the Greys had, were produced by the husband. The Greys were not standing very far away from us. I had the feeling they were going to use the younger husband for something very important, either on Earth, or with them, on the ship.

Why the entities used me in that scenario as a "stand-in" for them, is unclear. Maybe the Greys felt that human contact with this human man was necessary. Maybe they thought that, being human, I would be better able to relate to the alleged abusive husband.

Though I was given a lot of information about the man, I do not remember what I was directed to tell him. That part of the memory was wiped clean by the entities. I do remember that when the young husband was allowed to speak to me, he had no respect for me as a woman.

At first, he used a lot of derogatory language and harsh statements when responding to what I was saying to him. After awhile, his attitude changed and he spoke with some respect. He did a lot of crying. He told me a lot about himself and his life. I remember him telling me he had suffered much physical and verbal abuse.

His mother had made life very hard for him when he was growing up. She had expected too much from him. He had grown up with the idea that physical and verbal abuse was a way of life. He thought that was the correct way to treat people, especially when it came to his wife and children.

When I woke up from this experience, I remembered the whole dream. I did not understand why the Greys had put me through such an experience. I asked myself, "For what purpose or benefit had this been done? And who would benefit from it?"

I was not aware at the time, that the entities put people through various kinds of tests. That experience had been a test for me. Many parts of the dream have been wiped from my memory. I do remember that the Greys continually observed what was transpiring between the young husband and myself in that one conversation. I was led to believe that the alleged abusive husband had had a very rough life. That fact contributed to the way he treated people.

At the time, I did not understand that I was the authoritative, the stern and aggressive personality during the test. I was angry about the young husband's abusive treatment of his wife. However, once I understood his life experiences, I was compassionate toward him.

At one point in the scenario, I looked for approval from the Greys. To this day, no one can tell me they have no emotions. I seemed to have accomplished what they wanted of me, because my friendly Grey, Raytheon, smiled at me with his tiny mouth. Then, in unison, both Greys spoke to me and gave their approval of what I had done.

I had completed the test in the way the situation was to be resolved. They expressed to me how happy they were with me at the conclusion of the test. I do not remember what transpired after that.

Later, when I woke up, I was in my own bed. I was exhausted. I saw Fred lying next to me and I was glad. I tried to wake him up, but only got a mumble out of him.

158

The next morning, the first thing I did was attempt to remember the entire dream. It seemed as if it was rapidly fading away from me. Fred was already awake and in an agitated mood. I asked if he had been in bed all night. I received no answer from him.

As the day wore on, he became even more agitated, to the point that he upset me. We did not speak to one another. This lasted for a couple of days.

When Fred and I finally spoke, I asked him if anything had happened to him the night I had been "tested." He said that as far as he knew, he had been in bed asleep all night. I wondered why he had been in such an agitated state for two days. I shared the dream with him.

THE CASE OF THE MISSING BRAS

June 21, 1995

On June 15th, I opened the armoire drawer to get a clean bra. I had just purchased five new bras that month. My five new bras were not in the drawer. From that day until the 21st of June, I searched the entire house, including other bedroom drawers, garbage cans, shelves, even between the towels and bedding.

I tore the house apart looking for those bras, thinking maybe Fred or Michelle was playing games with me. I asked them more than twice if they had seen my new bras. I also asked my other daughter, Vanessa, to please check her drawers, in the event the bras had somehow been mixed in with her things. There were no clues as to where they could be.

The morning of June 21st, after Fred left for work, I went upstairs to use the bathroom. There on the bed, was a neatly folded new bra! "Okay," I said, "Fred and Michelle are playing games with me!"

When they got home that evening, I accused them of playing a joke on me. I asked them to please give back the other four new bras. They said they did not have them and that they had not placed the new one on the bed!

Later that evening, Mary and Ray Rowlison came to visit us. During our conversation, Mary asked me how I was feeling. Fred and I began to laugh hard. I answered her by saying that we were a little tired and stressed out.

Fred then explained that during the last two weeks there had been a number of weird occurrences. I had lost pens, pencils, anything in my hands just seemed to disappear. None of the items could be found. Ray asked Fred why he was laughing so hard.

Fred looked at me and told me to tell them what else I had misplaced and couldn't find. He eventually told them about my missing bras and about the one that had turned up on the bed that morning. Ray told us, in a very serious voice, that the Greys take things, including clothing! Little did I know how true that statement would turn out to be.

In a future experience with the Greys, I would walk into a room, on board their ship, and see one of my new bras. Winsha would be wearing one of my new bras!

ROSWELL FESTIVAL

July 4, 5, 1995

The Rowlisons had asked Fred and me to join them and another couple on a trip to Roswell, NM. The event was the UFO Festival. We were all going to meet at the Rowlisons the morning of the 4th. The plan was to take two cars to Roswell.

When we pulled into the Rowlisons driveway, a dark-haired woman was wiping down their car windows. As I approached the lady I immediately felt as if I knew her from somewhere. We said casual hellos and I went on into the Rowlisons house. As I came through the door, Ray walked out of the den with the woman's husband. I thought to myself that the man also looked familiar to me. I couldn't think where I would know them from. I figured I must have bumped into them while grocery shopping or some such thing.

The couple was introduced to me as Louise and Mike Riveria. I did not say anything to them about how familiar they looked to me. The Riverias rode in the Rowlison car to Roswell. Fred and I took our car. As we pulled out of the driveway, I mentioned to Fred that I knew those two people from somewhere, but I didn't know where. The topic was soon forgotten.

While having lunch together in Roswell, the Rowlisons saw another one of their friends from Albuquerque. I later found out from the Rowlisons, that the other lady and her family were also abductees. Over the course of the weekend, the other lady and I seemed to have accidental encounters with one another.

That night at dinner, I asked the Riverias what their affiliation was with Mufon and what their interest was in UFOs. Louise told me they thought Mike had some experiences and that possibly so had Louise. Then they asked what my interest was in UFOs. I hesitated to answer because I could not come out and say what I truly wanted to say. I looked to Ray and Mary for support. Suddenly I blurted out, "I think I am an abductee."

The conversation became very informative. Mike told me when he and Louise had met me early that morning at Rowlisons, Mike had told Louise, Ray and Mary that he knew me from somewhere and that he *knew* where he knew me from. Louise said she also thought we knew each other and that it was not from some store here on Earth. They had both shared that information with Rowlisons as soon as they had gotten into the car to leave for Roswell.

On Sunday morning, after seeing the other lady again, I began to feel as if there was some connection between us. The Rowlisons had not introduced me to her. They had insinuated that she was a lesbian. I later found out that was not true.

The woman and I formally introduced ourselves to each other at a gathering held by the Rowlisons. Her name was

Sharon. I found out she lived approximately one mile from where we lived and that she was also an abductee. Ray and Mary said they were not sure if Sharon was an abductee. She appeared to be sad, thoroughly unhappy.

I had wanted to hug her and tell her that if her sadness was because of her abduction, I understood. I did not hug Sharon. I was afraid of a negative response from her. Seeing her sadness brought up emotions of self-doubt about my own situation as an abductee.

The speakers we heard at the Roswell Festival were Linda Moulton Howe and Stanton Friedmen. I was just beginning to learn about the vastness of the whole subject of UFOs. In the park, booths had been set up with UFO wares and information on various UFO topics. Young and old made costumes for the "alien" parade. The weekend proved to be interesting, as this was something new for me. I found the whole event exciting because I was able to gain some knowledge regarding UFOs.

After that weekend in Roswell, Sharon and I spoke to each other on another occasion, at a holiday party given by the Rowlisons. Sharon shared a few of her alien abduction experiences. She never spoke of her family. That part of her life seemed to be held secret. Because of the negative information I had been given about Sharon, I was even more intrigued with getting to know her. Our lives would eventually grow apart until another chance meeting later, in 1998.

The only contact Fred and I had with the Riverias was when we, or I, visted the Rowlisons. The Riverias and Rowlisons had a close relationship. We were invited to dinner at the Riveria's home and discovered that they also lived quite close to us. At dinner, I was shown a video that Mike had taped of two UFOs flying above their Florida home. We shared some experiences to explore where we may have met each other, but the sharing soon became one-sided. I opened up more and more about my experiences, while they remained silent about theirs. I finally stopped talking about my experiences and gave no more information about myself.

In the meantime, the Rowlisons and Karen were trying to locate another hypnotherapist who worked with abductees in the New Mexico area. Their search was unsuccessful.

One evening, we had a small group of people over to our home for dinner. I shared my drawings with the Riverias. When we came to the symbol I had been given by the Grey, Louise and Mike recognized it. They both said that, even as children, they had drawn the very same symbol with the two dots. It was identical to mine. They also said that, for some unknown reason, even as adults, when they doodled on paper, they both unconsciously drew that symbol over and over again.

Mike and Louise had not known each other as small children. Neither of them knew where they had learned to draw the symbol. They also did not know its meaning. We all agreed it could very well be an Egyptian hieroglyph.

During the time of our friendship, the three of us shared a lot of comparisons on UFOs and the abduction phenomenon. Mike communicates telepathically with the Aliens. It was during one of his communications that he was told to live in Albuquerque near the mountains. I too had felt a strong urge to live close to the mountains.

THE BUGS

July 10, 1995

I woke up during the night, feeling as if something was biting my upper right arm. I quickly rubbed the arm to brush off whatever bug was on me. I turned on the table lamp to see what had bitten me. My arm, where the thing had bitten me, had a strange feeling that radiated throughout the arm. I noticed a large, strange-looking welt where I had been bitten.

I checked the bedspread, top sheet, and blankets for the dead insect. There was nothing there. I pushed back all the bed covers and discovered something black and fuzzy on the lower part of my gown. The "thing" appeared to have curly long hair on it. It was larger than a quarter! At first, I thought it was just fuzz. I tried to brush it off my nightgown and discovered that the center of it was hard. It seemed to have a hard body within the curly mass of hair. It had attached itself very firmly to my gown. I had never seen anything like it before.

I noticed movement on the floor and saw another kind of bug I had never seen before. This one was yellow with black markings on it. It was quite aggressive and was trying to crawl back up the bed toward me. I kept pushing it back down to the floor as it crawled up the sheet. I could not identify the bug, but I was certain that it was not native to New Mexico.

Fred woke up because of my movements on the bed. He asked me what I was doing. I told him that something had bitten me and I didn't know what kind of bugs were on my gown and on the floor. He got up and walked around to my side of the bed to see what kind of bugs they were. He did not recognize them either and thought they were very unusual looking. The one on the floor reminded him of a very large ladybug. That one was very aggressive and just wanted to get onto me! Fred brushed the black, hairy bug off my nightgown. It fell to the floor.

He knelt down to kill the aggressive "lady bug" and in doing so, he now thinks he knelt down on the hairy insect. He could not identify that one either. That is all we remember. Fred does not remember going back to bed. I do not remember turning off the lamp or Fred going back to bed. Our minds are blank as to what happened after Fred tried to kill the bugs.

The next morning, we woke up and Fred was on his side of the bed as usual. We just looked at each other, then immediately jumped out of bed. He came to my side of the bed and we both looked for the two weird bugs. Fred remembers squashing the yellow bug. Where had the insects gone? We could not find them anywhere on the floor or in the bedding. We removed the mattress and checked the box spring and the floor under the bed as well. We moved furniture to see if we could locate the insects. They were not to be found.

Later that morning, the back of my right leg began to hurt. It was a strange sensation. As I rubbed the area, I felt something like a small crust of skin which I peeled off my leg. It had a strange appearance that did not resemble human skin. It had a whitish color to it. That afternoon, Fred noticed a welt on the back of my leg and asked what I had done to it. He looked at the leg and discovered another round welt in the same place where I had pulled off the white substance.

The welt and redness on my upper arm disappeared after a week; but a scar remained for days. The back of my leg, where I'd pulled off the substance, became quite red. The welt remained but became smaller as the days passed.

I went to the library to research insects that are native to our area of New Mexico. I could not find anything that resembled the insects that had been in our bedroom. We were unsuccessful in finding the dead bugs and never did find out what type of insects they were. I contacted several exterminators in Albuquerque and described both bugs. No one could identify the black, hairy bug. The large "lady bug" type, I was told, could be found in the northern United States, but they were not aggressive.

A POEM AND A MAP

July 22, 1995

I was awakened at 2:40 a.m. by a voice calling, "Mom, Mom." It continued repeatedly until I was fully awake. The voice told me to go outside on the balcony. I did not leave my warm bed because I did not know who was talking to me. I cautiously looked around the room in the dark for the source of the voice. I stayed quiet and very still. I was fearful because someone was in our bedroom calling to me, yet I saw no one.

As I lay there in bed, the voice began repeating over and over again. I finally decided (or was told) to get a pencil and paper and write down what I was being told. It was as if someone was watching me write the nine instructions because each sentence was repeated until I had it completely written down. The first thing I was told:

165

1.*Only as a child she knows…*
2.*They ate alive…*
3.*Only she knows…Only she knows…Only she knows…*
4.*What do you know…*

Then I heard an electronic clicking sound in my ears, as if someone was tapping on a microphone. This was done three times. The sound was loud.

5.*Five alive now…Five alive now…*

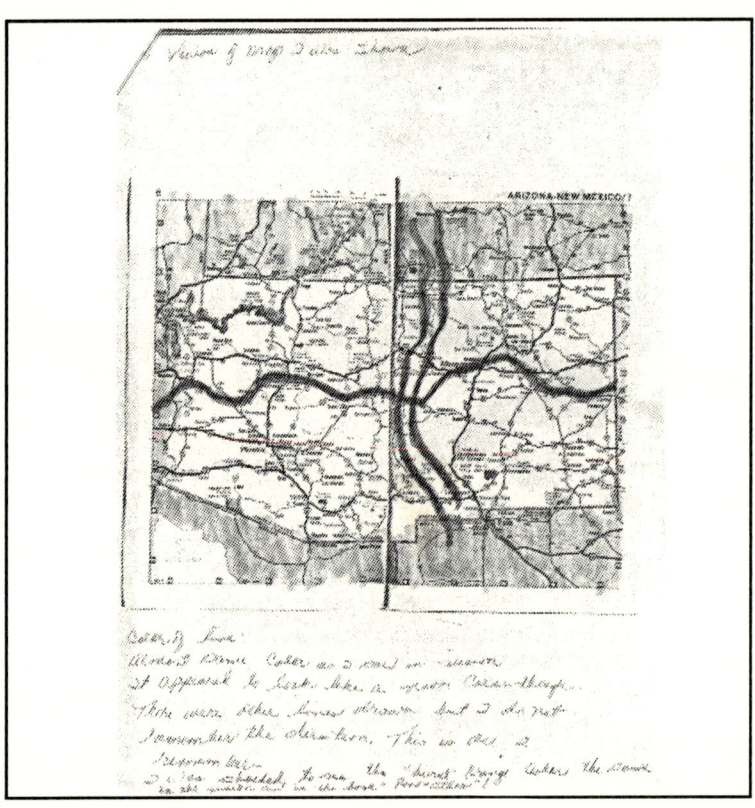

The Map

Again, I heard the clicking or tapping sound, as if someone was on a microphone. I was hearing it through my head. I felt a strong pressure in my ears which caused a slight headache. A voice then said a couple of words that sounded like

6.*Naw-Naw*
 I can do it...I can do it
7.*Run down a list...Run down a list...April 4th.*
 See map...see map...

I was then somehow shown a vision of a map. The map remained with me until I understood what was on it. It was a map of New Mexico and Arizona. Drawn on the map were two neon green lines that extended into the southwest corner of Colorado, through the western part of New Mexico, and into the northwest corner of Texas. One neon green line extended from the eastern border of New Mexico and continued on to the western border of Arizona. The lines were not straight lines.

8.*Go Outside...Go Outside...*
9.*Can anyone see, Can anyone see at 3:15 in the morning?*

Needless to say, I did not go outside as instructed. I almost did, just to see what might be going on, but fear kept me sitting up in bed. Since that early morning in 1995, and every year since, on April 4th, I still wait for news of a happening. To my knowledge, so far, nothing has occurred.

FRED'S ABDUCTION

August 26, 1995

Before going to bed that evening, I felt very nervous. I had a strong feeling of apprehension that something was going to happen. I had come to recognize the symptoms that preceded a visit from the Greys.

After getting into bed, Fred and I watched the nightly news, then a short program after the news. We turned off the lights before going to sleep. I tossed and turned in bed and was unable to go to sleep. I planned to stay awake as long as I could.

There was a lot of thunder and hard rain that night. I was awake through three different thunderstorms that raged after we had turned off the lights at 11:30 p.m. I would start to doze off, then suddenly wake up. Finally, I turned my body toward the balcony door and bedroom window. I laid there, wide awake.

I don't know what time it was because the clock was on Fred's nightstand and I was too lazy to turn over and look. I didn't really care what time it was. Fred was not sleeping comfortably either. He tossed and turned and woke up several different times.

I was breathing very fast and hard. I tried to calm myself, but my breathing would slow down only for short periods of time. As I lay in bed, looking at the balcony door and the window, something happened. There was a light on the balcony! There was a shadow! The shadow came into the bedroom; not just one shadow!

I quickly turned over and began to yell at my husband, "Fred, Fred, they are here. Fred, wake up, they are here!" Fred did not wake up. I shook him hard as he lay on his right side. I turned my head to see if the movement had reached our bed. They had stopped and were just watching me go ballistic, trying to get Fred awake. He would not wake up. I was very frightened and did not want to go with them that night. I clung to Fred's body very tightly. I was almost in tears. I kept hollering for Fred to just wake up!

All of a sudden, I felt as if I had cotton in my mouth. The words that came out were not intelligible. I don't remember hearing myself after that. As I clung to Fred, I saw his yellow walking shorts being lifted about a foot above his bedroom chair where he lays his clothes every night. Someone was shaking his walking shorts in mid air! Then they took the corner or the leg of Fred's shorts and began rolling them up very tightly.

The result was something that looked like a snake! They turned and pointed the replica of the "snake" at me. Evidently, they were having fun scaring the hell out of me. When they'd had their fun, they unrolled the shorts and placed them on the seat of the chair.

Fred also had a white dress shirt laying across the back of the chair. The entity picked it up and seemed to be examining it. As I watched what was going on, something made me look toward the open door to the hallway.

High above the door, close to the ceiling in the northwest corner of our bedroom, I saw a dim, circular light approximately five inches in diameter. The light was white with a lot of orange in it. As I looked at the light, something took hold of my body, forcibly turned me, and slammed me back onto the bed. Lying on my back, I tried to fight with my hands, but soon discovered I could not move my hands anymore. I was only able to move my shoulders and hips to form an arch. I did this twice, then realized that my body felt as if it was paralyzed. I could no longer move any part of my body.

I thought I had been yelling loudly while all this was going on. What I actually heard coming out of my mouth was not intelligible at all. Suddenly, it felt as if someone was sitting or lying on top of me! Then I heard Fred say, "There is something going on in here!"

At that point, Fred got up. He said he needed to go to the bathroom. I thought I was yelling at him, "No! No! Don't get up! Don't go!" but it was as if he could not hear me. Fred got up and left the bedroom. As he walked away from the bed, it seemed as if he was fast asleep and being led out of the bedroom toward the connecting bathroom. A shadow appeared to be leading Fred and holding onto his right arm, as if to assist him walking.

I thought surely Michelle and Vanessa would wake up during all the commotion, and come into our bedroom to see what was happening and help us. The girls did not come.

After Fred and his shadow guides disappeared, I remembered that Karen had told me I could call if I needed her during the night. I repeatedly told myself out loud, that I had to call Karen, Mary, and Ray. I kept trying to reach for the telephone but could not do so. I could not move any part of my body, though I kept trying.

I continued to repeat my desire to call Karen. The more I tried to move, the more drugged I felt. I noticed that Fred was not in bed with me. He never came back. I fell asleep repeating to myself that I needed to call Karen, Mary, and Ray.

I woke up at 3:00 a.m., immediately sat up and looked toward Fred's side of the bed. He was there, next to me. I woke him up and asked him, "Where did they take you?" He was very sleepy, as if he had been drugged, and would not respond to my questions.

Instead, he asked, "What's going on?" I assumed he was fully awake, so I began to tell him what had happened. I asked him again where they had taken him. Before I could finish telling the story, I realized he had fallen asleep on my chest. I felt very peaceful then and fell into a deep sleep.

When I woke up that Sunday morning, I could hardly get out of bed. I felt very weak, nauseous, and tired. My head was spinning. Fred was already up and downstairs making coffee. When he came back upstairs to our bedroom, he went directly into the bathroom without even speaking to me. That was unusual for him. He got into the shower.

Fred was not talkative that morning, so we just quietly got ourselves ready for 9:00 a.m. Mass. He seemed to be doing okay physically. He wanted me to ask him later "if anything went on last night."

When we got home from church, we did not discuss the previous night's events in detail as I had thought we would. Fred basically wanted to know what I had seen and what I knew. He did not remember anything that had happened

170

during the night. He also did not feel well for most of the day. We both took a long nap.

When I woke up, I called Karen about the incident, hoping she would know who the "shadows" were. I also informed her that they had taken Fred and that we were not feeling well. Karen listened to my story. She had no answers for us other than the possibility that the shadows had been Reptilians.

Fred became very agitated as the day wore on. He could not understand why he was so agitated or why he was not feeling well. He was not very happy about the turn of events and wanted to know where he had been taken and by whom.

NOTES

August 27, 1995

I did not sleep well this night. I could hardly sleep. My back, shoulders, and arm were hurting. Again I had felt a strange presence in the bedroom, but saw no one in the room or out on the balcony. The added agitation of the night before had been too much. Fred and I were still on edge.

August 28,1995

Again, I was unable to sleep. I felt very nervous and scared. I felt the unknown presence in our bedroom, yet I saw no one, in the bedroom or on the balcony. I finally drifted off to sleep. I awoke in the early morning hours to find myself sitting up in bed.

August 29, 1995

I was able to get a little bit more sleep this night, but kept waking up. The last time I woke up, I was lying on my left side, looking toward the east bedroom window and the open balcony door. I suppose I was meant to see what was out there. I saw long flashes of white and orange streaks of light near my side of the bed. The streaks of light passed me, traveling from north to south.

I lay there in bed, watching the flashes of orange and white light, until I fell asleep. I experienced pain in my back and shoulder again. I felt a presence in the room, yet saw no one.

In the morning, after waking up, I wondered what the lights had been. They did not seem to harm anyone, but what was their purpose? I never did find out what the lights were or what their purpose was.

August 30, 1995

The morning of August 30th, I went to my armoire to get underwear as I dressed for work. I had finally replaced the missing bras. That morning, three out of five new bras were missing again! They had been in the drawer the day before.

I felt apprehensive and somewhat nervous that night. I was exhausted from lack of sleep. I tried to fall asleep and eventually was able to achieve a very light sleep. I woke up during the night, not caring what time it was. I found myself lying on my left side. I stayed in bed, very scared, and looked out the window.

I saw some kind of movement out on the balcony but there was not enough light from the moon to illuminate the area. Through the window, I saw a small black vehicle rise up from the floor of the balcony. It went straight up into the night sky. For some reason, I just did not care enough to jump out of bed, run to the door, and watch the vehicle take off.

I became very upset with the Greys. Obviously, they had just brought someone home. Fred was lying there, as always, fast asleep. The vehicle appeared to be the same one I had ridden in before. The question I asked myself was, had Michelle or I been taken that night?

August 31, 1995

I slept a little better, but woke up in a sitting position, in bed, again. When I woke up, I kept brushing something off my arm, or I was trying to hit at something in the dark. I struck out at the unknown thing several different times. The white and orange streak of colored light appeared near my bed again. To this day, I do not know what the light was or where it had come from.

ANOTHER OUT-OF-BODY EXPERIENCE

October 18, 1995

Sometime between the evening of the 18th and the morning of the 19th, I woke up lying on a table in the Greys' ship. While on the table, looking up, I suddenly felt as if I was above and looking down on the table. I recognized the woman on the table as myself as had happened once before to me. I did not know how I was able to do that. I was not sure if I had clothes on. My right leg was hurting and very uncomfortable.

The two Greys who were standing on my right allowed me to move my leg.

From above the table, I saw that my right leg was bent at an angle and my knee was bent outward. My right foot was up against my left leg, which was straight. I was somewhat uncomfortable.

I did not know what type of examination was being done to me. My vision was very blurry so I could not see very well. Normally, the Greys do something to my vision that allows me to see 20-20 without my glasses or contact lenses. That did not seem to be the case this time.

The Greys who were working on me were not the friendly Greys. Their attitude was different from the other Greys I'd had contact with. When they spoke telepathically, they seemed to be more demanding and terse. I got the distinct impression they regarded humans as inferior beings. There was some communication but I do not remember what was said to me.

I seemed to be floating above myself in a well-lit room that looked like an operating room. I floated and saw myself down below without understanding how I was able to do that. When it was time to return to my body, I felt myself float directly over my body. I was somehow turned face up, then went back into my body. I experienced a strange sensation when that happened.

The Greys caused me to go back to sleep. I woke up again and the next thing I remember was standing in a dimly lit room. I was standing in a straight line with other humans. There were two other humans on either side of me. I did not know if they were male or female. My vision was still very blurred. One of the Greys passed in front of us. I could not turn my head to look at who was standing on either side of me. I felt paralyzed, so I tried moving my eyes from side to side in order to see who was standing next to me. I saw that those humans were nude, as I was.

I was telepathically asked to step forward, which I did. I was afraid. I felt as if I was being singled out from the group of humans for some unknown reason. I was taken forward about six feet in front of the other Grey who had been standing in front of us. By that time, another Grey had joined the Grey who was now in front of me.

I began to cry because I did not want to be separated from the other humans. I had a feeling the other people who had been standing on either side of me were Fred and Michelle. I felt as if something bad was going to happen to them. I said, "I don't want to go. Let me go with them." (meaning Fred and Michelle).

My memory of the event ends there. I don't know what happened after that. Maybe the experience was too traumatic to remember.

The next morning when I woke up, I was very confused. The Greys would normally let me see them bringing us (or me) home. That was not the case this time. I was also quite depressed and did not know why. My own little world seemed to be spinning very fast that day. I became irritable. I felt faint and was not very coherent or conscious of my surroundings. I had a horrific day.

October 19, 1995

October 19th was Mary Rowlisons birthday. I had bought her a birthday present. I went home and wrapped it, then went to visit with her. Mary noticed something different about me and knew something was very wrong. She asked, and I told her what had been happening. I told her I had felt that way all day because I was certain the Greys had hurt Fred and Michelle. As we talked, Mary convinced me that Fred and Michelle were okay and well. Mary continued to speak to me but I still could not figure out why I felt so sad and out of it.

When I got home that evening, I called Karen. She had told me many times to call her when things were not right. Karen and Mary were both very comforting. Karen tried to help me remember what might have happened with the Greys, but the memory would not come back.

Fred and Michelle appeared to be okay physically and mentally, but neither one of them remembered being taken that evening. Neither of them had any memory of the experience we had shared. They both thought they had spent the night at home in bed. I wondered if maybe the people standing next to me had been someone other than Fred and Michelle.

I remembered something else about that experience. The night before I was taken, I had seen black helicopters flying near and around our home. At the time, I was not aware of the connection between the black helicopters and Alien abductions. I just found it weird that they had been circling our home that evening.

BODY MARKINGS

October 20, 1995

After showering and drying myself, I noticed three very red, inflamed, small circles on my upper knee. If the area had been injected with a needle, it would have been a very large needle. It was quite painful to the touch. The markings seemed to be done in a pattern. To this day, the markings remain on my knee. Was this another way of identifying me to someone?

THE TEST

October 21, 1995

I am not sure I was actually taken on the evening of October 21st. I think it may have been a memory that was revealed to me about the October 18th experience I'd had. I think my subconscious mind was helping me to remember what had happened that night.

The memory began with the line-up of the other nude humans and myself. I was singled out and taken forward to the Greys. I was taken from the line-up and walked down a hall to a viewing room. The Greys discussed the H-bomb with me in detail. They told me how it was constructed and about the terrible devastation it would cause when used to bomb a country. They spoke of the controlling power one country has over another when threatened with the H-bomb. They spoke of the destruction that would occur should one be used.

That teaching was the first of many lessons I would have about nuclear fission and nuclear bombs. I would be taught how to help save human life. In future teachings, the Greys said they would tell me why I was being given their teachings.

The first lesson did not seem to be a lesson. It seemed to be a very real experience that I actually lived through. The scene was set on Earth. I thought I had been taken back to Earth by the Greys. It was a cloudy, misty day. I recognized the fact that I was in a large city outside the United States. I seemed to be the only westerner in that strange country. I did not see any other people from the United States. I was by myself.

The people I saw were oriental. I was somehow told that a large bomb was going to be dropped on those people. With the knowledge from my prior teachings, I would know what actions to take to save some of those people. Immediately, I was again shown the process I had to go through in order to save those people.

The bomb was dropped and hit its target. There was fire everywhere and the fire was being carried by a strong wind that was hard to stand up against. I could smell burnt skin. People were falling in the streets, everywhere. Buildings were breaking apart and falling to the ground. The air was thick with smoke and debris.

I began to run, stepping over burnt bodies. There were many, many bodies. People were dropping dead immediately. The blast effects were horrendous. I saw people stumbling over bodies. Men, women, and children were falling over and trying to escape the devastation as they ran. The smell was sickening. The power of the bomb was unbelievable.

I was somehow able to pick up and help people who could hardly walk. I found demolished gray buildings that seemed to be falling apart. I led the people to those buildings and ran back into the street to find more children, women, and men. I don't know where the strength came from, but I carried those who were still alive and laid them down next to each other.

It's a mystery to me how the medical supplies were made available, but they were there. I used them to bathe the people with a smooth substance that would save their lives. I wrapped their burnt faces and bodies with a type of clear cellophane. I heard their moans and groans of pain. There was blood everywhere. I had to work quickly to save as many as I could. There was so much noise and confusion and crying! The devastation and death were too much for me.

The memory ends there. I was brought out of the scene and woke up in my own bed. I was devastated. How could that be? I wondered how I could experience such a thing. I asked myself where the Greys had taken me. How had they been able to accomplish such a scenario? And why? Why had they told me that another nuclear bomb, stronger than the H-bomb would be exploded somewhere in our world? Could it be Russia? Or China?

I asked myself often, what the reasoning behind the test had been. How had the Greys made the test so genuine? Had I been taken back in history to the bombing of Hiroshima? Or had I been shown the future? Why had I been given information about the making of H-bombs? I was full of questions that I had no answers to.

I shared the information with Fred and Michelle that evening at the dinner table. I asked them if they had any knowledge about the H-bomb. Michelle said there was a lot of information on the internet.

After dinner, she opened Microsoft Encarta and found information on the blast effects of both the A-bomb and the H-bomb. She printed out copies of the information for me to read. When I saw the articles, I nearly fell over. The information I had been given by the Greys was the exact information I was reading on those pages! How had they instantly put all that information into my brain?

I did not understand the purpose of their test or where it would lead. Was some kind of nuclear attack going to happen somewhere in our world? Did the entities know about it? Were they trying to prepare people for that type of devastation? Or was the whole experience created to see how I would deal with and work in that situation?

The Encarta experience was too much to completely comprehend, but supplied me with information that dove-tailed with my October 18th and 19th experiences. It answered my question about why I had been so depressed on the 19th. I felt as if I had been given much more information on the subject, but the input was so overpowering, my subconscious mind would not let go of specifics.

October 24, 1995

I called Karen that evening about the bomb "Test Dream." The experience was bothering me quite a bit. We spoke at length. Again, I thought I must be going insane, and it was difficult for me to come out and tell her about that particular dream. I thought for sure she was going to think I was insane!

Karen coaxed me into telling her the whole story and she listened intently. She explained that this had been a form of psychological test the Greys or other entities use on many humans. She told me they use a devastation scenario (such as the one I had experienced) to see how a particular abductee will react when it comes to helping other humans. Would the abductee run away, or help? She said many other abductees had reported dreams of bombs, earthquakes, and floods. One scene even involved two women with the last glass of drinking water! The entities were very interested in our reactions to such situations and the way we would handle them in light of future training for those individuals. Karen also noted that Budd Hopkins and other investigator/researchers did not know why the entities gave these particular psychological tests to abductees.

Karen was concerned about the fact that I had not called her immediately after my experience. She reminded me not to wait, but to call right away. She also reminded me that the Greys had *told* me they were going to be testing me. She instructed me to pay attention and listen closely to what I was being told by the Greys. I must listen very carefully to every word. To help me feel better about the experience, she related some of the tests she had gone through with the Greys.

To make me feel more comfortable, Karen shared some confidential information with me. She had worked in Mr. Hopkins' office, putting information from cards into the

179

computer. She had worked on the cards from Albuquerque and the state of New Mexico for the years 1993-1994.

She had seen my card and remembered that she had not heard anything about Wade Valdez since they had received so many complaints about him. She again asked me the name of the doctor I had seen who was working with Mr. Valdez. I told her the name was Dr. Carolyn Miller. Karen was certain she had seen information on Dr. Miller. She said she would recheck the information.

She also told me that during 1993 and 1994 there had been a total of twelve people who had had contact with an alien entity or ship in Albuquerque and elsewhere in New Mexico.

Karen was very understanding, helpful and compassionate. By the time our conversation ended, she had me laughing and feeling 100% better about my first psychological test by the Greys.

November 1, 1995

The needle marks on my upper knee area were still red. The circles are perfectly round. Each circle seems to be indented. The area was still very painful to touch.

November 15, 1995

The perfect circles were still very red. The swelling that had developed was not so puffy now.

November 23, 1995

I read in bed until 11:00 p.m., then turned off the bed lamp. About five or ten minutes later (while I was still awake), I heard a noise that sounded as if someone was turning the doorknob on the front door. It sounded like the clicking noise the double bolt lock makes when you unlock it.

I asked Fred if he had locked the front door before coming upstairs to bed. He said that he had. He then went to sleep. I lay still, listening for the front door to open and for other noises from downstairs. Seemingly within the next minute, there was a noise inside our bedroom.

It sounded as if someone had picked up something from our dresser. It sounded like something had been opened, then closed, then put back down. In the bathroom, where I had crystal jewelry boxes on a mirrored tray, I heard a sliding movement. Then one of the crystal boxes was opened, closed and set down again. A moment later, I heard a rustling sound coming from Fred's side of the bed. There was a glass bowl on Fred's nightstand filled with potpourri. It sounded as if someone was searching, feeling around, and looking for something.

The next noise I heard was on my nightstand where there was a small wooden box, also filled with potpourri. The lid was lifted, then put back on top of the box. Then the box was set down again on the nightstand.

I was awake while those things happened, partially hiding under the covers. I heard no footsteps. The entity seemed to exit through the wall when he finished investigating. The sound of his exiting was different than what I had heard before. The exit noise was like a long, quick, low-toned boom. It was as if I was hearing the actual materials of the wall being separated.

The following are my feelings and thoughts during this event:

> *Approximately half an hour before turning off the light, I felt edgy.*
>
> *I had the feeling of anxiety I usually experience when the Greys come.*
>
> *I followed the movements with my eyes after hearing each noise. I lay very quietly, pretending to be asleep.*
>
> *After the "exiting" noise, I heard nothing else. I lay there for awhile longer, feeling very uncomfortable,.I suspected*

that one of the entities was looking for something. I remembered hiding the cameo Priscilla/Patricia had given me. I knew I had placed it in the glass bowl of potpourri on Fred's nightstand.

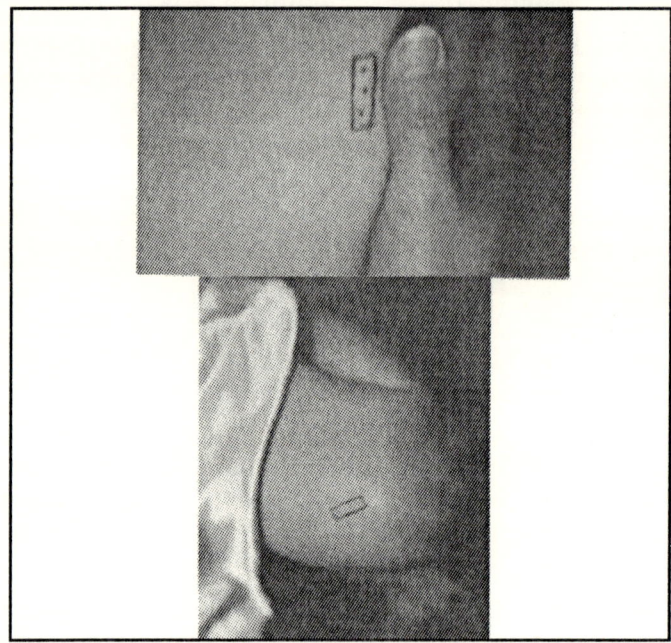

Photo enhanced red circles

December 1, 1995

After showering and drying, I again discovered two more, very red, swollen circles on my right leg on the side of my knee. The two circles were connected by a straight line, which was also very swollen. (Right knee circles 0---0). The circles on my left knee looked a lot better. The swelling had gone down and the color was not so red. The circles on my right knee seemed to be turning brownish.

I assumed the markings on my right knee were from an abduction, though I had no memory of having been taken the evening before. Otherwise, I felt fine and happy. So how did I get the other two circles?

THE GREYS TELL ME OF ILLNESS

December, 1995

Once again, I had feelings of anxiety, nervousness, and unrest. The symptoms began early in the evening. I knew something was going to happen but didn't know what.

I tossed and turned in bed and hated when Fred finally turned off the bedroom light. I waited in anticipation, but nothing occurred. I don't know what time I finally fell asleep but surprisingly, I awoke on their ship! My friendly Grey, Raytheon, was there by my side. I had the feeling they had already done something medical to me and I had not been allowed to be awake for the procedure.

My next memory was of standing up. Raytheon was telling me to walk with him. I did as he instructed. Even though I had been abducted by the Greys many times, I still had a lot of fear about what was going to happen to me. It was so hard to move my legs and follow the instructions that were given. My head would spin harder each time, making me want to fall to the cold floor. The Greys never seemed to listen to me when I protested. It did not matter if they had me paralyzed on a table or not.

I wondered why they had given me the freedom of being able to walk around with Raytheon when I had seen other human beings either strapped to or paralyzed on examining tables as they endured God-awful examinations. Some humans appeared to be dead while others thought they were screaming wildly (just as I did each time).

Why had I been granted the privilege of being able to walk to other areas of their ship? Why was Raytheon assigned to me? Why was he always my guide, pretending to be a "safe," knowledgeable friend to me? When Raytheon had verbal encounters with the mean Grey (who seemed to be the "boss"), he would always win in "our" favor. Otherwise, I'm certain there would have been much worse experiments and treatments in store for me.

As I walked with Raytheon, I felt very weak. I took each step with caution. We walked down a familiar, lighted, circular hallway. I was not told where we were going. Raytheon was speaking to me as we entered a room I recognized. I had been in that room before. Another Grey was present in the room. He was standing next to Winsha, who was sitting on a small silver chair. Her body appeared to be limp. She was being supported in the chair by three dark gray (or black) bands that went across her body.

Winsha recognized me immediately. She kept trying to reach for me and her large almond-shaped eyes were on me constantly. I felt she was happy to see me. I asked Raytheon what would happen to Winsha if the bands were removed from her body. We walked over and he took the bands off her body. She suddenly fell forward in the chair, but did not fall to the floor. Her body was very limp.

She lifted her head and looked directly at me. I heard her trying to call out to me in a low, scratchy voice. Winsha had a voice! I was filled with excitement at the thought of being able to communicate with her verbally. She said what sounded like "CT" and "DT." Raytheon knew what Winsha was trying to ask me. He told me she was asking about our cat and dog.

We'd had only one dog, a Carin Terrier named Queenie. Queenie had died in 1987. The cat we'd had was a Persian, named Princess. Princess had died in 1988.

More incoherent words came out of Winsha's small mouth. The Grey that was standing by her chair left so we could be alone. Raytheon continued to speak to me telepathically. I do not remember the full conversation we had. Winsha was also trying to speak to me. Because Raytheon was better able to understand what Winsha was saying, he acted as interpreter for me.

Apparently, Winsha had been in our home and played with Queenie and Princess. She described both pets. I found out she had "visited" us more than once! Since then, we had adopted two other Blue Persian cats.

That small bit of conversation told me that Winsha must have been older than I originally thought she was. Maybe the other small girl I had seen put into the silver tank was not Winsha, but a younger hybrid daughter I may have had. I felt very confused.

The mean Grey came up and joined us. He stood directly in front of me. He told me they were going to keep me and not allow me to return to my home. They needed to train me and use me. Raytheon immediately responded with "NO! Let her go home for her Christmas."

Winsha in Silver Chair

A confrontation seemed to be taking place in front of me between the two Greys. The mean Grey was dominant over Raytheon. Somehow, I heard part of their argument. The mean Grey quickly turned to me and I could sense he was very upset. Sternly, he told me, "Get your affairs in order!" Those were not his exact words, but that is the jist of what he said to me.

Next, he told me I was going to become very sick and I had better go to what we call a hospital if I wanted to live. He told me what would eventually happen to me after my Christmas.

I clearly remembered those two statements the next day after the "dream." The mean Grey always spoke as if he was angry. Every time I encountered the mean Grey, he was angry. That always increased my fear when I had to deal with him.

The next morning, after waking up, I was afraid and worried about the mean Grey's statement. I asked myself, "What exactly does he know? How does he know I'm going to become quite ill and have to be hospitalized?"

My health had never been better. I had been feeling very well. I prayed and pleaded just the same, to Our Lord, for His intervention. I prayed all day long, hoping that the threat was just a threat and would not really happen to me.

I had recently undergone many medical tests, preliminary to seeing Dr. Carleson for my carpal tunnel that was not healing. I had even been tested for gallbladder problems because some of the medications Dr. Carleson had me on were causing me to throw up. All the tests had come back negative, except for the carpal tunnel. So I knew I was in good health.

I did not tell Fred and other interested parties everything about that last visit with the Greys. I did not want anyone concerned and worried about me. I continued to pray daily about the prediction of the mean Grey. Every day I told myself, "How dare he do such a thing to my life!"

As Christmas drew near, I became cocky. My health was perfect except for the carpal tunnel. Dr. Carleson was going to avoid surgery at all costs and see if he could heal my wrist without surgery.

Christmas came and went. I began to laugh at the mean Grey and his pronouncements. Fred had planned a small trip to San Francisco, California. It was to be a get-away for us since we had not had a vacation in a long time. I was very excited about the trip. Three days after Christmas, I decided the mean Grey had been wrong.

At 2:00 a.m. Thursday morning, I woke up with severe pain in my lower right abdomen. I was very nauseated. Some of the carpal tunnel medications I was taking did not agree with me. I assumed the reason for my stomach pain was the medication. I was in and out of bed that night. I spent the majority of my last hour at home, sitting on the bathroom floor, doubled-up with pain. I was very weak. In the end, I could not walk or even sit. By 4:00 a.m., I was ready to go to the emergency room.

Fred drove me to Anna Kaseman Hospital. I remained in the emergency room until about 10:00 a.m. that morning, when they admitted me to the hospital. The ultrasound test for gallbladder showed no problems. My blood and liver enzyme counts were very high and I had a fever. The pain was intense and returned with a vengeance every time the pain medication wore off. They ran other tests that afternoon to find out what was happening. All tests came back negative except for the blood and liver enzyme counts. The doctors repeated the tests and got the same results: negative.

Thursday night, a gastroenterologist came in to examine me. He was looking for digestive or liver disorders. The doctor told me I would have to undergo nuclear testing on Friday morning. If those tests came back negative, I would be transferred to Presbyterian Hospital for another procedure. I would be asleep during the procedure. The doctors would look for cancer of the digestive system, the liver and for tumors in those areas.

Later Thursday night, the nurses came to put me on the bed pan. (I could no longer move my body.) As they turned me on my left side, I heard familiar male and female voices in both my ears. I had heard the voices many times before, as that was the manner in which they contacted me (whoever they were). I did not let them get three words out of their mouths before I told them in a loud whisper to "Go away! Leave me alone!" The voices did not leave. I was embarrassed because the nurse thought I was speaking to her.

My thoughts then turned to a much greater fear of the unknown. I experienced typical symptoms of anxiety, nervousness, and the feeling that "they" were coming to get me that night. Had *they* done something to me that would make me die?

On Friday, the nuclear test came back negative, so I was taken by ambulance to Presbyterian Hospital early that afternoon. That night, I was taken back to Anna Kaseman Hospital with another negative diagnosis.

I was awake when they took me into the operating room at Presbyterian Hospital. I saw the medical testing equipment. The operating room itself was small, with walls the same color as those on the Grey's ship. I became very frightened because it so closely resembled the room I had been taken to on the Greys' ship so many times.

The doctors had given me general anesthesia but I came out of the anesthesia during the procedure. When the anesthetist realized I was conscious, more anesthesia was administered. I remained asleep for the rest of the procedure.

Late Friday evening, I woke up with my family standing around my hospital bed. My condition was worse. I was told that the doctors would perform exploratory surgery early the next morning, Saturday, New Year's Eve.

During surgery, two stones in my gallbladder were discovered. The stones and my gallbladder were completely covered with a substance that appeared to be thick, black, oily sludge. Some time later, after my recovery, I heard of other abductees who'd had the same condition as mine.

The doctors told my family I had been very "uncomfortable" during surgery. My family would not tell me everything I had said or done during surgery. When I questioned them, they simply exchanged furtive looks. They told me the doctors had just said that I kept repeating "I have to wake up." The body language of my family told me much more had actually transpired.

I immediately felt a lot better New Year's Eve and New Year's Day. I became jaundiced as the liver enzyme count continued to climb. New Year's evening, after everyone went home, I was prepared for sleep.

I was awakened during the night by the door to my room being slammed hard. I heard the door being locked. Outside, I heard a male voice along with other female voices arguing that the person could not enter my room. I heard security alarms go off in the hallway. Evidently, some man was trying to enter my room.

It seemed as if the nurses were in my room checking on me every 15 minutes after that. They continued their checks until morning. I asked what had gone on the night before, but my question was avoided and never answered.

Monday evening, a blond nurse came in to take a blood test. That was the second blood test in twenty minutes. As I lay there resting, I thought that was questionable. Then a dark-haired woman came into my room to let me know she had come to take blood. I told her another nurse had taken my blood about twenty minutes ago.

The dark-haired woman said she was the first to take my blood and that she had just begun her rounds. She told me no one else had been there before her. I described the blond nurse to her and she did not recognize the description of the other lady! We never did find out who the other lady was.

A couple of days later, I was accidentally released from the hospital with a high liver enzyme count that was never resolved. I do not know when it became normal. I had to go back to the doctor's office after being home for only one day.

It had been discovered that before I left the hospital, the most recent vials of blood taken from me were missing. I was so fed up with the paranormal activities and all the poking and prodding, that I never followed through with the additional gastroenterologist appointments. I knew I would get better on my own.

Approximately four weeks after surgery, I arrived home from a doctor appointment to find a message on our answering machine. The phone call was from a surgeon who had been in the operating room when I was in surgery. He wanted to speak with me about something that had occurred during surgery.

I called him back several times, using the number he'd left on our machine. The receptionist at his office told me repeatedly that she had handed him the message. The doctor never returned my phone call.

I still wonder exactly what transpired in that operating room. I asked the surgeon in charge if anything unusual had happened while I was in surgery. His answer was "No."

January 6, 1996

I could not fall asleep due to the anticipation and anxiety of knowing the Greys were going to come. I really did not want to turn off the table lamp. Many times I would fall asleep with the light on, then wake up later and turn it off.

I went through the aggravation of tossing and turning, and in the end, finally reached over and switched the light off. Half an hour later, I was still awake in the dark bedroom. Bright moonlight was the only source of illumination. I was looking toward the south bedroom wall where there was a doorway to the bathroom. I heard the familiar sound of the wall breaking up.

I had finally figured out how to identify the noise I heard when the entities made an entrance. It sounded like a hand running over a venetian blind. As soon as I heard the familiar noise, they came through the wall. I was shocked to see four of them. Something about them felt different this time. I realized what it was: they were Greys, but they were taller. I did not remember having seen these taller Greys. It scared me even more than usual.

Silently, I asked myself, "What do they want from me?" As I looked toward them I saw that their skin was bathed in moonlight. I could feel my body turning cold with fright until I was frozen stiff. Fred was in a deep sleep and was snoring. Suddenly, the snoring stopped and I heard him breathing heavily.

190

The Four Greys

Apparently, I was taken that evening by the Greys, but I have no memory of leaving my bed. When I awoke, I found myself lying on the familiar silver table in the hospital-like room, staring straight up at the medical tools that would probably soon invade my body. The room was brightly lit. After my usual rebellious outbursts of screaming, fighting for my life and trying to get away from those controlling creatures, I felt the cold numbing hand over my forehead and up into my hair. I knew at that point, I would know nothing more and everything would turn black.

I had been having a lot of pain in my right leg. During the previous month, I'd had sharp pains in both my legs.

The next memory I had, was of leaving my body again. I felt as if I was becoming an expert at this, but did not understand how I could do it. As I looked down, I saw my body lying on the silver table. I wanted to turn and look at the room I was in. On the wall opposite the silver table, I saw clearly, something I had not been able to distinguish from my position *on* the table. I floated close to the black wall and saw a

191

long row of some kind of medical equipment that appeared to be attached to the wall. Next to the medical equipment were many small, black boxes with various knobs on them. I saw some kind of unusual writing on the black boxes. Two of the smaller Greys were standing by the black boxes. There were many of the same size boxes along the wall.

I turned back to see what they were doing to my nude body. I was shocked to see tubes coming out of my uncovered body. Many times before, they had covered me with a smooth, soft, warm blanket that felt almost like silken rubber. I looked toward the floor of the room. The floor appeared to be the same shade of yellow as the walls. The room was circular.

Out of Body again

I was told by the Greys that they had to take whatever they take from me to give to Winsha. I was told I would have to eat a lot of foods that contain a lot of sugar to enhance the substance the Greys removed from my body to give Winsha. I was given that instruction as I floated above the Greys and my

192

body. I don't think the Greys knew I was having an out-of-body experience.

This was the memory that remained with me when I woke up the next morning.

THE MISSING CASSETTE TAPES

January 16, 1996

I wrote a letter to Karen regarding a trip I had taken with Ray and Mary Rowlison and Mr. and Mrs. Dustin. We had gone to Santa Fe and Alcalde, New Mexico. I had sent Karen copies of the cassette tapes I recorded of Ray Rowlison and Ray Marrow. They had been guests on Fox KASA radio on January 9, 1996.

On January 23, 1996, I received a phone call from Karen. She was very exasperated about the events that took place after she received the wrapped tapes I'd sent her. Here is what she told me.

When she went to collect her mail on Saturday, my package, along with another package, was in her mailbox. She opened the envelope I had mailed the cassette tapes in, and saw the two audiotapes wrapped in pink bubble wrap. I had wrapped the two cassettes together and made a pocket out of bubble wrap. I then put the tapes into the pocket and secured the bubble wrap with packaging tape.

Karen said she put the package into her large carrying bag, along with the other mail she'd received, and walked to a copy store. She put her purchases into her large bag and then went directly home. When she arrived home, she took out my package and put it on a table. She removed the tape and looked inside the bubble-wrap pocket. She noted that there were two tapes still in the bubble wrap, and put them down on the table. She then left the room for a brief time.

When she returned five or ten minutes later, intending to listen to the tapes, she saw only one cassette in the bubble wrap. She searched the floor and under other items that were close by, thinking she had accidentally dropped the other cassette. She could not locate the missing tape. She then called the copy store to find out if the missing tape had somehow slipped out of her bag. They had not found a cassette tape.

Karen definitely remembered seeing two tapes in the bubble wrap. She also remembered that she had put both tapes down on the table before walking out of the room. She retraced her footsteps in the apartment to see if she could locate the missing cassette. It was nowhere to be found.

Next, she picked up the one remaining tape and put it into her recorder. The audio was not clear at all. The tape had country music on it! She said she could barely hear a man's voice on the tape, but it was unintelligible. Karen played a portion of the tape to me over the phone. All I could hear was country music.

She was very upset about the missing cassette and the fact that the remaining one was messed up. I had played both tapes before mailing them to her and they had been just fine. Both had been clearly audible recordings of Ray on the KASA radio program and the small convention we had attended in Alcalde, NM.

Neither Karen nor I know what transpired in the five or ten minutes she was gone from the room that day. Neither of us knows what happened to the missing tape, or why the remaining tape was recorded over with country music. We both felt someone did not want her to hear those two tapes. The missing tape was never found.

During that same phone call, Karen confirmed that she had received the package of snapshots I had mailed to her. They showed the round, red circles on my left leg.

Through her research over the years and through contact with other investigators and researchers, Karen said many other abductees were also marked in the same way. It seemed to signify that the Greys or other entities belong to the Orion Belt, and that possibly, I come from there as well. She said the Orion Belt has been reported to be a beautiful place.

She went on to describe the location of the Orion Belt, so I could locate it in the night sky.

BRUISES

January 21, 1996

I didn't always check my body for bruises after an abduction. Many times while dressing in the morning, or undressing at night, Fred would notice bruises on my body. I was getting used to having bruises after an abduction. It was becoming the norm for me. When I could, I documented every incident of abduction or unusual bruising that had not been self-inflicted.

While dressing on the morning of January 21st, I noticed another unexplained bruise on my left thigh. It was located on the right side toward the middle of my thigh. The bruise was a half-inch long and a quarter-inch wide. The shape was irregular. I also had two other bruises on my right leg toward the left side of my upper right thigh. The bruises were circular. They were different than the bruises on my left thigh. Half an inch above my knee, I found a small, raised dot that resembled a needle mark. When I touched the spot, I felt slight pain. It felt as if I had a sticker in that area on my leg. The needle mark became red and irritated as the day wore on.

THE WHITE STREAK

January 22, 1996   Wednesday a.m.

I had been sitting on the edge of the bed for some time, just waiting. I did not know what I was waiting for. Fred had been in the bathroom for awhile and I finally heard him turn on the shower. Our bathroom consisted of two rooms with two doors.

I turned my head toward the door of the outer bathroom where the two sinks were. What came out of that room as Fred turned on the shower shocked me. I saw a white streak approximately two feet long and about a half-foot across. It was about two feet above the carpeted floor. It moved quickly from the outer bathroom toward the bed where I was sitting. Then, it just disappeared into thin air! As it disappeared, I suddenly felt a very strong presence standing in front of me in our bedroom. The presence remained with me for the duration of the day.

January 24, 1996   Friday a.m.

I still had faint bruising from Tuesday. On January 24th, I located three more slightly raised, very red dots. They were on my right thigh, above the original bruises and close to the vaginal area. The three new, red dots resembled needle marks. To the right of the three needle marks was a larger red dot, approximately one inch away. The color of the larger, single mark was reddish blue. My skin was very irritated in that area and appeared strange. I knew I had not had those marks on that part of my body before I went to bed the previous evening. I had pictures taken of my legs.

WHO IS CALLING ME?

February 15, 1996

It began on February 15th. I was not asleep when I heard someone calling, "Mom." When it first began, I thought it was Michelle or Brian calling from their bedrooms. I got up and went to each of their rooms to see what they needed. I discovered both of my children sound asleep in their beds. I searched my bedroom for the unidentified voice that called out to me. This continued for many nights and only happened at nighttime.

The scenario was played out every night. Someone would start calling out, "Mom." Even when I was asleep, I would be wakened by the voice calling, "Mom."

After being awakened by the voice for several nights and realizing it was not Michelle or Brian, I would stay awake. I laid in bed, listening. Soon after being awakened, I would hear some kind of movement along with a quick sound, like wind passing through the bedroom. The sound seemed to exit through a wall. As I listened to the voice and paid more attention, I began to realize that sometimes it sounded like a male voice, and other times, like a female.

Whoever was calling "Mom" at night, soon afterward began to call out during the day as well. Again, it was either male or female. I heard it constantly and clearly, calling me. I would be driving down the street with the car windows rolled up and the radio turned off, and suddenly, I would hear my name being called out: "Gloria."

This happened more than once. Sometimes it would happen in a crowded grocery or department store. I would turn and search for the unknown person who had called out. I would find no one I recognized. The voice was very loud and very clear.

I became somewhat paranoid. I began to look around for the owner of the voice. I also began to look up, but was never able to see anyone or anything.

THE SMALL LIGHT

March 6, 1996

Something woke me late in the night or in the early morning hours of March 6th. I found myself lying in bed on my left side, facing the east wall of the bedroom. For some unknown reason, my eyes were drawn toward the carpet. Approximately 1 to 1 ½ feet away from the bed, in front of the nightstand, was a very bright, circular light. It was approximately 1 ½ to 2 inches in diameter and was shining on the carpet.

I lay still, looking at the light, trying to figure out where it might be coming from. It was not a reflection from outside because I looked out the window and it was cloudy. The circular light was a very bright, white spot. I was afraid to get out of bed to investigate the source so I just laid there for some time, looking at it. The light did not flicker or move in any direction. It simply remained in the same place.

I decided to slowly take off one of the white socks I was wearing and throw it into the light. As I threw my sock into the spot of light, it seemed to travel throughout the whole sock like lightening or an electrical charge. The entire sock was illuminated!

I sat up in bed, awe struck, and afraid to move or touch the sock. I became more brave and got out of bed. I walked slowly toward the lit-up sock, grabbed it, and quickly threw it. It landed on the bed, by my pillow. I remember thinking I would have to remove the sock from the bed if I wanted to get back into bed. I thought that whatever had happened to the sock might possibly harm Fred as he slept. I had to remove the sock, and quickly.

As soon as I picked up the sock, it was no longer illuminated. I turned around to see if the circular, white light was still on the floor, and it was. I kept my eye on the round, white light. It seemed to dim from white to orange. Then it became even dimmer and flickered out, just as a candle would. I could not fall asleep right away, but did eventually.

When I woke up the next morning, I immediately investigated the area. Where the light had been on the carpet, was a dark, circular spot. It appeared to be the same size as the light had been. The spot was a darker brown than the rest of the carpet. The stain remained on the carpet until the 14th of March.

Though the stain faded back to the original color of the carpet, the carpet appeared to have been burnt. Eventually, the carpet fibers did regain their normal appearance and no longer looked as if they had been burned.

THE END OF A FRIENDSHIP

April 8, 1996

April 8th was the day I realized that certain people who had been guiding me through the UFO and alien abduction phenomena were creating much distress in my life. The people I had confided in were attempting to control and manipulate me into a belief system I was not comfortable with. The friendship had broken down.

By then, I had become very intimidated by those who proclaimed I had better react to their given directives to get rid of the entities. They demanded I share their belief system and told me I was not to listen to any other authorities on the subject. The friendship culminated in a dictatorship that came close to destroying my peace of mind.

In the beginning, I had been caught up in the friendship because they seemed to be so knowledgeable and had supposedly helped other abductees. I felt they were very understanding and compassionate. I was under the impression that their knowledge of the subject was more extensive than my own, and that they would help me.

Having been in the friendship for many months, I overlooked the hurtful and negative things they presented to me each day. I overlooked all those things because they professed to care about me and the direction my life was taking.

I finally realized what the friendship had grown into: a relationship that was paranoid, delusional, denying and guilt-ridden. I was constantly made to feel guilty about myself. I was told that I *allowed* the entities to prey upon me and that I was not doing anything to stop the abductions. Every day, I was subjected to their accusatory, opinionated, and ego-ridden overtones.

The low point came when I was told that I had a psychological problem. That was when I decided to break off the friendship. What I did not realize at the time, was the extent of the entrapment. I had begun to feel as if Mary Rowlison was a mother figure whose advice had to be obeyed.

An example of this was when she decided I had had enough visitations from evil entities. She told me I should not have to put up with them. I was instructed by Mary to give the entities verbal orders to leave my family and me alone. I was to do anything in my power to accomplish that. I was instructed to pray daily and constantly for the entities to be removed from my life. Repeatedly, I was told that the entities were no good and were destroying my life.

I diligently followed my "orders." When Mary's many suggestions did not work to produce the correct outcome, she accused me of *wanting* the horrific entities in my life. She said that maybe I was reaping joy from the attention I was calling to myself.

I slowly began to see a difference in her attitude toward me. After a year had passed, her control over me had become even stronger. I foolishly perceived it to be a "safety net" of love and concern for me. I finally understood that our relationship was *not* a healthy one. Mary accused me many times, saying that I must enjoy being abducted, since I was not doing anything to stop the abductions. There were many other demeaning accusations as well.

She told me she was going to act on my behalf, through her new belief in angels and her new club of angel friends. They would pray one evening, and call the angels in to save me and my family. A candle would be burned for me that evening. Apparently, I was prayed upon all evening. Their prayers were not answered because the abductions actually increased.

During that time, a lot of false empathy was shown toward me. The accusations continued about my not doing anything to stop the abductions. I was told that I must *certainly* enjoy being abducted, brutally tested, and come home with bruising and sores all over my body.

Mary Rowlison then suggested I seek help from a psychiatrist or psychologist to find out why I did not want the abductions to stop. She thought I had gotten to the point of insanity with this.

I was still included in the Rowlison's restaurant gatherings and a short trip to hear Ray speak on a Santa Fe radio station. As part of that same trip, we drove to northern New Mexico, where Ray was to give a lecture on UFOs to about ten or twelve people in Alcalde. I deeply regretted that trip. The evening was full of anger and intimidation that was vented on me in front of a couple of mutual UFO friends.

The one woman I had met through the Rowlisons continued to be my friend. She remained friends with the Rowlisons, but ended her relationship with them some months later. Through my lady friend and some other friends who knew the Rowlisons, rumor was, that they had been speaking of me and my experiences in a derogatory manner.

The Rowlisons themselves were not abductees. They used to tell me that they would both love to experience alien abduction. If they had truly listened with compassion, they would have realized the trauma abduction causes in one's life. If they had been motivated by genuine concern for abductees, I don't think they would have wished that for themselves. I felt there was some jealousy on their part because they were not abductees.

As the years went by, I saw and heard of other abductees who were treated in the same manner I had been treated by the Rowlisons. I spoke with some abductee friends whom I'd met at a later date. They told me of their own situations and experiences with the Rowlisons.

The Rowlisons' knowledge seemingly came from the many books and videos they owned about UFOs and alien abduction. I'm guessing they felt knowledgeable and compassionate in their role of controlling and "helping" abductees.

Because of the actual accusations made by Mary Rowlison about my being insane, Karen had her work cut out for her. She led me from questioning my sanity to the healing process I would need to deal with my experiences.

I had been so gullible that I believed all the negative things I was told about myself. It wasn't until I separated from those people and ended the relationship, that I was able to find healing and growth within myself.

On the same day I left the friendship behind, I received a letter from Karen. The letter contained the names of two UFO investigators living in the Albuquerque area. It was planned that I would contact these two ladies. I called Joan Duce-Ashe and Sue Minshall and arranged for us to meet at my home.

Joan and Sue presented themselves as concerned, warm and caring ladies who had worked in the UFO field as investigators. They listened intently to my stories of dreams and experiences with the entities. They gathered their information. They told me to call them when I needed someone to talk to regarding this phenomena. Both women stayed by my side until 1998. They comforted me when I called about the strange phenomena that occurred in our home, both during the day and at night.

What was happening were the first occurrences of abduction by an "entity" that looked human, and wore white lab coats or camouflage military uniforms. It also seemed that some kind of scare tactics were being used on me.

For example, one morning while I was downstairs, I suddenly heard a very loud noise. It sounded as if a large piece of furniture was being moved and dropped several times. There was a sound of metal hitting wood. The vibrating noise seemed to have come from upstairs. I ran up the stairs and checked the two bedrooms. The furniture appeared to be undisturbed.

I walked out onto the balcony to check the arroyo for any activity that would explain the noise, such as men working to clean up weeds. No one was around and none of the neighbors were out working in their yards. I walked back into my bedroom from the balcony and looked down at the carpeted floor. I noticed that something was different about the wooden armoire. It was out from the wall about two inches more than it should have been.

I saw the long crease in the carpet behind the armoire where it had set for many months. I also noticed the crease in the carpet that ran under the front of the armoire. The armoire had been moved. I was not capable of moving the armoire myself. It was over five feet high and about four feet long. Yet someone had moved that heavy piece of furniture. But who?

I asked Fred if he had moved the armoire and he said no, why would he move it? He had no reason to move it. By coincidence, the armoire has metal pulls on the large doors. I believe that *someone* moved it that morning.

Many times when the outside balcony door was closed, the inside bedroom door would slam shut by itself. Other doors in the house, though not any particular one, would also suddenly slam shut.

Some invisible person would walk down the wooden stairs. You could hear each step creak as they walked. Yet no one was there.

Airplanes and helicopters would fly so low and close to the house, I would run outside to look. When I got there, I saw no planes or helicopters. But I heard them, just the same.

Dishes and glasses would bang against themselves. I would hear the front door open and close, as if someone had walked into the house, yet no one was there. I would hear knocking on the inside walls of the house. For a fraction of a minute, I would see a man in the house, then he would be gone. This occurred many times, but never long enough to recognize the person.

I would feel tapping on my shoulders, and when I turned around to see who it was, no one would be there. I would hear footsteps, or water being turned on in the upstairs bath, or the toilets flushing.

These phenomena occurred at any time of the day or night. For awhile, I felt as if they had succeeded in making me so paranoid I did not want to remain in my house. I would get ready for work very quickly and would try to leave early. If I knew I would have to be alone at night, I did not want to go home. When I'd had enough, I would call Sue and Joan. They would come sit with me, calm me down, and the three of us would then try to reason it all out.

MY EYES

April 20, 1996

I opened my eyes in the darkened bedroom, not knowing what time it was. I rolled onto my back and closed my eyes. Suddenly, a very strong, bright light shined directly onto my closed eyes. I struggled to open my eyes to see where the bright light was coming from, but found that I could not open them at all.

At the same time, I heard a loud "POP." At that point, I was able to open my eyes. I saw no one. I saw nothing unusual in the bedroom. I immediately experienced a sharp, deep pain in both eyes.

For two days, the pain was intense and constant. The pain made it difficult to wear my contact lenses. I did not know if someone had done something to my eyes, or exactly what had happened. After two days of this, I decided I'd better make an appointment with the ophthalmologist.

I could not get in right away and had to wait several days for the appointment. Two days later, my eyes felt a lot better and I cancelled the appointment. The reason I was so quick to cancel was my reluctance to explain my Alien abduction to the doctor, should he find no reason for the pain. I knew he would not believe me. I was certain the entities had something to do with that experience.

April 26, 1996

I awoke, lying nude, on a movable table. The room was small and circular. The walls were yellowish or ivory colored. I thought I recognized the room because, to my right, I could see a partition that divided the moveable tables they had us laying on.

To my right, also lying on a table, was a very young lady. I thought she must be twenty or twenty-five years old. She was able to raise her head and chest up from the table. She looked at me with a very fearful face. She was crying and she told me she was afraid. I think I told her not to be afraid, that it would be over quickly, and to lie down. I thought she was a very pretty young woman, and the drawing I later made of her does not do her justice.

I was able to move my head and look on the other side of the partition. At the far end of the room, lay a heavy-set woman. Her voice was deep and she was very upset and angry. She kept voicing her opinion of the situation quite loudly. She used foul language repeatedly, then continued to say something else under her breath. I could not hear what she was saying. The heavy-set woman kept yelling at the young lady and the woman who was on a table in front of me. She told them to just shut up and kept cussing at them because they would not stop crying.

I could not see the face or upper part of the heavy-set woman's body, because the partition had been pulled forward to where I could not see around it. The woman had her right leg bent at the knee and her left leg out straight.

The lady on the table in front of me and to my left, had short, black hair. I noticed that she too, was nude. I could not see her face, so I do not know what she looked like. She continued to cry to herself.

Soon, three Greys walked into the room from the right side, walking past the heavy-set woman. They went directly to the table where the lady with the black hair lay. My body began to tremble. I thought they were coming for me because they had looked in my direction. I had no idea what they were going to do to the four of us women.

The Greys stood at the head of the table, blocking my view of the black-haired lady. I wanted to see what they were going to do to her so I could prepare myself for what was coming. I could not calm myself down. The other two ladies were crying and the heavy-set woman kept cussing and yelling.

The black-haired lady began to moan and cry harder when the Greys began to work on her. This made me even more upset and more afraid. I wanted to yell out loud for everyone to just shut up! The black-haired lady moaned and cried again.

Then something happened that I did not understand. Another entity came into the room. The entity was not a Grey but appeared to be human, like me! He had on a white mask that covered his nose and mouth. He wore a white cap on his head. He was taller than the Greys. It was very shocking to me to see another human being come into the room and work along with the Greys on us!

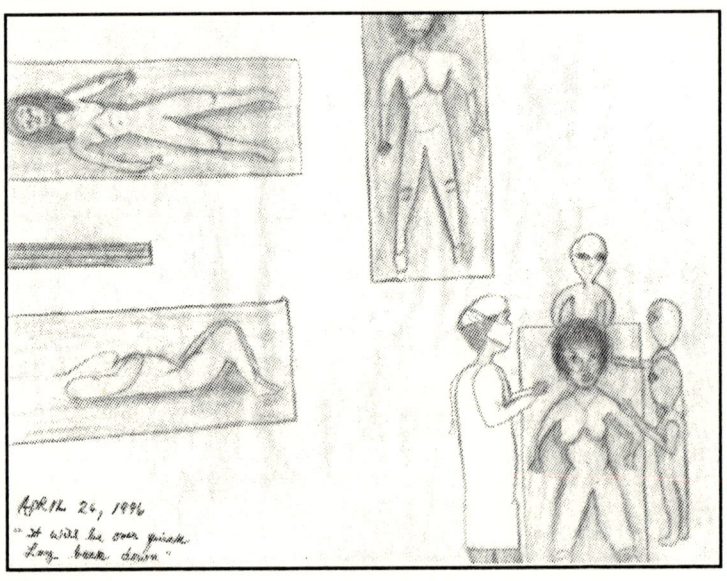

APRIL 26, 1996
" It will be over quickly.
Lay back down."

It will be over soon

He stood at the foot of the table I was lying on with his back toward me. I saw his arms moving as if he was doing something to the black-haired lady's head. Then he moved to the opposite side of the table. When he did that, I could not see very well what they were doing to her. She began to moan and cry a little bit louder as they worked on her.

206

The heavy-set woman became more agitated at hearing the black-haired lady moan and cry. I became very nervous and I trembled. I kept telling the young lady not to cry, to just close her eyes, and that she would be okay.

I don't know if I passed out or what happened next. This is all I remember of the dream.

I woke up half an hour later than usual the next morning. When I tried to get up out of bed, my back and shoulder blades were in pain up to my neck. I had a terrific headache. The pain seemed to be pinpointed in the center of my forehead.

April 26, 1996
young lady who
was on table to
my right side

The young lady

I had severe pain from my right shoulder to the tip of my fingers. I also had pain from my right hip to my toes. I lifted myself up as I bent my body to sit on the side of the bed. As I stood up, there was a sudden, sharp pain on the right side of my body where my good ovary was. The pain shot through me.

When I walked, sat wrong or just turned the wrong way, sharp pain would shoot across my lower abdomen where the uterus should be. My lower abdomen seemed to be swollen. The severity of pain diminished slightly in the early evening, but when I went to bed that night, I had pain in my back, arm, neck, hip and leg.

The next morning when I woke up, I began to experience the morning-after symptoms that come when I have been abducted the previous night. My head would not quit spinning, causing me to feel nauseated. Deep down inside, I just wanted to cry. I cried most of the day. I was still feeling muscle pain in my arm, as if someone had pulled hard on my arm. I found no bruising on my arms, legs or back.

PAUL BUNYAN

June 2, 1996

In this night's dream, I found myself being guided down a hallway by a human woman with blond hair. I had never seen her before. I was unsure if I was on an Alien craft or not. The woman did not speak to me except to give directions. She spoke verbally, and in English. That was how I heard her communications to me. I was unsure if she was a hybrid. She wore a silver uniform. She led me to a small, very well lit room.

As we entered the room, I saw cubicles that reminded me of clothing store dressing rooms. Each cubicle had a door. I counted three cubicles in the room, arranged in an "L". There were two small cubicles on the long side of the wall and one large cubicle on the short side of the wall. The walls were all the same yellowish-cream color.

I was taken to the middle cubicle and told to go inside and wait. Then the woman closed the door to the cubicle I was in. I stood there, dressed in my nightgown, and realized I was not nude. I wondered what I was waiting for, and for whom I was waiting. I was the only person in my cubicle. I heard footsteps followed by the outer door opening and closing.

Waiting felt like an eternity as I stood there, glaring up at the ceiling and looking down at the floor of that strange place. It was deathly quiet in the room. It seemed like many minutes before the outer door opened again.

I heard a male voice talking to someone. The voice was loud and deep. The man was asked to step inside another cubicle. I did not hear the door to his cubicle close. Whoever brought the man in must have also left the room. The room became quiet again and I could hear the man breathing deeply. No communication took place between us.

The outer door opened again, and I heard footsteps walking toward me. The door to my cubicle opened, and the blond woman told me to follow her. Out of curiosity, I looked to my right because I wanted to see the man who had been brought into the room. The door to his cubicle was not closed. I stopped walking. To my amazement, there was a giant of a man standing in the small cubicle. The upper half of his body seemed to tower over the top of the door to his cubicle. He appeared to be anywhere from twelve to fifteen feet tall! It is possible my visual perception could have been off and that in reality, he may have only been seven feet tall. I had just never seen such a tall person before.

His body frame was very large. I wondered how his oversized body could fit into the small cubicle. He was indeed, a giant to me! He had a dark beard that extended well below his chin. He had dark, shoulder-length hair.

The man said "hello" to me in English. He told me not to be afraid of the tests they were probably going to give me. He said he had had the same tests and they did not hurt. He said that they were very gentle with him. He asked my name and I told him it was Gloria. He then told me his name but all I could think was that he looked like Paul Bunyan. I did not hear what he said his name was. The man wore a blue and white, plaid shirt with jeans. The blond woman told me to continue walking and I was led out of the room.

My memory blacked out then, and I don't remember what took place next. I don't know who conducted the tests or what type of tests were performed on me. Evidently, I was not allowed to keep those memories; or, I was injected with something that put me to sleep immediately. I do not remember lying on a table or what the room looked like.

THE CATACOMB SHIP

June 20, 1996

I was standing at the kitchen sink. It was 8:00 a.m. I was rinsing dishes and thinking about everything I had to do that day. A very bright light came out of nowhere and suddenly engulfed me. I had previously experienced those lights on many nights, while sleeping. I felt as if my whole body was being controlled as I was led into a vision while I stood at the kitchen counter. This is the vision I saw:

I was taken to a large city where I was placed on a crowded sidewalk on a street that was located in an older part of the city. Many of the buildings were made out of brick. The brick was dark, brownish- red and appeared to be old. I saw many tall buildings as well as shorter buildings, in what seemed to be an older part of the city. Some of the buildings appeared to be ten stories high or taller.

Directly in front of me, were three specific buildings that caught my eye. They were identical to each other and stood in a row. They were of different sizes and had gold, dome-shaped, metal roofs. The metal was not bright and shiny, but old looking. The sky was clear and cloudless. The sun shone brightly. I was standing on the edge of a sidewalk, facing the street, with an unknown person by my side. People were walking hurriedly and going on about their business.

While I stood on the sidewalk, some of the people began to panic. I noticed they were looking up into the sky and to their left. From where I stood, I had to turn my head to the left to see what was happening. People began to scream and the looks on their faces were frightful. The majority of people began to run in different directions, knocking others down to the concrete sidewalk. I saw small children screaming and crying while holding tightly to the adults they were with. Some people simply froze in place and would not move.

As I looked in the direction everyone else was looking, I saw a large, strange-looking spacecraft hovering over us. The ship made no noise. It was approximately twenty feet high and twenty feet wide. It had the color of dull aluminum. The craft was about thirty to forty feet above us. As it hovered, metal panels began to open from the middle of the craft. Each panel folded onto itself until the ship was half-way open. From where I stood, I was able to look inside the ship. I saw no Aliens or anyone who could be controlling the craft.

I was told telepathically that the craft was called a "catacomb craft." I looked into the open part of the craft and saw strange individual compartments. The compartments reminded me of a honeycomb. The honeycomb compartments were white. The ends were clear so that you could actually look into each one. There were several rows of the padded compartments.

There was more screaming from the crowd. A slim, young, Caucasian man who appeared to be about twenty-five to thirty years old, almost fell to the street where he had been standing. The man had black hair and was wearing a blue, dress shirt, black pants, and black shoes. What transpired next was eerie.

His body folded from the waist and was lifted up into one of the hexagon honeycomb compartments in the ship. Seconds later, another man who was standing close by in the street, was suddenly lifted from a standing position. His body folded the same way the first man's body had, and he was gently lifted and put into a horizontal position, floating upward toward the craft. He was placed in another honeycomb compartment.

This process continued until all the sections of the honeycomb were filled with women, children, and men. The people who were taken seemed to have fallen asleep immediately after being chosen from the street. Their bodies became relaxed and they did not fight to get away. The people who were still standing on the sidewalk and in the street were screaming hysterically. They shouted, "They are taking us! They are taking humans!"

Through the mayhem, I heard someone calling my name, "Gloria! Gloria!" I looked around to see who was calling out to me, but saw no one.

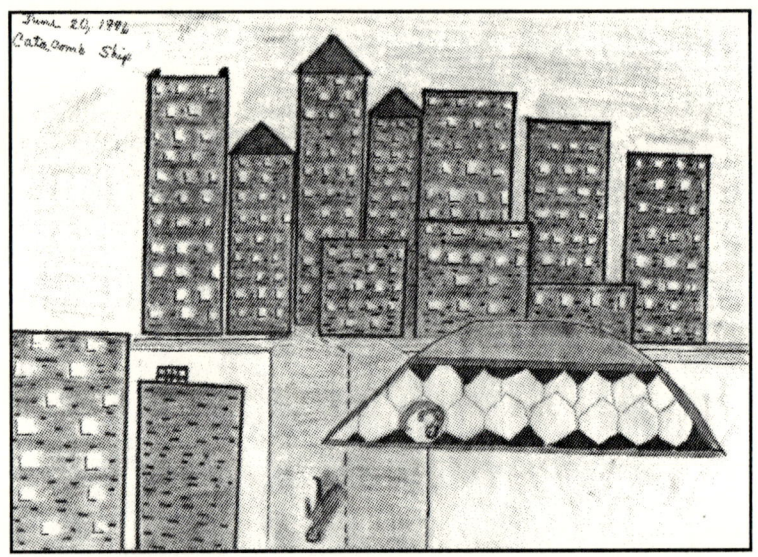

The Catacomb Ship

As quickly as I had been drawn into the vision, I was taken out of it and returned to my kitchen. I was standing with my hands in the sink and water was running from the facet. I felt as if I had awakened from a bad dream. No one else was in the house with me. My body began to shake and I had to sit down.

I was mentally confused and did not understand what I had just experienced. I felt as if I had been shown a movie. I suddenly remembered being shown another type of "movie" previously, but did not understand how the visual process had taken place.

That night, I called Karen. I could not answer many of her questions. We thought the description of the three buildings might indicate where the activity could take place, if it had not happened already.

Over the next several days, I went to the library and located some architecture books to learn about domed buildings of the type I had seen. Many of the books showed buildings from various cities in the United States. I searched further and found books with pictures of buildings that had been built in other countries around the world. I found buildings that had the domed, gold-metal roof I had seen in the vision, but could not find three similar buildings, side-by-side, as I had seen in the vision.

I looked up the definition of catacomb: *any of a series of galleries in an underground burial place; usually used in plural.*

THE HISTORICAL ROOM

July 9, 1996

I woke up on board the Greys' ship. I was being helped up from the table I had been lying on. I was escorted out of the room by a Grey and a human and led down a hall to another room.

In the room, I was shown a light-green, glowing, square panel. On the revolving panel were kept the histories of abductees. On each record was the abductee's height, weight, color of hair and eyes, and a small digital photo of the person. Also listed were the number of times they had been taken, the purpose, and which tests had been done to that particular human. The record specified if the human was assigned to a particular position and who they were working with.

July 13, 1996

While lying awake that evening, an electronic male voice began to speak and give me information about the catacomb space craft. I was told that the craft was used to transport human beings from Earth to a particular alien planet. The humans were put into a "near-death mode" for transport. They would remain that way until they (the aliens) thought the time was right to awaken them for our survival or the survival of the entities. We would then share one world (planet).

I was told that the catacomb space craft was real and had been used by other entities in the Federation that come to Earth. I was not told how long the humans are "stored" or when the catacombs would be reopened. Many humans of different races and nationalities had been taken. My feelings were such that I did not know if the humans that had been taken, and the ones that were going to be taken, would survive to re-populate the world.

I was shown one way the entities can take people off the streets when their other means of abduction fail. I soon realized that there are many millions of missing people in our world. Had they been taken by various entities of the Federation for that purpose? Were they being stored on an unknown planet for the purpose of re-populating our world?

SUSPECTED IMPLANTS

In the early part of 1995, when I was abducted and lying on the Greys' table, I noticed that they frequently worked on my ears or my nose. They seemed to work on the left ear more than the right. After they had worked on my ears, I would come back after the abduction suffering from an earache. Many times, the earaches would turn into ear infections.

Other times, my nose would bleed so profusely it was difficult to stop the flow of blood. Some of the nosebleeds would last for two days. My nose felt as if it had been cut open or stretched wide open. The tissue in my nose felt as if it had been poked and prodded. At the time, I did not connect those symptoms to implants having been put into my nose and ears.

I had an uncomfortable sensation of bugs crawling deep within my ears. I was continually digging in my ear with my fingernails or a q-tip to rid myself of the "bug." My efforts produced nothing but ear wax. Many times I asked the doctor to "please look closely. I think I have a live bug in my ear." I was not aware of the fact that the crawling sensation could have been caused by the vibration of the implant. At the time, I knew nothing about implants. Implants were something that happened to other people, not me.

One day, the crawling sensation became extremely bothersome and continued for several days. It felt as if the bug were crawling toward the opening of my ear. I thought that finally, the bug was going to give up its home in my ear. As it crawled closer to the opening, I quickly reached into the ear canal with my finger and brought out not one, but two unusual "bugs!"

To my amazement, they were small and round but not live bugs at all! I got a magnifying glass to take a closer look. They appeared to be made of paper-thin material. There were whitish lines going throughout them. I tried to cut one of the objects with my fingernail to see if it would split in two. It did not. It would not bend as I put it through various tests. When I looked closely, I could see something like small hairs attached to the unusual object.

I was terrified. I did not understand what I had just pulled out of my ear and I did not know what to do with them. Could these be implants? I felt the need to protect the objects and hopefully, hide them so the entities could not find them. I wrapped the two small objects in a tissue. Then I put plastic wrap over the tissue and stored the packet in a safe place.

The crawling sensation had stopped immediately after I removed the objects from my ear. A week later, the sensation began again! This time, it was deep within my ear. I could not reach it with my finger or a q-tip. I eventually got some relief from the sensation when the object quit crawling or vibrating.

Many months went by and the objects seemed to crawl close to the opening of my ear again. I decided that was my chance to grab them again. After using my fingers and q-tips many times, I was finally able to grab two more of the strange objects.

I examined them very closely. They appeared to be the same type as those I had pulled from my left ear months earlier. I laid the objects out on the same Kleenex I had stored the other two in. I got down close and my breath blew one down into the brown carpet. That is how light the objects were. I searched through the carpet but never did find the object that had been blown off the Kleenex.

That same evening, I was again abducted. I awoke the next morning with a much stronger crawling sensation in my right ear. The vibration of the new bug was a lot stronger. It seemed to remain in place and did not crawl around as the other four objects had done.

Each time the vibration began, I would use my finger or a q-tip to dig deeply into the ear, hoping to stop the sensation. I was not able to do so. Next, I pressed the front of my ear with my hand in an attempt to make the sensation stop. I was beginning to believe the object had a mind of its own. At any time of the day or night it would activate. I was resigned to the fact that the Greys who had put the objects into my ear were determined to make them stay there.

About a year later, the object began crawling around in my ear just as the other ones had. I poked and prodded, digging deeply into my ear to get the thing out. Again, I was able to grab two objects with my fingernails. These two objects appeared to be much different from the other four I had previously pulled from my ear. The current variety was still round but came to a point at the top. These also had small hairs on them. Maybe it was the small "hairs" that allowed it to attach to the inside of my ear. The objects were hard to the touch. I attempted to penetrate them with the tip of my nail file and my fingernail, to no avail.

I put the two objects into a small bottle I had. When they fell to the bottom of the bottle, they made a clink, like metal hitting glass. I then dropped an older version of the object into the bottle and it too, made the same sound. I experimented by dropping them into the bottle several more times. Each time I heard the same sound of metal hitting glass.

I began searching through various UFO books to see if I could locate pictures or information on implants. I did not find much.

I was abducted again and came back with another crawling "bug" in my left ear. This new object did not vibrate as much as the others, but when it did, I knew it was in there. The electronic, high-pitched voice that came through seemed to be clearer and much louder when the device activated. I would hear a high-pitched tone or electronic voice that seemed to communicate with me. I had been told that implants were used as locator devices as well.

If I did have an implant in my nose, it did not bother me, aside from causing my nose to bleed profusely. I speculated that the electronic voice I often heard and the high-pitched tones were indeed, coming from the objects I now thought to be implants in my ears. Whoever was monitoring the objects seemed to be able to turn them on and off at any given time.

In 1988, when the Greys finally made me aware of their existence in our lives, I began to notice a high-pitched tone in my ear. I also experienced a crawling sensation in each ear. The tone was not constant, but rather, would be turned on and off like a radio. I would suddenly hear the electronic sound in either my right or left ear, but mostly, in the left ear. Through the electronic sound, I would hear an electronic male or female voice talking to me. I believe that is how I heard my name being called out by whomever was calling to me.

In the Spring of 1999, I attended a UFO conference. I had the opportunity of being scanned by a small machine that resembled a Geiger counter. The machine was designed to pick up radiation counts from an abductee, to determine whether or not there were implants in their bodies. The range of the Geiger counter was from 1 to 10. When it was passed over both my ears, it registered between 9 and 10. When it was passed over an area of my left shoulder, it registered 9.

RED URINE

November 11, 1996

On Monday, the 11th of November, I experienced many emotions. I felt uncomfortable, anxious, and irritable. I felt as if there was an invisible presence following me around the house; as if I was going to bump into one of the Greys at some point during the day. The feelings stayed with me until I retired around 10:30 p.m.

I had been taking an over-the-counter sleeping pill because I would wake up many times during the night and be unable to go back to sleep. Some nights, I would have trouble just getting to sleep. In spite of the sleeping pill, I continued to automatically wake up at 3:30 a.m., which I did on that particular night. The resulting anxiety became so cumbersome I could not go back to sleep.

As soon as my eyes opened, I had the feeling something had happened. I did not immediately remember having been abducted. I lay there in bed for about an hour before finally falling asleep. At 6:50 a.m., I got up to use the bathroom.

I stood up from the commode and turned to flush the toilet. I noticed that the water in the commode was dark. I turned on the light and took another look. The water appeared to be bloody. Since I no longer had a menstrual cycle, I could not understand why I was seeing blood. I had not felt ill during the night or that morning.

I was depressed most of that day. I had a feeling that I had been abducted but had no memory of it. The only evidence I had was the blood in my urine that morning.

By Tuesday evening, the feelings of anxiety had returned, along with depression and general discomfort. I still felt a strong presence and something inside kept telling me the Greys were going to come. The feeling was constant inside me. I verbally argued against the feeling, telling myself I was going to be all right. The more I did that, the more nervous and upset I became. I prayed for safety.

I had taken my sleeping pill early and was ready to retire for the night. I awoke again at 3:30 a.m. with the impression that I had not been in my bed all night. I had no memory of abduction while I lay there in bed. I finally fell asleep.

I woke up at 7:00 a.m. feeling very agitated. My usual trek to the bathroom produced shocking results for the second time. As I turned to flush the toilet, I looked down and saw bloody red water. I screamed to myself, "What is going on?"

Clearly, it was time to make an appointment with the doctor. Something was seriously wrong with me. As I stumbled out of the bathroom, my legs felt as if they had been torn from my body. I thought to myself, "My God! I feel like a split pea!"

I never made the doctor appointment because the next time I used the toilet, my urine was normal. I still had no memory of having been abducted. However, the typical post-abduction symptoms of nervousness and dread stayed with me the rest of the day.

I don't know why I sensed this, but all that day, for some unknown reason, I also knew that my abductor would show up, either at home or at work! I do not know why I said that.

November 15, 1996

I noticed more low-flying airplanes and dark helicopters circling our house several times a week. It happened during daylight hours as well as late night.

November 17, 1996 Sunday

I have documented this to let the reader know that nosebleeds can happen at any time with abductees.

I was eating dinner that Sunday night in November when my left nostril began to bleed for no apparent reason. It felt as if someone had punched me on that side of my nose.

I would have nosebleeds at least twice a day, sometimes profusely. At other times it would bleed as often as every day or as rarely as once a month. The nosebleeds seemed to coincide with abductions that included something being done to my nose by the entities. It was not uncommon for my nose to bleed from both nostrils.

As of the date of this writing (November 17th), my nose bled every day for most of the year. I do not know what the entities have done to my nose. I keep thinking it is a defective implant that has been in my nose for quite some time now.

A BLINKING WHITE LIGHT

November 20, 1996

The night of November 20th, I did not take a sleeping pill. I lay in bed, tossing and turning, trying to go to sleep without the help of medication. I tried everything I could think of to get my body to relax. I prayed for love and peace. I prayed for God to be near us and keep us safe. I prayed He would help me sleep peacefully.

As I prayed away the long, quiet nighttime hours, my thoughts turned to memories of military/government abductions. I tried to reason out those particular abductions. The more I thought about the subject, the more nervous and fearful I became. Sleep was far from me that night. I turned toward Fred and held onto him. I looked at the clock. It was nearly 3:30 a.m. I turned and faced the east bedroom window. In the window, I saw a large, blinking light.

I jumped out of bed, grabbed my glasses and ran to the balcony door. The light was airborne and seemed to travel faster than an aircraft. It emanated from a round object that was not an airplane or helicopter. The light was very close to the east side of our house. It traveled away to the south very quickly.

I jumped back onto the bed to wake up Fred so I could describe what I saw. He barely woke up, so I turned away from him and faced the window again to see if the object would make a second pass.

I don't know if it came back or not because the next thing I knew, I was awake and it was morning. Fred and I discussed the large, blinking light. He had no opinion as to what it was I had seen.

November 27, 1996 Wednesday Night

I was sleeping soundly. I thought I was dreaming, hearing someone call out my name. Abruptly, I woke up and heard my name being called as I lay in bed. "Gloria."

My eyes were open. I saw some flashes of bright white lights going across the room.

November 29, 1996 Friday Morning

Fred's sister, Roni, and her daughter, Lisa, had come to spend some vacation time with us. I had gone upstairs to my bedroom to get dressed. I closed the bedroom door. Alone in the room, I went into the bathroom and began to put on make-up while sitting on the bathroom chair.

Suddenly, I felt a presence close by me. It was as if a real person was standing behind me. There was no one in the room with me. Then I heard a lady's voice begin to whisper something to me. I did not hear her message in its entirety. What I heard was, "Psst --- Come on. Come over here." The other words she said were unclear. When she whispered, I could feel her warm breath on the back of my neck.

I turned around quickly and thought I saw a real person standing in the bathroom with me, but I was alone. The presence seemed to go into the bedroom. I felt as if the presence wanted me to follow her.

Instead, I ran out of the bedroom and stood quietly at the top of the stairs, looking down toward the living room. Vanessa, Roni, and Lisa were sitting there, talking quietly. I was somewhat hesitant to go back into the bedroom and close the door. I left the door open. The presence had evidently left.

WINSHA

January 6, 1997

At about 9:30 p.m., I went upstairs to take a shower. While I was in the shower, I either had a flashback or I was abducted. Whatever occurred, I was thinking of Winsha and Raytheon. I was thinking that it would be nice to be able to see and visit with Winsha. It seemed that immediately after thinking the thought, I felt a powerful presence on the other side of the shower door. I saw no one in the bathroom with me.

I looked through the glass shower door and suddenly, my vision went black. I found myself walking down a hallway with Raytheon, my friendly Grey. As we walked down the hallway, I asked him if I could see Winsha and visit with her. He was taking me to another room but said that he knew where she was. She was in an "activity room."

Raytheon took me to the activity room. As we stood in the doorway, I saw about twenty Greys sitting at and standing by silver-colored tables. There were some items on the tables. The Greys were using their hands to work with the items. I looked around the room. To my right, approximately fifteen feet away, I saw a silver-colored chair and the back of a Grey who had hair like I'd had as a child. I knew it was Winsha. A Grey was standing by her side.

Winsha was sitting there, watching the other Greys work with the items on the tables. The Grey that stood next to her quickly looked toward Raytheon and me, then turned Winsha's chair around to face us. When Winsha saw me, she produced a large smile with her small mouth! I expressed much excitement over her response to seeing me.

Somehow her chair floated toward me as the other Grey walked with her. Winsha was still tied to the chair, the black belts supporting her. The Grey touched a button on the top belt and released the restraints around her body. The belts fell to Winsha's side. I moved toward her and picked her up from the chair. I walked to another chair by one of the tables and we sat down. I held her tightly.

I do not remember if we talked or just sat quietly, looking at one another. Raytheon and the other Grey left the room. I don't know how long Winsha and I visited. I apparently "woke up" some time later, to find myself sitting on the closed lid of the commode. I do not remember if the water was still running in the shower. I do remember sitting in a stupor on the closed commode lid.

SCENARIOS BEING REPEATED?

February 1, 1997

During the summer of 1995, this same incident occurred, just as it did on this day.

Lying awake in the dark bedroom, I heard movement on the outside balcony. It sounded as if a person was either rubbing their body up against a wall, or moving something on the balcony. A few minutes later, I heard movement downstairs, as if someone was walking and rubbing against or scratching on the wall.

I quickly and quietly went to check on Michelle. She was sound asleep in her room, directly across from our bedroom. I did not see anyone moving around from my vantage point at the top of the stairs. I was afraid to go downstairs.

February 2, 1997

I woke up again during the night. My right nostril felt runny. I started to clean my nose and noticed a lot of blood. I went into the bathroom with a full-blown nosebleed that would not stop. The blood was going down my throat. I finally got it to stop bleeding.

When I went back to bed, I noticed a lot of blood on the pillowcase. I laid down on the bed and the nose bleed started up again. I pinched my nose, causing a profusion of blood to run down the back of my throat. I turned on my side and pinched my nose until the bleeding stopped.

February 3, 1997

I was working at the computer on my desk, in our office, when I felt something wet on my lips and chin. When I looked down, I saw a lot of blood on my clothing. I ran to the bathroom to get tissue and to wash up. It took awhile for the nosebleed to stop. I had to take off my blouse and wash it. The nosebleeds occurred every day, twice a day until the 15th of February.

As of this writing, I am still having nosebleeds. It is my understanding that abductees experience quite a few nosebleeds because of the implants inserted into the nose by the entities. Nosebleeds also occur when the entities have been working on an abductee's nose.

THE SNAKE

February 9, 1997 Sunday

Saturday evening, February 8th, I went to bed feeling uncomfortable, tossing and turning until I finally fell asleep. I felt very confused. I did not remember being with or seeing the Greys that Saturday night.

I woke up. Or was I still awake? I had a horrible dream. I heard noises again in the house. This was becoming a regular occurrence. I did not hear the rippling sound the wall made when the Greys would come. I heard instead, a low-pitched, quick pounding.

The dream seemed very real because it felt as if I was wide awake at the time. Michelle now slept in one of the downstairs bedrooms. I heard her calling to me from downstairs. Her voice was soft, but loud enough for me to hear her. Our bedroom door was open. I thought I also heard her bedroom door open.

The next noise was a heavy swishing sound. Michelle continued to call for me. She said, "Mom." and "Mommy." Her voice became clearer and sounded closer to our bedroom. The stairs leading to our bedroom creaked. I then heard an unusual swishing, or something rubbing against the wood. It sounded like something was crawling.

I do not remember getting out of bed but I must have, because I found myself at our bedroom door, looking down the stairs. There was a dim light coming from somewhere. It lit the stairs. What I saw coming toward me was a very large, brown snake with a long, wide body. The body was approximately 1 ½ feet around and about five feet long. It slithered up the stairs!

I cannot describe the terror of what I saw next. I stood frozen in place, shocked, and screaming. No one heard my screams. What I thought I saw was the snake, carrying Michelle in its mouth. As it slithered closer to me, I could not see its head. Instead of a snake's head, the creature somehow had Michelle's head attached to its body! She was calling out to me, "Mom, Mommy, help me!"

I could not comprehend what was happening. The realization was too powerful to see and understand. Initially, I thought that a large snake had somehow gotten into the house and was eating Michelle. It looked as if her head was the last part of her body to be swallowed. But this was not the case. Michelle's head was actually attached to the body of the huge snake. She was looking straight into my eyes. I looked into her eyes and saw they were filled with much pain.

At that point, I think I fainted, or my mind simply blacked out. Whatever happened next, transpired without my knowledge. The experience of that terrifying episode was unforgivable. Whoever had used it for their benefit, whatever the reasoning, be damned! If that was meant to be some kind of sick test for me, may that entity be damned for what they did to me that night!

I don't remember anything more of that night except waking up in bed at some point and feeling paralyzed. I was not even able to sit up. My body shook and I felt as if I was out of my mind. I knew the experience had not just been another terrible dream. It had felt very real.

I lay in bed, wide-eyed, fighting against the paralysis. I could not even run to Michelle's bed to check on her! Something would not let me up. The house was very quiet. I could not even turn or raise my arm to wake Fred. I cannot explain this, but I was forced to go back to sleep.

When I awoke on Sunday morning, I was very disturbed! A thought came to me when I discovered I could get up from the bed; was this some kind of horrible psychological test from the Greys or another entity?

It was 8:00 a.m. when I got up. I raced downstairs to Michelle's bedroom where I found her in bed, sound asleep. I thanked Our Lord that her body was intact and that she appeared to be fine. Normally, Michelle would wake up when she sensed my presence in the room. She did not respond to my presence this time. I decided to let her sleep.

Later that morning, when Michelle got up, I told her about the terrible dream, hoping she could share something of it with me. I dearly needed to know if the event had indeed occurred. Michelle said nothing, simply listened as I told about the event.

Whoever had done this to me knew about my fear of snakes. I detest snakes. They had used someone I loved and superimposed her on the deadliest, most feared thing on earth! For the sake of my sanity, I buried the event in my subconscious; but as I wrote about it, I wanted to cry and shake all over again. I had absolutely no reason to have had such a strange dream as that one.

I got through the day pretty well until that evening, when we watched *The X-Files* on television. The episode was about abductees and agent Scully's alien experiences. One scene took place in a lab with Fox Mulder and the cloned men who worked there. In the lab were large, square aquarium-style containers that held other clones in various stages of development. The aquariums were the same type I had seen on the Greys' ship. The tanks I had seen contained body parts and babies. I have documented this in the section titled "The Laboratory."

Also shown in The *X-Files* episode, were the small black boxes stored against the wall. On The *X-Files*, the boxes held vials of eggs taken from many female abductees. I don't know what was in the small, black boxes I saw (and subsequently documented) on the Greys' ship. The entire scenario really upset me.

I had a hard time getting to sleep that Sunday night because of the previous night's events and The *X-Files* episode. I read until 11:00 p.m. I turned off the light, tossed and turned and finally fell asleep. I was suddenly awakened during the night. I was very restless, agitated and fearful. I recognized the symptoms of an impending Greys visit.

I heard movement downstairs but could not tell if it was someone walking around or banging something against the walls. I heard the stairs creak outside our bedroom door. I was very frightened for Michelle and myself. All I could think of was the snake from the night before. I turned toward Fred and started hitting him to wake him up. When he woke, I told him that they were coming back and coming into the bedroom, or that they were already in the room! He turned to me and held me tightly as he always does.

At that moment, I felt an invisible presence come into our bedroom. The presence came toward the foot of the bed. I told this to Fred and he kissed me and went to sleep! I could not see the presence but I felt it there. I had a strong urge to sleep. I fought the urge but was overcome by it.

When I awoke, it was still dark outside. I had stomach pain. There was a very sharp pain in my anal area that shot upward. I could not move. I tried to wake Fred to tell him about the pain. I also wanted to ask him if I had been abducted that night or if he had knowledge of what had taken place. I could not wake him. I again felt very tired and began to experience a lot of fear. I then fell asleep.

When I woke around 6:30 a.m., Fred was already up and getting dressed for work. I dozed off and on until 7:30 a.m. Fred had already gone to work. I sat on the edge of the bed while my whole body shook inside. I felt very disoriented. I felt as if I wanted to fall to the floor and black out. The anal pain had subsided. When I stood up, I felt very weak. I felt that way all day.

When Fred came home for lunch around 1:30 p.m., we spoke about the night's events. He remembered me hitting him and waking him up. He told me that he was going to ask me if he could go with me during the night.

I was still bothered by all of this, even after talking to Fred, so I called Karen around 6:00 p.m. that evening. She listened as I cried into the phone and told her the story about Michelle, the snake creature, and the previous night's experience.

That night I learned from Karen that the entities use holograms for the psychological testing they do on abductees. I knew very little about holograms and their use. Karen was sure the scenario with Michelle was a psychological test by the entities. She had to do a lot of talking and convincing to get me to understand what had happened.

During our conversation, Karen asked me if I had ever experienced a crash on a Grey's ship. I recalled some of the dreams I'd had. I initially thought I'd had three dreams of being on the Grey's ships that had crashed, on three separate occasions. Sometime later, however, I was certain it had only been two times that I'd been on a ship when it crashed. I never discussed those incidents with Karen because I felt they were simply strange experiences that had not really happened.

As I recalled this incident, I remembered making notes that I had not dated but had written up and stapled to the February 9, 1997 documentation I had made. My notes follow:

228

In this dream, about three weeks ago, Raytheon (my friendly Grey), took me to the so-called cockpit of their spaceship. He walked me down a narrow, rounded hallway into a dimly lit room. When I entered the room, I saw about five other Greys sitting at what appeared to be a control panel. The panel was a half-moon shape.

The chairs were made of silver-colored material and seemed to have black cushions on the seats and backs. There were small round and square colored lights that the Greys pushed constantly with their fingers or hands. The lights were strange shades of bright green, orange-yellow, and red. There were many of these lights and I was told that they were controls.

When they used their hands, the Greys would press on a control that was in the shape of their hands. I don't remember if that control lit up or not.

Raytheon sat me down in one of the two chairs located behind the Greys who were seated at the control panel. I watched them work with their fingers and hands, pushing the various control lights and moving other black objects. I did not recognize the black objects.

I remember joking and laughing to myself the next day about a small steering wheel that one of the Greys had been using. It was as if he had been steering an automobile. I saw three or four small windows above the control panel.

Another Grey came to the door and told Raytheon he had to leave the room. I did not know the reason I had been taken to the cockpit of the ship or why I was left alone with the other Greys; nor do I remember how long I sat in the chair before the following events began.

The Grey on my right looked at the Grey sitting to his left. In unison, they looked at each other. The Grey on my far left, whom I believe was the head "pilot," quickly stood up and walked to the right side where the other Grey was sitting. He spoke to the Grey in a language unknown to me. Somehow, I understood him to say, "Slow it! Slow it."

The head pilot seemed to be excited and emotional. He was waving his arms and his body movements were quick. All the Greys became emotional and reacted very fast. I felt a slight vibration in the floor. Within a short time, the vibration increased and the walls and control panel began to vibrate as well.

I can still hear the sound of metal hitting metal. It seemed to be caused by the vibration. I felt pressure against my body. The head pilot kept telling the others to slow it more and more. I knew something was terribly wrong, but did not know what.

Then it felt as if we slammed into or hit something like a large rock or wall. Or it could have been the result of suddenly slowing the ship. We all landed on the floor. I saw some of the Greys lying immobile on the floor. I too, was thrown to the floor. I heard someone say we crashed. I saw broken metal parts from the inside of the ship, and what appeared to be broken glass on the floor. A piece of black metal slid and covered a window.

A Grey came to the door of the cockpit. He had a hard time opening the door. He said that someone had gotten hurt. I don't know why, but I felt as if we had crash-landed in a mountainous area. It felt as if we had hit a large rock. There was a lot of confusion and disorientation on the ship.

I do not know if this was an actual occurrence or not. It may have been another psychological test to see what I would do and how I would react in a crash situation.

When I woke up in bed the next morning, I remembered the dream and the experience. I do not remember seeing anyone bleed, nor do I remember any of us getting up off the floor. I do not know the extent of the injuries or how severely the ship was damaged.

I had a second dream of a crash about two or three months after the first one. The dream was not documented as an abduction, because I did not see or hear the Greys as I usually did when they came to get me. I passed it off as just a weird dream. The following is a recount of the second crash dream I had.

> *I was lying on a table in a well-lit, familiar room. There were two other human females lying on metal tables as well. A Grey came into the room and spoke to another Grey who was there with us. I do not know what they said to each other. At that moment, the walls began to vibrate and I heard a sound like metal hitting metal or like a riveting of metal. A Grey began to get the other two females and me down from the tables. We were instructed to stay right there, to stand beside the tables, and not move.*
>
> *The two Greys then ran into an adjoining room or hallway. I felt a lot of hard vibration on the floor. I was jolted against the table I had been lying on. I reached across the table with my arms and held onto it until it felt as if the ship had stopped or landed. It was a hard landing. I heard a scraping noise, like sliding metal, coming from the floor. The ship did not roll, but it felt as if we had hit the ground. I saw a Grey open the door to the room the three of us females were in. We were asked to "Come over here, quickly."*
>
> *We did as we were instructed. We went into another room where we saw three other Greys opening a door that led outside. The three Greys ran outside of the ship. I looked outside through the door. When I looked upward, I saw sky. It was twilight outside. I did not know where we were or how I was finally brought back home. I woke up in my bed, next to Fred, the next morning.*

I did not suffer any extensive injuries. The next morning, I did have bruises on my legs and upper body. Again, I am unsure if this was a real experience or a dream. I would think if we'd been in a spaceship that crashed from high in the sky, we would have all been killed. I don't understand this dream. Maybe it was just another psychological, holographic test. Perhaps the craft had been landing or taking off and had crashed from not very high up.

PREPARING FOR THE TRIP TO NEW YORK

February 22, 1997

I had made plans to travel to New York to meet with Karen and Budd Hopkins. On Sunday afternoon, the 22nd of February, I went to the mall to shop for birthday presents and last minute items for the trip.

While in the men's section of a large department store, I had the distinct feeling I was being followed. I looked around and everything seemed to be fine. Ten minutes later, while still in the men's department, I noticed a large, red-haired man staring at me. I did not recognize him. He was with a blond-haired lady. I could not figure out why he was staring at me, unless perhaps, he thought he knew me from somewhere. I thought nothing of it and continued on with my shopping.

I then remembered having seen the same man in another store where I had shopped the past week. What a coincidence to have encountered him and the lady he was with, in other departments and stores I had shopped in recently. I thought it was odd.

February 28, 1997

I was living with the anticipation of actually going to meet Karen and Budd face to face. Early that Friday morning, I boarded flight 1854 and settled into my seat with much excitement. A large, heavy-set man who looked very familiar to me, walked up the aisle and took a seat in my row. He sat in the aisle seat, leaving the one between us empty. As he settled in, he introduced himself to me. I couldn't get over how familiar he looked to me.

I experienced a flashback of being with the Greys when they had introduced me to a young lady named either Priscilla or Patricia. In the memory, I was supposed to eventually meet one of the government men who was looking for the young lady. In the flashback, I saw the face and body of a dark, heavy-

232

set man. The man sitting at the end of my row was identical to the man in my flashback.

I was uncomfortable with this knowledge and wanted to change my seat. But then, I thought it might be interesting to find out more about the man, so I stayed put. I watched the other passengers as they came on board.

Walking down the aisle were the large, red-haired man and the blond-haired woman! As they walked past my row, we made eye contact. I thought to myself that this was no coincidence! I turned in time to see them take a seat near the back of the plane. My first thought was to just get off the plane, but I told myself to quit being so paranoid.

The man sitting next to me was talkative. Before we had landed in Houston, he had told me he'd spent the last week working at Sandia Base and the Los Alamos Laboratory. He also said that he worked for the Pentagon and lived in Virginia, near Washington, D.C. I was careful not to give him any vital information about myself. I told him I was going on vacation to visit a couple of friends in New York.

The man changed planes in Houston. I did not see the red-haired man and the blond-haired woman get back on the plane headed for New York. It seemed I was not being followed after all. I felt safe and that made me more comfortable.

A young lady took the aisle seat that had been vacated by the big man when we stopped in Houston. I remained in my window seat. We introduced ourselves and she told me she worked for Continental Airlines. She was on her way to visit her boyfriend who worked in Manhattan.

I told her that I too, was going to Manhattan to visit friends. She asked what part of Manhattan I was going to and said she was also going to the west side. She inquired about the street I was headed for and told me that her hotel was on the same street but further up.

She asked if I would consider sharing a taxi with her and splitting the cost, since we were going in the same direction. Before the plane landed, I felt I would be safe riding with her in a taxi, so we traveled together from the airport to Manhattan.

We reached my destination first. I thought it strange that she told me not to be so quick to believe people, because you never knew how trustworthy they would be. She said, "Don't accept rides with people you don't know."

After hearing this, I felt very stupid. I wondered if she really was who she had said she was. I mentally questioned her intentions as well. Was she working with the red-haired man and the heavy-set man? Would I encounter her again while in New York?

After meeting Karen, I told her about the heavy-set man and how I was certain he was the one I'd been warned about during the Priscilla/Patricia experience. I told her about the red-haired man as well. She thought the whole thing was strange. Because of my reason for being in Manhattan, she advised me to be cautious and on guard. I did not encounter the young lady from the taxi or the heavy-set man while in Manhattan.

I met with Budd Hopkins the next day and spent most of the day with him. He worked with me through hypnosis for many days after our initial meeting. I found him to be a very caring, understanding person. He was definitely knowledgeable in his field. He answered many questions that came up after the hypnotherapy sessions.

One afternoon, when I left Mr. Hopkins' home, we said our goodbyes and he locked the door behind me. I walked down the stairs and noticed a red-haired man to my left. He was attempting to lock his bicycle to a rack in front of Mr. Hopkins' home. I was shocked when the man looked up at me. He was the same red-haired man I had seen in the stores in Albuquerque. He was the same man who had gotten onto the Albuquerque-Houston flight with the blond lady!

I stood there, hesitant to take another step. He stared at me and fumbled with the bicycle chain. I turned my head to see if Mr. Hopkins was standing in his enclosed porch, but he was not. I intended to go back up the stairs and ring his doorbell to be let back inside. I did not know what the red-haired man was up to or why he was following me. It had been several days since I'd seen him. The last time was on the flight to Houston.

I thought to myself as he stared at me, "I am not going to let him intimidate me like this. If he tries anything, surely Mr. Hopkins will hear my screams." The red-haired man appeared to be having problems with the chain so I took advantage of that. I boldly stood in front of him, buttoned my coat, and put my scarf around my neck.

I began to walk. I walked close to him, staring back. I looked up toward the windows of Mr. Hopkins' home, hoping that perhaps he or his wife might be looking out, but they were not. I then became fearful, thinking that the man was going to grab me as I walked past him.

Then I had another thought. Maybe he too was going to see Hopkins. Did Hopkins know this man? As I went by, keeping my eye on him, he finally got the chain locked and stood up. He turned to look at me again. I walked faster, knowing there was a pay phone close by. If this man followed me, I would go into one of the stores and call either Mr. Hopkins or Karen.

I looked back toward the man and thought he was going to go up the stairs to Mr. Hopkins' house. Instead, he walked past the house. I had a feeling I should be cautious.

Not far away from Mr. Hopkins' house was a strong-looking, black man sitting on a fence. I noticed him watching me as I walked down the street. He seemed to keep looking as I went past him. I was getting closer to the pay phone. I was going to call Karen at work. Something did not seem right. I was afraid. As I got closer to the pay phone, another big black man rushed to the phone and dialed a number.

I stood at a distance and watched the red-haired man, thinking he was using some kind of ploy and that something was going to happen. While I waited for the phone, the red-haired man walked further away from me, down the street. I could not understand why he would lock up his bike in front of

Hopkins' house and then walk such a distance in the opposite direction.

The black man never did get off the phone. I saw a policeman standing across the street where I needed to catch the bus back to Karen's. I walked to the main street and crossed over to where the policeman was. I felt safe. I was thinking I could ask his help if either of the two big men or the red-haired man showed up. Or, I could go into a nearby coffee shop and call Karen or Budd Hopkins for help.

The city bus I was waiting for came promptly and I arrived at Karen's without further incident. As I unlocked the door to her apartment, the phone was ringing. It was Karen. I told her about seeing the red-haired man again and she said to make sure the door was locked. She would be home immediately.

I did not encounter the red-haired man again, even while touring the sites of New York and going to my last session with Mr. Hopkins. Whoever he was and whatever his purpose, we thought his appearance in New York was more than just coincidence!

March 2, 1997

Late Sunday evening, I arrived back at Karen's apartment. I'd had a day out by myself because Karen had spent the day with a friend. When I unlocked the door and stepped inside, I felt a strong presence - something I recognized as "normal" for me. My attention was drawn to a large mirror that covered most of one of the walls in her apartment. In my ears I heard, "They're coming. They're coming!"

Standing in the entryway, I felt uneasy. I began to experience the symptoms that happen when the entities come. I left the door open until I checked the other rooms to make sure no one was in the apartment. For about an hour my attention was focused on the mirror.

When Karen got home, late that evening, I discussed my feelings with her that someone had been in the apartment. I told her about the voice I'd heard and how my attention had been drawn to her large, plate-glass mirror.

The symptoms disappeared the next day and I felt better. I had not slept well the night before because of having been told, "They're coming." No one had come and the evening had been quiet.

While I was getting ready to go to another hypnosis session, an abductee whom I'd met over the phone, called twice for Karen. That evening, Karen spoke with the lady. This is the story of what happened.

The woman and her family were abductees. Her youngest son, who was four years old, was apparently taken every night, to be with his "teacher" who was a Nordic or a Grey. He attended a school that was set up for him and some other young children.

Her son had told her all day that Sunday that he wanted to come to New York and visit with Karen. When his "teacher" arrived that night, the boy asked to be taken to New York to visit a friend. The teacher had complied with the boy's request.

On Monday morning, the boy told his mother that he had gone with his teacher to visit Karen. They had gone through a large mirror. The teacher had told the boy they were going to go *through* the mirror but they would not be hurt transporting through it.

Before they went through the mirror, they had seen the room I had just entered when coming into the apartment. The small boy had said there was another lady in Karen's apartment, so he had not wanted to come into the room.

Later that night, the small boy asked to come back to visit with Karen. They returned and came through the mirror. He was allowed to tickle Karen on her face and arms. She was not supposed to know she was being tickled. He then walked over to the couch where I was sleeping and took a good look at me. He looked at my hands. He told his mother he had picked up one of my hands, then picked up the other soft hand that had a pretty ring on its finger.

On the phone that night, he described my large opal ring. He described it as an oval shape, pink and swirly. He said it also had a jewel in it. This was an accurate description of my ring! When he described what I looked like, he was correct again! He described some dishes and rocks that were sitting on a table.

During the night, I had awakened because Karen was restless and moving around on the floor, where she slept on a mattress. It was as if something was bothering her. The boy's mother, Karen, and I, just sat. We were perplexed.

March 4, 1997

During the night, I woke up. The room was filled with red light. I put on my glasses to see what was going on. Karen was sound asleep. I sat up on my couch. I looked toward the large windows and saw a bright, red light that illuminated the courtyard and surrounding brick buildings. I stood up and walked to the window. The red light was suddenly lifting up toward the sky. I saw no object and heard no helicopter or airplane noises. The mysterious red light soon disappeared.

I walked back to the couch and called out for Karen to wake up. She did not move an inch. I walked over to her and tried to shake her awake. Still, she did not move. I went back to the couch and laid down. Then I remembered. They had just brought us back!

I remembered being on a spaceship with Karen and the Greys. The Greys had Karen and me do something like fold some type of material or papers on a silver table. The table had been connected to a round wall. I could not remember much more than that and hoped Karen would remember our abduction in the morning.

When she awoke the next morning, I asked her if she remembered being abducted the night before. She could not remember anything. I told her my memory of what had happened and about the red light that had illuminated the buildings and the courtyard.

238

ANOTHER SHARED VISIT

April 15, 1997

I woke up in a familiar, very well-lit room where I had been many times before. I knew where I was, but had no idea when I had left my bed at home. I was lying on a table. A Grey told me to get down from the table. I may not have had any clothes on. I could not feel the short pink nightgown I'd put on before going to bed that night.

The Grey walked me about two or three feet away from the table and told me to stop. Another Grey came and stood by my side. I was unable to turn my head in either direction, but could move my eyes to the right.

As I did this, I noticed a lady with long blond hair standing on my right, just within range of my peripheral vision. She was a lot taller than I was. Suddenly, I could move my body so I turned toward the blond-haired woman. We were shocked to see each other! It was my friend, Christine, who lived near by me. She had on a short pink or white sleeping gown. She was also an abductee!

The Grey I was with handed me a silver pail and told me to carry it. The substance in the pail was light green. The Grey told me that the substance was mucus. He told me I would become ill with a very bad sinus infection and that I would have flu-like symptoms because of what was in the pail I carried.

One of the Greys began to walk Christine and me out of the room and into a hallway. As we walked down the hall, I felt something on my lower left leg. I looked down at my leg and saw a brown substance there. It was round and mushy looking. I bent down to inspect the substance and try to remove it from my leg. I was told telepathically not to touch it, to stand up straight and to walk!

Christine was several steps ahead of me. As I straightened up, I looked at her legs. She had two brown, raised spots on her left leg also. The brown spots were elongated.

We did not know who had put the brown spots on our legs. Nor did we know why or for what purpose they were put there. Our memories about where we were taken and what our duties were concerning the green mucus were blocked.

I had been feeling very healthy the night before. When I woke up the next morning, I had a severe sinus headache and my body ached with pain. I felt as if I was coming down with a cold or the flu. I blew green mucus from my nose, just as I had been told I would. I was very ill for about a week and a half. I remembered the dream and I remembered seeing Christine with me on the ship.

Before our shared abduction, I had not heard from my friend Christine for about three weeks, so I was anxious to call her. I did not know exactly how to approach the subject of our shared abduction. I wanted her to confirm our mutual experience and to find out what she remembered.

The second day after our experience, I called her. She said she felt like she was coming down with a sinus infection or a cold. I asked if she'd had any "experiences" or "dreams" lately. She said that she'd had a very weird dream the previous Sunday night and that I had been in the dream with her, on the Greys' ship. Then we both said, simultaneously, "We were together the other night!"

I then asked her if there had been something wrong with our legs while we were on the ship. She said that we'd had something like "poop" on our left legs! Brown poop!

She asked me where they had taken us and if the green stuff in the pail had really been mucus. As we spoke that morning, we confirmed the information about what had transpired. I asked Christine if I had been wearing anything or if I had been nude. She said they had put my pink nightgown back on me.

Her memory was also blocked, so she did not know where we were taken or what we did with the green substance I had carried in the pail. On the third day after our shared experience, Christine became ill with the same symptoms that I had!

MORE BLOOD

May 8, 1997

I woke up during the night to go to the bathroom. I had pain on the right side of my head, from my ear to my cheek. My right hand also hurt. On the way back to bed, I stopped at the open balcony door and stood there, looking out. I got back into bed and lay awake for awhile before finally falling asleep.

Sometime later, I woke up. My right nostril was clogged, but runny. I grabbed a Kleenex and blew my nose. It continued to run. I looked at the Kleenex and saw that it was bloody. I pinched my nose to stop the flow of blood. Several Kleenexes later, it stopped bleeding. I was too tired to get up and throw the Kleenexes away, so I just dropped them on the floor by the bed. I went back to sleep.

When I woke up the next morning, I looked over the side of the bed at the bloody tissues I had dropped during the night. I was shocked to discover that my nose had bled more profusely than I'd thought. I picked up the Kleenexes and went into the bathroom to dispose of them.

As I came out of the bathroom, I looked down and saw several spots of blood on the lower leg of my silk pajamas. The spots were approximately ¼ to ½ inch in size. As I removed my pajama bottoms, I noticed that they were inside out and backward on my body. I distinctly remembered putting them on right side out, with the tag in the back when I'd dressed for bed the night before. Who had removed my pajama bottoms during the night? How had they gotten turned inside out and backward? I certainly had not done it!

I examined my right leg and foot. On my ankle I noticed an irregularly shaped, small sore. The sore was scabbed over. The sore had not been there the night before! Other than the odd sore, there were no other cuts on my leg.

Looking down at my ankle again, I noticed blood spots on the carpet between the wall and the bed. The pulsating pain in my right ear and cheek radiated upward to the right side of my forehead. The pain intensified

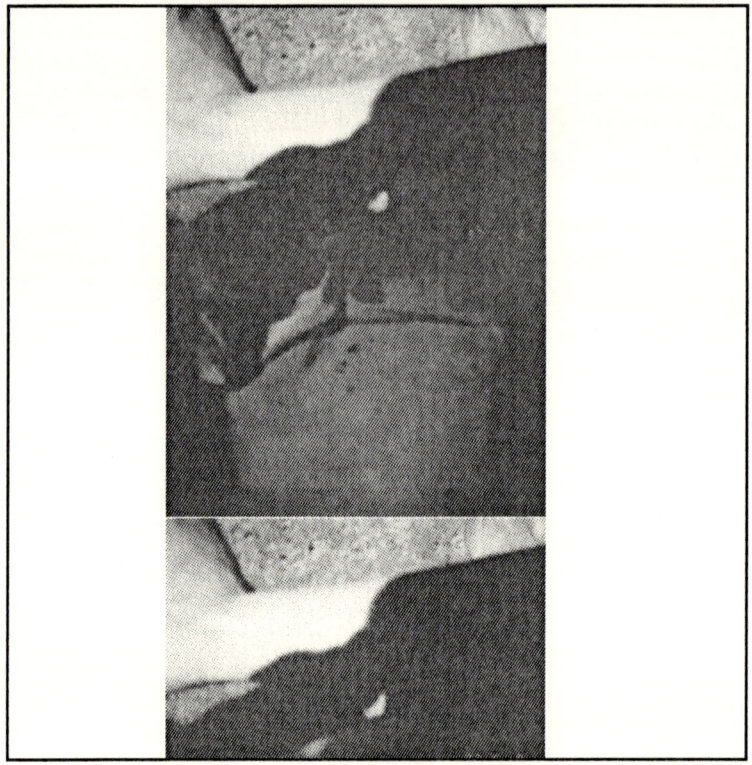

Blood Spots on carpet and silk pajamas

Later that morning, I called my doctor. His schedule was full and he could not see me that morning. The receptionist asked if I wanted to see the doctor on call. I did not want to do that as I needed to see my own doctor. I told the receptionist I would call back if I felt any worse.

242

WHY IS THIS ENTITY HIDING?

May 11, 1997

We had made a weekend trip to Lubbock, Texas to visit our son Brian, who was attending college there. We arrived home from Lubbock around 5:00 p.m. I was the first one to walk into the house.

As I came inside, I felt a presence, as if someone was in the house. Tired from the five-hour trip, I quickly went from room to room, checking to see if anything was out of place or missing. Everything seemed to be okay. The feeling of a presence grew stronger. I did not bother to mention the feeling to either Fred or Michelle.

I walked into the kitchen, went to the sink and turned on the water. I caught a glimpse of something out of the corner of my left eye. I thought it was Fred or Michelle standing in the doorway to the kitchen. I turned to look in that direction.

I saw an entity who was not in solid form. It seemed to be transparent as I looked at it. It did not have human form. It stood about five feet tall. It was fat and brown in color. I saw no face. It disappeared as quickly as it had become visible. It seemed to walk or float north, into the living room. I assumed I was just seeing things because I was tired from the trip.

Thirty minutes later, I was in the upstairs bedroom, sitting on the bed, facing the TV. The bedroom door was open. Michelle came in, followed by Fred. Michelle sat down on my right and eventually laid down on the bed. Fred laid down on the left side of the bed and closed his eyes to take a cat nap.

I did not focus on the TV after they came in, but instead, looked straight ahead into the bathroom. Again, my right eye caught a glimpse of something. I turned, and was dumbfounded to see the same entity enter through the bedroom door! It appeared more solid than before, not as transparent. It was not brown this time. Instead, it appeared to be holding a brown blanket over its body. The entity now appeared to have a large body. It's right hand was wrapped in the top of the blanket, but I could see that fingers were holding onto the inside of the blanket that covered it's head and body.

It stopped briefly at the end of the bed and seemed to be looking at the three of us. Then it passed right in front of me and walked *through* the east wall of the room!

I could not move or even holler out to Fred or Michelle. I don't know why I could not move. I sat there, frozen in place on the bed, my eyes feeling as if they were glued open. I stayed that way for quite some time. Then I heard Fred and Michelle stirring and waking up.

I tried to tell them what had happened, but the words did not come out of my mouth correctly. They could not understand me and told me to just go to bed!

TELEPHONE CONVERSATION WITH
BUDD HOPKINS

May 21, 1997

In a phone conversation with Mr. Hopkins on this day, I accidentally blurted out information about some military /government experiences I'd had. Karen had asked me not to discuss this topic with Budd Hopkins.

I was curious and seeking answers to my questions about remote viewing. The question I had asked Budd Hopkins was, "Is it possible, if you are the person being remote viewed, to see the person or entity that is remote viewing you?"

The question opened a can of worms. It was that question that led us into a discussion of government and military abductions. I'm sure Mr. Hopkins had a suspicion that my question had something to do with my own government and military abductions. He asked me detailed questions regarding the abductions and I wanted to answer him truthfully. I fidgeted and was afraid to talk about the subject. I also wanted to honor my understanding with Karen about not discussing the topic with Mr. Hopkins.

I began to tell him about my experiences. I described each government and military abduction to date. I was afraid to give him specific names of abductors at the time. I waited until he came to Albuquerque before naming my government abductors.

As we explored the topic, Mr. Hopkins told me that he saw no reason why the government or military would abduct me. He reminded me that I had not spoken out publicly about my experiences. Nor had I done anything against the government or military.

He then told me about a person who was close to him, that had been an abductee. The person was in a branch of the U.S. military and had been abducted by the United States Air Force. Mr. Hopkins' friend had been drugged by people in that branch of the military in order to gain certain information.

Mr. Hopkins said he wanted to speak more with me about this topic. He became quite upset with me for not mentioning the government/military abductions when I had seen him in New York. I explained to him that I had honored my verbal agreement with Karen not to mention it.

In actual fact, Karen had told me that Budd had no belief or interest in government/military abductions and not to bring up the subject at all with him.

June 18, 1997

I was awakened at 2:00 a.m. by a repetitive statement in my head. What I heard was, "It is time." The statement repeated over and over again until I finally got up out of bed and went to open the balcony door.

At that moment, I heard a strange, unfamiliar noise coming from outside. I immediately experienced the symptoms that occur when the Greys come. I looked outside. I saw nothing up in the dark sky. The voice I'd heard while lying in bed, began its recitation again. "It is time."

As I stood in the open doorway, I heard a cry come from my stomach area! The cry was not the sound of a human baby.

It was the sound of a deep, throaty voice. I heard it two or three times. As I jumped back away from the door, I realized the sound was coming from inside my body! With each cry, my stomach vibrated a little bit. I thought I now had an answer to one of my questions.

During the month, I had felt movement within my stomach. The sensation was like the movement of a baby during pregnancy. It felt like a fetus moving inside of me. I looked at the clock radio. It was 2:45 a.m.

I had extreme pain in my neck so I took one Ibuprophen and went back to bed. As I lay in bed, I heard the same strange noise outside again. Then the noise seemed to come indoors. I heard it downstairs. I was very frightened. I closed my eyes.

While my eyes were shut, I saw the number 7. The number 7 repeated again and again. Then I had a vision of a small, white, pitched-roof house. The shape of the house was square. To the left of the house was a small, attached porch that was covered with some kind of green vine. The number 7 was written in black letters all over the back side of the house.

Then another scene followed. I found myself in a small room in the house. Laying on the floor was a large, black, leather book about 10 inches by 12 inches in size. I picked up the book. The leather felt very soft and smooth. I thought the book must be very expensive. The book was about three inches thick. I looked at the edges of the pages without opening the book. I noticed that some of the pages were pink and white. I noticed an unusual inscription or initials on the front of the book. I tried to open the book, but as I did that, everything went black in my mind. I then heard a voice speaking to me.

I felt as if I had heard the voice before. I thought it either belonged to a Grey or a human male. The voice repeated to me three times in a very demanding way: "Do not look for Paul! Quit your search!" Then there was another voice in broken English, Spanish or Mexican.

I recognized the voice as belonging to the man in the lab I had been taken to. It was Paul's voice! He started to tell me, "I'm ..." Then it sounded as if someone was threatening him, but he got the rest of the sentence out: "Look in Mazatlan, Matamoros --- Rose, Rose, Rose" I think he also said, "Help me find..." I could not remember all of what he said to me.

Then the other voice began to repeat its message again. "It is time." The sentence repeated until I was put to sleep again.

When I had met Paul in the lab, he had told me his name and where he lived. He had asked me to find his wife. Now, I knew this had been a second message from Paul.

A SIGHTING

October 31, 1997

I was on my way to our office, traveling west on Montgomery. I moved into the left-turn lane that would take me south on Carlisle, and stopped for the red light at Carlisle and Montgomery. There was a fire truck in front of me with six firemen inside.

While waiting for the light to change, I happened to look up at the sky, a little to the northwest. It was a clear, sunny, fall day. What I saw in the sky nearly caused me to jump out of my seat! There in the sky, over Albuquerque's north valley, was a round silver disk.

At first, I thought it was an airplane circling overhead. But this was no airplane. Nor was it a weather balloon. The disk tilted in the sky, reflecting a burnt orange color as well as silver. About two seconds later, it flew west, then turned and flew east of my location and just disappeared. I had never seen anything fly so fast or disappear so quickly.

I speculated that if I had seen the disk in the sky, surely the firemen in front of me and the driver of the car to my right must have seen it as well. The fire station was on the same street as our office, just north of us. I saw the fire truck pull into the station. I was going to stop and ask them if they had seen the disk but I was running late for work. I decided to call them instead.

Later that afternoon, I put in a call to the fire station and spoke to the driver of the truck that had been in front of me. When I asked him if they had seen the silver disk in the sky that morning, he became very quiet. It was almost as if he was afraid to answer me. He then said that no one in the truck had seen the object.

I remembered an internet site called *UFO Sightings in New Mexico and the World*, where people can post UFO sightings. I logged on and posted my sighting, hoping someone would respond. No one answered my posting and as time went by, I only checked the website once a week. Eventually, I just forgot about the whole thing.

In late November, I went back to the website and discovered that my posting was still up. To my surprise, I had a response! I was very excited. The message was from a Mr. Martin. He too had witnessed the flight of the disk and described it as I had seen it! He had left his address for me to contact him, which I did.

Subject: UFO Sighting Reports
Below is the result of your feedback form.
It was submitted by ()
on Tuesday, November 4, 1997 at 20:37:27

location: ALBUQUERQUE, NM
date: 10/31/97
time: 11 a.m.

sighting: TRAVELING WEST ON MONTGOMERY N.E., FROM MY POSITION TO THE NORTH WEST (OVER THE IMMEDIATE VALLEY AREA) I SAW A SILVER ROUND OBJECT IN A CLOUDLESS SKY. AT FIRST I THOUGHT IT WAS AN AIRPLANE CIRCULING ABOVE BUT TO MY AMAZEMENT IT WAS NOT AN AIRPLANE. THIS OBJECT TILTED IN THE SKY, AND REFLECTED A BURNT ORANGE COLOR AS WELL AS SILVER. APPROXIMATELY TWO SECONDS LATER IT FLEW WEST OF MY LOCATION AND JUST QUICKLY DISAPPEARED. ALSO IT WAS NOT A BALLOON. DID ANYONE ELSE SEE THIS?

[UFO Sightings in New Mexico and the World]
[http://www.artesia.net/~jstvck/ufo.shtml]
[jstvck@artesia.net]

NEXT SIGHTING

When he contacted me again, I purposely left out some of the particulars, in case this was a person who was just looking for public recognition. I set up a meeting with Mr. Martin and took Fred along with me. I found out that Martin worked at Kirtland Base and traveled throughout the United States on work-related business. He was an environmentalist, so his job took him outdoors a lot of the time. Mr. Martin described the object exactly as I had seen it, right down to the color, shape, tilt of the craft, and the directions it had flown before disappearing.

UFO Sightings in New Mexico and the World

http://nmufo.simplenet.com/index.html

http://www.artesia.net/~kstrck/ufo.shtml

During our conversation he told me that when he was about five or six years old, he and another member of his family had experienced "missing time" in their lives. There were witnesses who had seen a UFO in the area around their home. He spoke of other friends whom he believed were abductees residing in Albuquerque and working at Kirtland Base and in Los Alamos. He confirmed that there were underground facilities out at the Base along with unusual activities that took place there.

To protect this person, I will not say more about our first meeting. We had said we would stay in touch with one another. Mr. Martin informed me that if they (meaning the government) knew he was speaking to me, he himself would be jeopardized.

We had one short phone call after the initial meeting and from that point on, I never heard from him again.

May 25, 1998

I did not look at the clock during this event, but it happened sometime Monday night or in the very early hours of Tuesday morning.

I heard the voice in my head. It was quite persistent. It told me to go north on Friday night. I was then shown a map from Albuquerque, north to Santa Fe, New Mexico. I said, to whoever was showing me the map, "That's Santa Fe!" According to the map, whatever was supposed to happen was going to happen north of Santa Fe and south of Espanola.

After I woke up, the persistent voice told me to "look down at the floor." I looked down at the floor. I saw nothing.

May 28, 1998

I was shown "Blanco, site 22" in a dream this night. I was told to remember it. I have no other memories of that dream.

June 12, 1998 Friday

I woke up with unusual bruising. On my upper right thigh, I found three circles and what appeared to be a triangle shape. I drew a picture of my leg. I have no memories of having been taken last night.

June 15, 1998 Monday

The round, circle bruises disappeared quickly. I woke up again with more irregular, individual bruises on my upper right thigh. The bruises appeared to be in a straight line 3 ½ inches long. There was no film in my camera, so did not take pictures of either incident. Again, I have no memories of having been abducted.

July 21, 1998

I met with Carrie Satter (a mutual friend) and Sharon Klein at my home for dinner. Sharon and I discovered that we had other mutual friends: Mary and Ray Rowlison. She had not seen the Rowlisons for at least two years. We had met briefly at Mary and Ray's home several years before. Neither of us could remember the exact date.

After dinner, Sharon and I spoke about our experiences and "dreams." Her daughter and son were also abductees, as well as many of her extended family. We discovered that some of our information and experiences were the same. Sharon revealed that she too, had a long, white object in her gums. The object that had come out of my upper gums had been as big around as a toothpick and about ¾ of an inch long.

Sharon had had the same problem I did, but was x-rayed by her dentist. The dentist had seen a long, narrow object embedded in her gum near the molars. I believe she told me she never had the object removed.

ALIEN OR HUMAN?

I was unable to keep up with documentation at times because of the frequency of my abductions. I had finally reached a stage in my life when I could accept the reality of other "entities" or creatures living in the vastness of the universe.

There are no words to express the horror, terror, and feelings of insanity I went through when the entities first appeared in my life. I lived on an emotional roller coaster with the knowledge of what was happening to myself and to my children.

The "why" and the reasons were never explained by the entities, nor had we ever been told why we had been selected to be the "chosen ones." In the beginning, I hated the entities for what they were, and for what they did to my children, myself, and other human beings.

Over and over again, I screamed at them to just leave us alone and never touch us again! I had been told by others that the entities were from Satan and I certainly did not want that to be a part of our lives. My belief in God and my love for God was so great that I knew He would protect me and be with me every hour of every day. Many times, I asked my God to remove the entities from our lives. I understood little of God's answer as to why he did not remove the entities. I told God, if the entities were not of His making but of a satanic nature, to intervene on my behalf and take them away from us.

My God's answer to that plea was to inspire me to ask the Greys a particular question. The question I should ask was this: Do these beings have a "higher power" (meaning a Supreme being) in their lives that they honor, love and are guided by? The majority of humans believe and are guided each day, through love for our Supreme being, the Lord God. Every waking moment, I constantly drilled that question into my mind so the next time I was abducted, I would remember that question in my conscious and subconscious mind.

I had the opportunity to ask that question during another abduction. Raytheon and I were walking down a hall on the ship. "The Boss," a Grey who seems to be the leader of the Greys on that particular ship, was walking down the hall in the opposite direction. The Boss is always present for any medical procedure or mind altering "operations" on humans. I hated that particular Grey because he had no respect for human life.

I asked Raytheon my question first because I knew he would answer the question. He said to me, "This is a question you need to ask [I don't remember the name he used for The Boss]. Then, Raytheon stopped The Boss in the hallway and told him I had a question for him. My whole body shook with fright at the sight of him. Somehow, I was able to get the words out of my mouth. His answer shocked me. This is what The Boss told me:

"Not even the most intelligent scientist, theologian, or human on Earth can know the Creator of All in the vastness of the galaxies. He is of the brightest light and most powerful energy that no one, including human, can comprehend until death. He is All's Creator."

I then put this question to The Boss: "If He is All's Creator and He is your Creator, why do you treat us badly and have disrespect for human 'Earthlings' and take us? My children and I do not like being abducted! We do not like being put through all your experiments and breeding procedures! Why are you doing it?"

I don't believe The Boss answered my second set of questions, but I remembered the phrases "lost world," "lost others," and "need you," when I was brought back home. If the memory was not from that abduction experience, then those phrases were said to me during a future abduction.

Raytheon (or The Boss) told me they had lost their world and a large population of their species because of their carelessness with the environment. Fighting amongst themselves had evidently led to some kind of vast chemical warfare that had quickly destroyed their world. Only a few managed to escape. Some had tried to rebuild their society by settling on other open planets. They incurred other problems also and soon discovered the need to interbreed.

Millennia ago, Earth had been discovered not only by the Greys, but by other species as well. The Greys were hoping to save yet another species (namely, humans) from destroying their home world. Their goal was to one day be able to grow, work with us, and live with us. The time would come, they said, when humans would evolve and be able to accept the presence of a more intelligent species in the world. I was told about a Federation of Worlds within the many galaxies, that included many different species.

The next time I was abducted after my questioning of The Boss, I noticed a difference in his attitude toward me. I don't know if it had anything to do with my question about the Creator, but we seemed to have come to an understanding of sorts. I was shown some respect as a human being. One of the good changes that happened was the way The Boss communicated with me telepathically. His tone was much calmer, less harsh, and his directives were not put so strongly.

As if all this was not enough for one lifetime, I now had to deal with another phenomenon that I was beginning to suspect was connected to the alien abductions.

I began having dreams and memories of government/military abductions. Soon after my encounter with The Boss, I was forced into some of the most fearful experiences of my life. These new abductions were even more frightening than those perpetrated by the alien entities because the fear I felt was generated not by aliens, but by other human beings here on Earth!

SCREEN MEMORIES AND SHAPE-SHIFTERS

Entities have the ability to use mind control on those they abduct. This has been documented not only by me, but by other abductees as well. The entities have been known to wipe out (or screen) an actual memory (of an abductee) and replace it with another memory that may or may not have happened. It is said that world governments and military organizations on Earth now also have this capability.

The entities have the ability to shape-shift. That is, they can change their physical shape at will, to resemble human form. Many abductees (myself included) believe they have experienced the effects of both mind-control and the shape-shifting of some entities.

PART II

GOVERNMENT MILITARY ABDUCTIONS

Or...as I have been told, "Screen Memories And Shape-Shifters"

The Author wholly believes in the truth of her experiences, but acknowledges the fact that Alien beings are capable of producing screen memories and illusion, thus the people mentioned in this section could very well be alien representations of said persons and therefore not a reflection on the actual person themselves.

There are millions of people who are not Experiencers but believe in this phenomenon. Because the truth is known to them, they give their support to these abductees. Yes, in the vastness of the universe, it is known that we are not alone, and that higher intelligence and greater technology do exist.

Great numbers of Experiencers have come to realize that their abductions also come from a source other than the alien entities. They have been rudely awakened to the fact that fellow humans can be extremely hurtful in the mistreatment of other human beings. Their purpose? Study and learning. Their reason? The false nobility of being the "first."

Are we, "the chosen ones," being used as guinea pigs for the survival of future humans and hybrids on this Earth and perhaps other planets as well? Are we the essential puzzle pieces that will precipitate the eventual coming together and living together of human and alien in peace and dignity? Does this ultimate goal *justify* the experimentation being done on human beings by fellow humans, right here in our world?

Military/government abductions do not just include Experiencers from the United States, but from all over the world. MILABS (Military Abductees) are abducted by high-ranking officials (dignitaries) of their own state governments for various reasons.

One of the qualifications for military/government abduction is prior alien abduction. The alien abductee is given credentials by a "supervising entity" who, along with assigned rogue military units, have painstakingly trained the abductee to work in various fields.

Those of us who are MILABS are traumatized and used as informants. We are used for medical and psychological testing. We are forced to work in chemical and medical laboratories; many times, we are used as experiments in chemical and medical laboratories. Some of us are used as high-clearance "workers."

Some abductees are repeatedly used sexually by high-ranking dignitaries. All this is being done against our will, without respect for our lives and our dignity as human beings. We are tortured, harassed and threatened with our lives if we try to speak out against these practices. I myself, have been victimized in this way.

There are well-known researchers who have studied, investigated, reported, and confirmed such cases. There is an over-powering and large "underground" secrecy maintained by our Earth governments with regard to these cases and abductions. It is our hope, as abductees, that perhaps one day, the truth of these atrocities will be made known to all humans.

Military abductees are threatened by their governments against speaking out. They are told there will be no life for them on Earth or on any other world if they do not maintain silence. A few researchers have spoken out and given a helping hand to protect the military abductee. They have done this knowing that their own lives are in danger. Yet, these courageous people take that chance because, they want to stop the mistreatment of humans and make public this horrifying phenomenon. Some researchers have lost their lives because of what they tried to report to the public. Many researchers remain anonymous, knowing the dire consequences of revealing the truth about their investigative studies.

257

Many military abductees are quietly and cautiously trying to make known their tormenters, in an attempt to stop the inhumane treatment of abductees. Here too, some have lost their lives because they knew too much and tried to expose the truth to the world. I have been asked many times, "What do you think the reaction would be, from the whole populace of Earth, if alien entities were to suddenly land and make themselves known? Sheer panic and human destruction would occur. What would the reaction be today, of the world populace, if they knew their own governments were working with alien entities, side by side, mistreating and killing humans of every culture? Just as Hitler did in the Nazi era?"

Perhaps, who cares? I feel that I can speak up now, because I have already been maimed at least a couple of times by our military/government. How long I have to live is unknown. If I can at least help other alien or military abductees who are living through this hell, unable to comprehend the reality and authenticity of what is happening to them, then my effort is worthwhile. I can give of myself, my love, and my caring to those abductees who need help. I can attempt to inform the populace, even though I am an unknown human in this large world.

The following is a chronology of my first encounter with what I believe were, people in our military/government.

May 20, 1996 Monday, 2:00 p.m.

I felt a presence standing near me and following me around the downstairs while I cleaned the house. While washing the kitchen floor, I felt the presence standing in the hallway door to the kitchen. It was as if it was watching me work. I stopped what I was doing and looked in that direction - about three feet away.

I had experienced another presence in the past who had made himself visible to me. I was becoming more accustomed to speaking to those entities whose presence I felt in the room with me, and May 20th was no exception. I was tired that afternoon. I told the entity to quit watching me work and to get off his butt and help me clean!

Every other Monday is a heavy-detailed house cleaning day for me. I would begin cleaning around 8:00 a.m. and finish up around 8:30 or 9:00 p.m. May 20th was a heavy-cleaning day. After I told the entity to "get off his butt," I continued on with my housework. I did not feel as if I worked any faster than usual that day; nor did I skip any of the cleaning jobs I normally did. To my amazement, I was completely finished by 6:00 p.m.!

My question is this: Did someone help me or give me the extra energy to finish up early? I thought it was weird that I could suddenly do the work faster than I normally did. It felt really great to have accomplished so much and be finished early. I thanked the entity for helping me.

May 20, 1996 Monday Evening

I fell asleep but kept waking up, feeling restless and uncomfortable. I heard footsteps again in our bedroom, but saw no one. I had a feeling the Greys were coming. The Greys did not come. I felt a presence in our bedroom and it was difficult for me to fall asleep.

Michelle was spending the nights that week, house-and pet-sitting at our oldest daughter's home. I was not worried about her because I knew she would be safe. Fred did not seem to be sleeping very comfortably. He too, seemed restless. He woke up several times during the night and we spoke to each other.

May 21, 1996 Tuesday Morning

I woke up feeling tired due to lack of sleep the night before. The presence remained with us and seemed to be following me through the house. I demanded that the presence make itself visible to me. It did not. I then began to communicate with it telepathically, but received no communication back.

The presence even followed me into the bathroom! I told it to go away and let me have my privacy. I seemed to have some privacy at least once. I was feeling uncomfortable about the presence because this was the first time a presence had remained with us for a long period of time. I thought it might have been a Grey.

May 21, 1996 Evening

I knew that night the Greys would come. The symptoms were so strong in me! Somehow, I fell asleep. I woke up several times during the night when a strikingly bright, white light penetrated my closed eyelids. I could see the bright light inside my closed eyes.

I had experienced the bright light behind closed eyes before. I did not know the reason for the light or where it was coming from. When I opened my eyes, all I saw was my sleeping husband!

Suddenly, I heard a popping sound that came from the direction of the east wall of our bedroom; yet no one came through the wall. I became agitated and restless.

I lay there in bed, trying to figure out if I was fabricating the whole scenario. Was the bright, white light really happening? What had made the popping noise on the wall? Had I been abducted that night and brought back with no memories of what had transpired? Was the popping noise on the wall their energy going through the wall as they left the house?

May 22, 1996 Wednesday 8:30 a.m.

It was my habit to get up early on Wednesdays, wash clothes, and do most of the ironing before leaving for work. I was working in the kitchen when I heard a loud crashing noise somewhere in the house. It sounded as if a large piece of furniture had fallen or something had fallen from up high.

I checked the rooms, one by one. I saw our startled Persian cats standing rigid by the stairway. Their eyes were opened as wide as they could be, their heads pointing in the direction of our upstairs bedroom. I slowly and quietly walked up the stairs and proceeded to check the upstairs bedrooms. I checked the closets as well. I did not find any furniture or object that had fallen.

I went outside to investigate and saw that nothing had been disturbed. I knew for a fact that the crashing sound had come from within the house. It had not been an outside noise because the ceiling and kitchen walls had vibrated with the impact of the crash.

May 22, 1996 Wednesday 9:00 a.m.

I was getting dressed for work. I sat down in my chair in the master bathroom to put in my contact lenses. I heard an unusual, loud, heavy pounding coming from the adjoining bedroom. It sounded like metal hitting against a piece of wood furniture. I suspected someone was in the house with me, trying their darnedest to scare me. It sounded as if someone was opening and slamming the large doors of the clothing armoire.

Because of the noise and the shaking of the floor, I thought maybe we were having an earthquake although that seemed unlikely for Albuquerque. I was afraid to move from my chair. I tried to look around the corner into the bedroom from where I sat.

I rose from the chair slowly. I took a few deep breaths. I quietly walked toward the bedroom and looked out at the north side of the room. I saw nothing. I turned my head to the left, where the armoire was located. I could not believe what I was seeing!

The armoire was actually being lifted *up* from the floor, one or two inches, and was being *shaken!* The metal latch pulls on the wood doors of the armoire were swinging outward and bouncing back against the doors. As soon as I observed this, whatever power that had caused it to happen, quietly put the armoire back down on the floor! The sudden silence was alarming. I stood there, staring in disbelief. My body was frozen in place by fear.

As I stood in the bathroom doorway, I listened for other noises in the house and outside the house. I heard no other noises; not children playing, aircraft flying, or cars driving by. Everything was deathly quiet. I felt as if my sanity had deserted me.

I did not understand where the vibration had come from. I could not accept the fact that I'd seen a large, heavy piece of furniture lifted off the floor and shaken. What was going on? Who had done this?

I realized I was trembling. All I wanted to do was run out of the house and get to the office as fast as I could. I wanted to be where other people were. I wanted to be with Fred.

As I continued to stand in the bathroom doorway, I felt the presence right in front of me, blocking my way out.

May 22-23, 1996 Wednesday Evening to Thursday Morning

On Wednesday, I experienced another night of not being able to sleep much. I felt lucky to have gotten three hours of sleep that night. I kept thinking and wondering who the presence was and why it had hung around our home for so long. What exactly did it want from me, or us? I asked myself, "Were all the weird happenings of the last few days caused by the Greys and whoever was studying my reactions?"

I kept wishing the entity would make itself visible to me. In an angry tone of voice, I told the entity I would not be afraid of him if he would only make himself visible. I also told him how uncomfortable and fearful he made me by remaining invisible. I demanded that he either go away or make himself visible to me. The entity did not honor either request.

On Thursday morning at 9:00 a.m., I was in the kitchen rinsing breakfast dishes. I heard what sounded like a large, low-flying helicopter go over our house. It must have been quite low because the walls of the house vibrated very hard. This type of activity is not unusual in our area because Kirtland and Sandia were in close proximity to our neighborhood. Quite often, we were in their flight path. We not only had military helicopters flying overhead on a regular basis, but other aircraft as well.

Usually though, even at a distance, one can recognize the sound of a particular approaching aircraft. The helicopter I heard that morning did not approach from a distance. It seemed to fly in circles over our house for several minutes, then sounded as if it were simply hovering over us. I could hear the blades of the helicopter going round and the walls and windows vibrated. It was that close.

I was concerned that something had happened in the arroyo to the east of the cinder block wall that marks our property. I stood in the kitchen, unwilling to move, just waiting. Waiting for what? I decided to walk toward the French doors in the dining room. As I did so, the motor of the helicopter suddenly quit. I thought it had landed in the arroyo, so I ran outside to look. I saw nothing. I heard nothing.

My first reaction was to look in the sky. I searched with my eyes but saw no helicopter flying in any direction. There were no noises coming from the arroyo...nothing. I heard no aircraft in the distance. I stood outside feeling stumped. While I was outside, I had the feeling of someone telling me not to go back into the house.

I eventually *did* go back inside. I went upstairs and out onto the balcony to search the arroyo for the helicopter I thought must have landed there. To my amazement, I found no helicopter in the arroyo!

May 23, 1996   2:30 to 3:00 p.m.

One of our employees and I were the only people in the office that afternoon. I was sitting at my desk. Amy (the employee) was sitting at Fred's desk, which was behind and to the left of my desk. We were both working at our computers.

The office was quiet except for the radio playing in the background.

Suddenly, Amy jumped out of her chair and screamed loudly, "There is a tool raising up in the air! Look, look! It's going back down!" She told me it was as if someone was there (meaning a human), lifting up the tool. She was very animated and scared.

I stood up from my chair and asked her which tool it was. She excitedly told me it was a black tool.

"Gloria, didn't you see it?"

At first, I did not know where to look. By the time I looked in the direction she was indicating, nothing was happening. To the south of our desks was an open space where we had set up tables to hold computers that were being repaired. There were many tools on those tables.

The presence I'd felt at home seemed to have followed me to the office. I did not mention that fact to Amy. I remained calm and tried not to show how nervous I truly was. What came out of my mouth sounded odd. I said to her, "Talk to him and ask him what he is doing, Amy."

She then turned toward me and we both just stood there, staring at each other. I slowly sat down in my chair and turned to my computer, not saying anything to her. I felt as if I was in another world or some other place. I was not aware of my actions. I do not remember comforting Amy. When I came out of my emotional daze, I just looked at her scared and puzzled face. I didn't know what to say to her as she sat down again.

The occurrence was not mentioned by either of us for the rest of the afternoon. The presence seemed to have left us. I experienced a sense of freedom at it's departure.

On Tuesday, June 4th, 1996, I approached Amy about the floating tool episode. By then she had recanted her story. She told me the tool was *not* up in the air, that she had simply heard movement of tools on the table, as if someone was working there. She said she had heard the noise twice. She appeared to be embarrassed over the questions I asked her about that afternoon. Watching her responses, I decided otherwise. Amy had a sad and strange look on her face. I let the topic drop and did not pursue it further.

I believe what transpired that Thursday really happened; but because of how it happened, Amy was too embarrassed to verify it.

May 23-24, 1996 Thursday Evening to Friday Morning

I felt numb about the occurrences of the past week. I had called Sue Minshall and Joan Duce-Ashe who were investigators and researchers in the Albuquerque area. I was nervous about meeting them for the first time. We had spoken on the phone several times before about my alien abductions. We had discussed the investigators who were helping me.

Our first meeting went very well. I found both women to be compassionate and concerned as they listened to my story about the previous week's experiences. They offered suggestions about what might be going on in and around the house. They explained it away as paranormal activity.

That night I had another experience of white light being flashed into my eyes. I fell asleep but was awakened sometime during the night by the bright light in my eyes. As before, I was unable to open my eyes. I struggled to open my eyes but they would not open.

Next, I was shown what appeared to be a video within the white light. The video was projecting some kind of information into my head. The information seemed to be going into my subconscious mind. I felt as if I was under the control of someone else during that time. My body was frozen and I could not move.

The video was in fast forward and I could not comprehend what I was seeing or what I was supposed to remember. I do recall seeing humans moving about, involved in some type of work. After the video was implanted in my mind, I was able to open my eyes.

I looked around the darkened room for any kind of movement, but saw nothing. As I turned my head from left to right in search of an entity, I heard a soft, male voice repeating to me: "Soon it will be." The words repeated over and over again.

I was uncomfortable and nervous. I questioned what had been said to me. I was trying to understand what the video was about. Who had shown it to me and how had they accomplished it? What did it all mean? What kind of information had been put into my mind? Who was *doing* this to me?

I tried to understand. I argued with myself for many minutes, trying to figure out if this had been a real occurrence or not. If it *was* real, then I needed to stay calm and try to relax. Maybe my subconscious would reveal the information I had been given.

I felt mixed up. I felt as if the information made me sad and I wanted to cry. I also felt afraid for someone or something that had been projected into my mind. It was not good. I wanted to know who, what, and why, and I had no answers. I felt a lot of anxiety. I did not want to wake up Fred, so I lay there until relaxation calmed my body and mind, allowing me to sleep.

May 24, 1996 Friday Evening

I was very tired, but felt happy and comfortable. I went to bed at 10:30 p.m. and fell soundly asleep. I had a very "real dream" that was (as it turned out), not a dream at all.

When I woke up, I was being lifted from a gurney. I was disoriented and incoherent. My head spun wildly. I was then made to walk down a dark hallway with my eyes covered. Someone was helping me walk because I felt support under my armpits. Someone was almost carrying or dragging me.

At that point, I thought I was in one of the hallways on one of the Greys' ships. When my eye-covering was removed, I looked around. The "Greys" on either side of me appeared to

266

be around six feet tall! Their body structure was quite large. It took awhile before I realized that two *human* men were forcing me to walk and holding me under my arms. I was able to see them in the soft light of the hallway. I panicked.

I don't know where I am! Who are these men and where am I being taken?

Soon we stopped walking and the men opened a door at the end of the dimly lit hallway. One man walked through the open door. I was the second person to go through, followed by the other man.

The area we entered had a lot more lighting. I had no idea where I was. The men let go of my arms and I stood on my own. I felt nauseous. My head was spinning and hurting. I was very afraid. I did not know where I was or how I had gotten there. I did not know what was going to happen to me. My underarms hurt from being dragged.

I looked at my abductors. I could not understand why they were dressed in camouflage military uniforms. The uniforms were the variegated green variety I had seen on military combat men. My abductors wore matching hats with a bill on the front. The men were hefty looking and each one had a large build. Both were Caucasians. One had blond hair, the other had brownish-blond hair. The two men were fair skinned. I turned away from them, still feeling nauseated and groggy. My whole body shook and I wanted to cry.

As I looked around the room, I thought I was in someone else's home. At the other end of the room, a woman was rearranging or doing something to a chair. I looked at the furnishings in the room and thought surely, I was in the home of a very wealthy person. For a moment, I thought I was in the entryway of the house.

I thought to myself, "I don't know where I am, and I am worried about the future. My future."

I did not pay attention to what the men said to the woman, other than hearing them say, "Here she is."

My mind was occupied with trying to figure out where I was and what was going to happen to me. When the woman stood up and turned toward me, I saw that she was an older lady. She appeared to be in her 60's or 70's. She was also Caucasian. The woman looked directly at me, then walked over to me with a warm smile on her face. She embraced me and told me I was going to be okay now and that I was safe. (Apparently, her job was to make me feel comfortable and safe.)

Ms. A.

She introduced herself to me but I don't remember what she said her name was. She looked familiar, but I could not place her. She walked me further into the room. As we walked, I thought, "Maybe...maybe she can help me."

My mind was clearer than it had been before and I was more awake by then. The woman appeared to be about my height (5'2"). I could not determine her actual height because she bent over slightly to hold me as we walked. When she sat me down in a chair, I thought she might even be shorter than me. She had a medium frame and her hair was shorter than shoulder length. Her hair was blond with some white mixed in. Her hair was combed nicely, the sides pushed back in a large wave. She had on little white earrings and wore small silver framed glasses. The woman was dressed in a light-blue patterned dress with a large, white, V-neck collar. There were four white buttons going down the center of the dress. The woman's voice was soft and she spoke with somewhat of an accent.

She told the two men she did not need them anymore. They exited through the same door we had used to come into the room. I looked down to see if I was dressed. I had on my pink, winter nightgown and I was barefoot. The woman made sure I was comfortably seated in the chair before walking to the far end of the room. I was left to survey my surroundings.

Directly in front of me was a half wall about 3 ½ to 4 feet high. In front of the wall was a French provincial, cherry-wood desk with a ceramic, rose-colored lamp on it. The lamp had a pleated, beige shade. The lamp was on. The desk was missing its chair. To the right of the half-wall, there was an entryway. I don't know what was in the darkened area on the other side of the half-wall.

A dark rose, French provincial armchair was located to my right. Above the chair was a small painting. I do not remember if the picture had an eagle in it or some type of old boat. The walls of the room were a light, cream color. I thought the room must have been done by an interior decorator. The furnishings and accessories appeared to be very expensive.

As I turned to look over my shoulder, I saw a hallway and another room. Through the doorway, I saw a sofa covered in flowered fabric. At the side of the sofa was a small, end table with another rose-colored, ceramic lamp with a pleated, beige shade. That lamp was also turned on.

The woman then walked in front of me and began to tell me that I was going to meet a very important person. She would not say who the important person was, but did say that he worked for the government.

Washington office

I know I tried to ask her where I was and how I had gotten there but she would not answer my questions. She cut me off by repeating to me the line about meeting the important person. She told me she was his wife. She repeated the same sentence at least three times.

The woman asked if I would like a glass of water and I said yes. She asked if I was warm and comfortable, but I don't remember answering her. She put a hand on my shoulder and told me not to be nervous and to quit shaking. She repeated to me that I was safe and need not be frightened. The important man would be arriving just any time now.

Before she disappeared into the room or hallway on the other side of the half wall, we heard two male voices talking and laughing outside the entryway. The woman then told me, "He is here."

I sat in the chair, afraid to even try to escape. I did not know where I was. If I got caught, I might be hurt. I also decided that maybe I didn't want to drink the water she was bringing. I had a hunch there might be something in the water. My stomach churned nervously as I heard the doorknob being unlocked and turned. As the slim man entered the room, the woman walked back toward me carrying the glass of water. She introduced him to me as Mr. Ralph Nader.

At the time, I did not know who Ralph Nader was. He walked over to where I was sitting and offered his hand. I shook hands stiffly with him. He was Caucasian and stood about 5'7". He was dressed in a dark suit with a white shirt and a dark, red tie. He had dark, short, graying hair and wore large, dark-framed glasses.

Nader said, "How are you doing, Gloria?" I noticed he was carrying a brown, legal-size folder under his left arm. While he shook my hand, I heard the door open. I had a glimpse of another heavy-set man. Mr. Nader moved to block my view of the man who walked down the hall to my right. Then he pulled the French provincial armchair in front of me and sat down.

As I watched him move the chair, I tried to remember if I had ever seen him on TV or in the newspapers. I was sure I had heard his name before but was not sure about the position he held in the government. Mr. Nader laid the legal folder on his lap. The woman, who had been standing on my left, handed me the glass of water. I held it, not wanting to drink from it, but she demanded I drink the water.

I took a sip then "accidentally" spilled the glass of water on the carpeted floor. The woman quickly left and brought back a white cloth to soak up the water. She then disappeared from the room.

Ralph Nader opened his folder and began interrogating me in a sharp, loud, and insistent voice. He questioned me about the contents of the file folder. The folder seemed to contain information about my life history. He wanted confirmation or a verbal reaction when he mentioned the species that was abducting three of my children, my husband and myself.

He asked me the same questions over and over again. I did not answer him. Some of the questions he asked were about where I lived, how many children I had, how long I had been married, and who I was married to. He knew that I had graduated from Valley High School in Albuquerque and that I had attended business school. He knew the positions I had held after business school. Because I would not answer his questions or confirm his facts, he answered them for himself.

Nader knew how long Fred had been in the military and when he had separated from the service. His folder seemed to have a lot of information about my whole life! I am sure I saw photographs of myself and the family in his folder. I did not know where all this was leading, so I did not answer the questions he was asking. Nader bent forward in the chair so he was right in front of me. He held onto the large, legal folder with his right hand. Moving quickly, he tried to get his right hand positioned on his lap.

Again, he began to speak loudly to me. He wanted to know about the aliens and what they were training me for. He wanted to know what type of work I had been doing for them. He mentioned the Greys specifically. I still did not answer any of his questions as he stared deeply into my eyes.

Nader called the woman, Maggie (or Madeline), and instructed her to go get the tray, saying, "She is not going to talk." The woman returned with the two military men in camouflage uniforms. She carried a silver tray that held two hypodermic needles.

One of the men grabbed my left arm. I tried to pull back, but the men were stronger than I was. They both held my outstretched arm so tightly I could do nothing. I tried to kick but that did not work either. One of them put his leg against mine and held it fast. Before I knew it, I felt the needle going into my arm. It was not long before I blacked out.

I heard a man asking questions and a woman answering back. I don't remember the details of the questions or who the woman was that answered the man's questions.

I woke up in the same room, groggy, lethargic, sedated, my head swimming, my body swaying. I felt like a limp, rag doll. My body was so relaxed I felt as if I wanted to sink into the chair I was sitting in. I felt disjointed because my body had fallen into the chair as I "slept." I knew I had been interrogated while under the influence of the drug I had been given. As I became more coherent, I remember seeing the man's unsettled temperament. I guess I had not answered the questions to his satisfaction because he was waving a stiff finger at me. He had removed his suit jacket. I heard him yell out to someone that I had awakened. Before I could move my body, the military men reappeared with another large hypodermic. They held my left arm out and I felt the needle pierce my skin. I blacked out.

I listened to the rational voice that demanded answers and heard the woman respond in a sluggish voice. The strange thing was, it seemed to be my voice I was listening to.

When I woke up again, I found myself lying on the floor. Ralph Nader and the woman were standing above me. I blacked out again. Inside my head, I heard myself repeating "Ralph Nader," over and over again. Then I heard my voice repeating the name out loud until I woke myself up. I was lying in my own bed.

Fred woke up at the same time and I asked him if he heard me repeating Ralph Nader's name. He said no, he had not heard me. He did not know what woke him up. I then told Fred about the very real dream I'd had. The experience had felt just as real as when the entities abducted me. More real in fact, because there had been human beings in this experience. I knew that it had not been a dream. I could not go back to sleep because of what I had just experienced.

What had happened to me that night was very traumatic and defies rational explanation. I could not understand the reason for it and I wanted to know how that experience was alien related. I could not remember the majority of the questions I had been asked. Who were these humans who had supposedly taken me? My thoughts were so mixed up, I found myself in a confused state of mind.

When the sun came up, my left arm was hurting. I looked and discovered what appeared to be three needle marks on my left arm. I knew then, that something had happened during the night. I had a horrendous headache and felt as if I would fall to the floor if I stood up too quickly or tried to walk. The whole episode was so traumatic and seemed so unbelievable! I had to have some confirmation of what had happened.

On Saturday morning, I planned to go the library and research Ralph Nader. I had to see a picture of Ralph Nader. During the night, I remembered having heard something about him being connected to the "Consumer Department."

When I arrived at the library, I found it closed for the Memorial Day weekend. I went to a local bookstore hoping to find books that contained pictures. I found nothing because all the books on Ralph Nader had been sold. My search would have to wait until the following Tuesday.

I returned to the library on Tuesday and my research was successful. Out of the four books I found, one had Nader's picture in it. As I stood at the library table, I could only stare in disbelief at the picture in front of me. I could not even move. I was frozen with fear, the events of the previous Friday night running through my head. I was in complete shock.

There was no mistaking the picture of the man, Ralph Nader, as the man who had questioned me during my abduction. I had many questions and no answers. I now definitely knew that my experience had been no dream. It had been an actual event.

I was oblivious to everything around me as Tuesday passed into Wednesday. I wrestled with the memory of my abduction and tried to reason it all out. Many times, I examined the marks on my arm and asked myself if they were really needle marks. I was glad the experience was over and in the past. I hoped to resolve my questions and felt that this kind of thing would not happen again.

May 29, 1996 Wednesday

I was somewhat more rested and thought that I would sleep well that night. I retired early, only to be rudely awakened at some point during the night.

I felt drugged, very disoriented, and confused. I did not know if I was standing up straight or walking down a dreadfully dark hallway with two hefty military men. They were holding me so tightly, I felt as if they were actually dragging me.

Or... was I lying down on something that produced a rolling sensation? My stomach churned and I wanted to throw up. I could see the side and backs of their bodies, up to the waist and part of the upper thighs. The ceiling (if that was what I was actually looking at) was dark. I saw dim light coming from somewhere.

Their hands held my upper arms tightly and they wouldn't let me go. God! I couldn't believe this was happening again! I thought I might be dreaming but because of what happened next, I knew I was awake and experiencing a real event.

There was pain traveling through my arms and body. I didn't know what was causing the pain in my body, but I knew the pain in my arms was produced by them holding me so tightly. I heard myself moaning and groaning, asking them to let go of my arms. I thought I was walking and looking down at the floor. Then I thought I was riding in something and seeing the ceiling. I felt so confused at that point, I didn't know if I was walking or riding! I couldn't tell what my legs were doing, they felt so numb. It felt as if I had tree stumps for legs.

If I was lying down, then they were dragging whatever I was lying on, by my arms. Their hands were holding me under the arms and the pressure of being pulled was causing pain under my arms. Suddenly, all motion stopped for me. I heard knocking, as if they were knocking on a door. Someone opened the door. I was not walking. I was riding on a table, like when you are in the hospital, going into surgery.

275

There was a lot of light and I could see clearly that I was in a well- lit room. The two military men sat me up on the table and turned my legs. I realized that I was in the same room I had been in last week! They helped me down from the table and helped me walk further into the room, passing by the original room I had been in the previous week.

They walked me down a short hall into the room with the floral sofa. I saw Ralph Nader again, standing by a cabinet that held books. He asked me to come and sit on the sofa. As I entered the room I saw a large, tall window. I walked to the window and moved the sheer white curtains to look outside. I saw street lights and tall, white buildings across the street. It was nighttime wherever I was. The street lights made it look bright outside.

"Go sit down on the sofa." Nader told me in a stern voice as he quickly closed the curtains. He practically pushed me down onto the sofa and turned off the light next to it.

The military men in camouflage were still standing there without their hats on. One man was holding a tray in his hand. I saw the needles. I stood up and tried to run to the other side of the room to get away, but I was caught and brought back to the sofa. Before I was injected and blacked out, I saw a fancy daybed on the other side of the room.

I was carried by the military men to the daybed. I heard the woman speaking in a low, sluggish voice, answering questions. I tried to look around and saw nothing but black. Inside my head, I did not realize that it was I who was speaking.

Ralph Nader interrogated me again. His temperament was unsettled. I don't know how long he interrogated me or how long I was in the room and gone from my home and my bed. I woke up as the two military men were lifting me onto a gurney. Before we went through the door to the dimly lit hallway, I was injected again.

I woke up in my own bed the next morning and experienced the same symptoms as the week before. I did not

Another room in the Washington Office

want to get out of bed. I laid there for some time, feeling quite ill.

I felt the need to talk to Karen, but knew that I would not be able to get hold of her until that evening. I did not know what was going on. Was I experiencing hallucinations? I felt so frustrated. There was so much to analyze and try to understand.

I thought I had been taken to Washington, D.C.! I had seen buildings like that when I was in Washington, D.C. I thought that was where I had been taken. I did not know what to believe at that point. I didn't understand what was happening. I found needle marks on my right arm with finger-like bruising.

Karen and Budd Hopkins worked with me on that experience. Under hypnosis, I discovered that, after being injected and blacking out, I had begun saying the words "Ra Chol Bra." I repeated the words quickly and loudly. I said those words to Mr. Nader over and over again.

After regaining consciousness, I remembered the words but not their meaning. I did not remember which entity had taught me the words. I knew that Ralph Nader knew the meaning of those words.

I was not able to discover the reason my mind holds onto particular pieces of knowledge. Therefore, I remained in the dark about the last two abductions by the military people.

Under hypnosis, I described the exact memories of my experience, and then some. When I described the first room (under hypnosis), I also saw a cherry-wood, antique clock sitting on the desk.

I was not able to contact Karen until the following week because she was out of town. By then, I'd had yet another abduction experience with the government men.

June 5, 1996 Wednesday

I had not spoken with Karen yet. The week was a blur of many emotions, including fear and being physically tired due to lack of sleep. As the evening wore on, I dreaded the thought of going to bed and trying to sleep.

My sleep was light and I woke up many times during the night. I felt restless, agitated, and nervous. I knew it would be another long night because I recognized the symptoms of the Greys coming. I thought they would appear that night. I tossed and turned.

I woke up with a most horrible-smelling cloth over my nose and mouth. Lying in my bed, I saw a man standing over me! I was unable to scream, but fought by pushing and trying to kick. I could not kick because the man was straddling my legs. The room was dark. I was quickly gathered up by two men and carried outside, through our balcony door! Whatever was on the cloth caused me to pass out.

When I awoke, I was being lifted out of a truck into the cool, night air. Two military men walked me through the large, open entrance of a building, then through another door that led to a dimly lit hallway. I was not as sedated as the last time this had happened. The two military men were not the same ones as before. Though not as large as the other two had been, they were just as strong. One of the men had blond hair, the other had dark brown hair. I believe the dark-haired man was Hispanic.

Though I still did not know the location of the building I was in, I once again found myself in a familiar room. As I was led into the room, I noticed that the gray curtains were already drawn across the large window. The room was well lit. Sitting at a desk to the right of the sofa was a black man who looked familiar. I thought I knew who he was but wasn't sure. He was wearing a blue, military, dress uniform. He had a lot of medals on his uniform. He wore dark-rimmed glasses. He was a larger man than Ralph Nader. I could not tell how tall he was because he was sitting at the desk.

On top of the desk was the same legal file folder Ralph Nader had referred to. It contained information about me. The file was open on the desk, as if the man had been reading it. He asked me to sit on a chair in front of the desk. The chair was directly in front of him. The man introduced himself to me as Mr. P..

Mr P. was apologetic and expressed regret at having brought me in like that. He apologized for the manner in which I had to be injected many times in order to be interrogated. He said it must be done that way for my own good, and to help our country. They needed the information that had been given to me by the aliens. He said the information was necessary to ensure national security. He told me that as soon as I gave them the information they needed (information that was buried deep within my brain), they would erase the knowledge from my mind, for my own protection.

Mr. P. spoke to me in a kind voice and a warm tone, but he spoke with much authority. He had a glass of water waiting for me and seemed to know that I was thirsty. I was afraid to drink the water, but he insisted I do so. I took a small sip of the water he offered. The woman who had been present at my two previous abductions walked into the room and said something to Mr. P.

My head was spinning very fast. I was trying to cope with what was happening and with what I had been told by Mr. P. I thought of many questions I wanted to ask, but the questions just swirled round and round in my head. "Why, why, why" and "where, where" were the only words that came into my head.

When Mr P. had finished conversing with the woman Madeleine, he turned his head toward me. He explained that I was going to work with them, but that they had to control my consciousness and memory. Apparently, whatever they had put in my water was making me feel relaxed and light-headed.

He began the interview by speaking about my life and the abductions by the entities. I was shown photographs of my family and myself. I don't know how they obtained those photographs. Mr. P.'s stern face made me even more nervous and fearful. Before I knew it, there were two military men standing on my right side, holding the familiar tray with needles. My vision blurred and Mr. P. faded away.

280

He asked me if I could walk to the day-couch by myself, and lie down. I asked him why I had to lie down, for what purpose? There was no way I was going to lie down! Mr P. said I would be more comfortable. Before I knew it, the two military men had their hands under my arms. They walked me to the couch, and forced me to lie down. Then, one of the military men administered the injections, one right after the other, into my right arm.

The world went black. I tried to focus on the lady with the sluggish voice who was talking about equations and bio-chemistry, nuclear warfare, and the green substance with its universal powers. I thought to myself, that lady seems to be very intelligent, but what do I have to do with all of this? I didn't understand a lot of what she was explaining or to whom she was giving the information.

I heard a man speaking as if he was interrogating the lady. I knew the lady was not myself because I didn't know the answers to the questions he was asking. I didn't know the technicalities of what was being discussed. Even the questions were far beyond any knowledge I had!

In my head, the lady with the sluggish voice repeated over and over again, "Mr. P.," until a loud whisper woke me up. I repeated the name over and over again as I looked around to see where I was in the darkened room.

I realized I was in my own bed, in my own home. My right arm was in such pain and my stomach so nauseated, I just wanted to throw up. I knew that if I moved, I would vomit.

I lay as still as I could and tried to close my eyes. The comfort and relaxation I was hoping for would not come because my mind was reeling with so many questions. I had no answers to help me understand what had transpired. I looked at my right arm and saw two needle marks along with (what I call) finger tip bruises. That was enough confirmation for me that something very real had indeed, happened to me during the night.

I was not able to document a second abduction with the man I knew as Mr. P.. My fear had outgrown my rational understanding of what I was going through. My fear was intensified because of the two men and the woman who had abducted me. What horrified me was the way they had abducted me; the techniques they had used to gain information; the mistreatment I had suffered at their hands; the physical and mental pain they had inflicted; the lack of concern for my dignity, and the lack of respect for my life and the lives of my family.

What truly horrified me was the fact that all these things had been done to me by fellow human beings! Who had given them the right to do these things? Is a human life worth the price of political power and being #1 on planet Earth?

I felt certain the two men and the woman knew a lot about the entities and that our governments were working side-by-side with them. I knew of many well-known military dignitaries who were involved in the role of abductors and who were working together to become the number one nation on Earth.

Many generals were destroying the lives of women MILAB's by sexually misusing them and treating them like prostitutes against their will. Not only women, but men as well, were being taken by certain dignitaries in our government. Those male abductees' lives, along with their families', were being destroyed. Truly, we have a long way to go as a species, before we can call ourselves civilized!

Didn't the military/government abductors understand that the methods they used on alien abductees was unacceptable and detrimental to human life? These people were being mistreated and abused for information they unknowingly held in their unconscious minds!

The statements I have made will surely be denied by our government. I have made these statements knowing that there will possibly be more threats made against my life by our government. They do not want me to speak out about these experiences. Where do our rights as human beings come into play? Our "freedom" is no freedom at all!

As long as I can, I will struggle to maintain my sanity through all the medical and psychological testing done to me by the entities and military/government abductors. I know the truth of what has happened to me.

With the information embedded in my subconscious, I may someday be able to help those who have not been coerced into working with the government abductors. I feel that a time is coming in the near future, when the abductees who have been trained by the entities for a specific task, will not only help them (the entities) in their survival, but help humans in our own survival as well.

The one thing that causes the most fear in me is not the entities, but our own human military/government. Whatever my destiny is, this is what I most fear for all humankind.

For me, television has become a good medium, especially when I see my government abductors there. To see their faces is shocking in more ways than one. I knew I had recognized one particular woman in the news on TV and in many newspaper articles. I did not have to study her face or listen to her voice twice to know that the intelligent woman I was seeing on TV was indeed, one of my abductors. Ms. A. I now knew that the last three abductions were in fact, real, not a dream. No definitely, the abductions were not a dream!

The following week, I researched the two men. I began my search at the public library. I wanted to obtain history on the men and find out exactly who they were. Somehow, somewhere, I needed to find out if the three of them (Nader, Mr. P., and Ms. A.) had been involved with the entities and if they had also taken other alien abductees.

I knew I would not find the latter information at the library. I was only able to locate a few books on the two men involved. I learned that Ralph Nader was involved with the Green Party. The books I found - <u>Collision Course</u>, <u>The Big Boys, Power And Position In American Business</u>, <u>The Lemon Book</u>, and <u>Old Age</u> - unfortunately did not contain the information I was looking for about Ralph Nader. The book,

My American Journey, about Mr. P., gave me information about his life.

I began to pay more attention to news spots on TV I was becoming more aware of articles in the *Albuquerque Journal* regarding either of the two men and the woman. As I watched them on TV, I knew they were the people I recognized from my military/government abduction experiences.

On any evening while watching the news on television, I would hear a story about one of my three abductors. I would sit there, in the safety of my own home, in my own living room, and re-live the terrifying things I had experienced at their hands. I would look at their faces on television and find myself shaking and holding my breath in fear. In my heart and mind, I knew I had correctly identified my abductors.

I kept thinking, this could not be possible, coming from three dignitaries who have so much "respect" for their fellow man. There was Mr. P., who portrays his respect for human life. How could he do such a thing as he did to me? It did not seem like the three of them could do something like that to other human beings, or even be involved in these abductions.

But if they weren't, then who *were* the men and the woman who had spoken in their voices, mimicked their mannerisms and moved about in their likenesses? Every physical feature, every action, mannerism, and tone of voice I saw in those three people on television was exactly what I had seen and heard in that room during my abductions.

The only question that remained was this: If the humans who abducted me were not Nader, Mr. P, and Ms. A., then who were they? If they were not the originals, then they were incredibly good copies of the three!

My story goes on...

July 13, 1996

Karen had me read the book, Lost Was The Key by Leah Haley. The purpose for reading the book was to familiarize myself with another abductee who had experienced similar problems with the government. As I read her book, I found many similarities between her abduction and my own.

I have retained many memories without the help of hypnosis. I remember working in a chemical laboratory as a "worker." I use the term "worker" because I do not know why I was chosen to work in a chemical laboratory. I have no knowledge of chemicals other than the household products I use at home. I don't even know the chemical make-up of the cleaning products I use. For the most part, I don't understand what I read on the labels of the cleaning products I use. I have a child who is a chemical engineer, but I certainly don't have that kind of knowledge!

If anything, I have an interest in medical things. So why was I not chosen to work on the medical side of this? How all this came about is unknown to me. I do know that I work with test tubes, side by side with other chemists and other human beings in a laboratory, either here on Earth or on a large alien ship. The chemicals are hazardous and we dress in spandex-type uniforms to protect ourselves. We wear helmets that have air moving through them.

My question is this: What knowledge does my unconscious mind hold that I am unaware of in my conscious mind?

THE GREEN PANEL AND THE BRONZE REACTOR

Date Unknown, 1996

After waking up, I was walked out of the room by a Grey and a human male. We went down a well-lit hall into another room. I thought I was being taken to the "school room," but when we entered the darkened room, I noticed that the opposite wall was lit from floor to ceiling in neon green.

As we got closer, I realized it was not a wall but a panel. This was apparently a panel I had worked on in the past. The green panel had rows of hot, wavy, black tubing across the

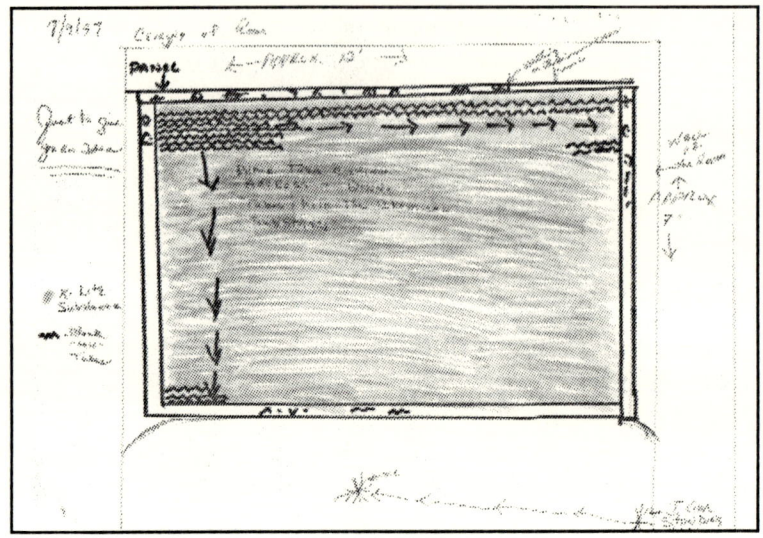

The Neon Board

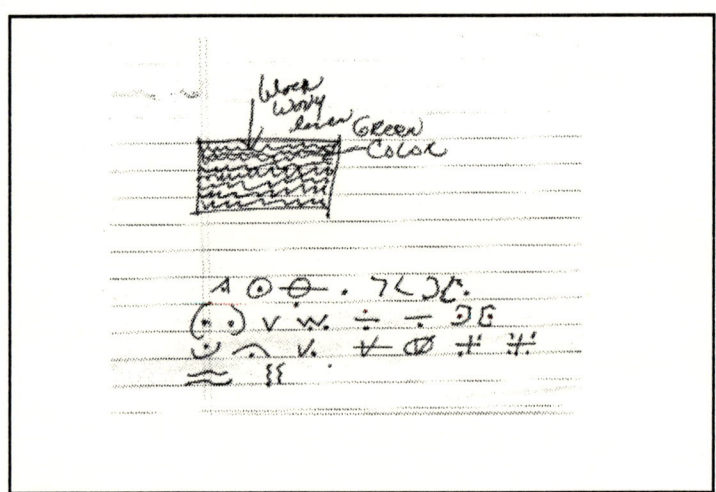

Alien Writing

length of it. I don't know if "hot" referred to a nuclear substance or if "hot" was used to mean "running hot." If the latter were true, then "hot" referred to keeping the neon green substance

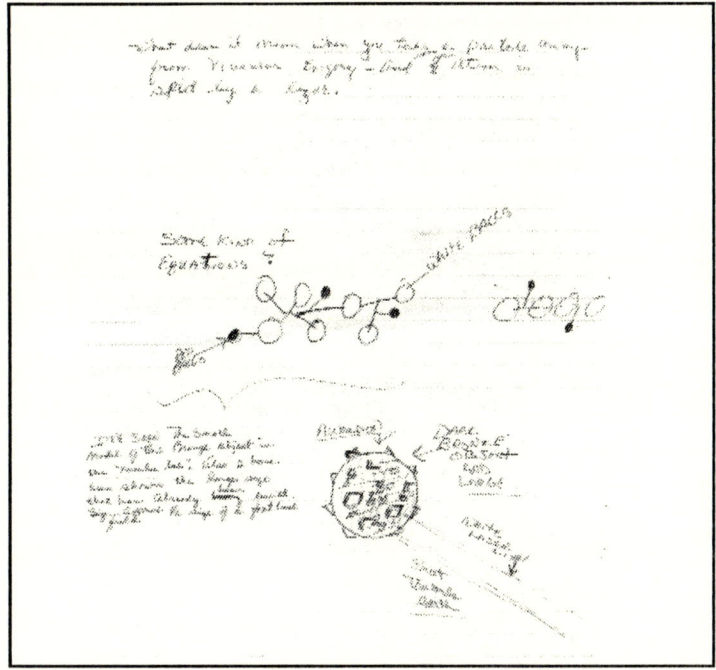

Equations drawing

from setting and letting it flow in its jellied form. The neon green was the substance I had worked with.

The green substance appeared to be in a jellied form under some type of container within the large panel. The panel was about twelve feet wide and seven feet high. Around the perimeter of the panel was dialogue written in the Greys' language.

After being hypnotized about this experience and seeing the large panel, I was able to sit down and automatically write out some of the dialogue I had seen. Somehow, I knew exactly the meaning of what I wrote; but in my conscious mind, I didn't know the meaning of any of this.

The panel was one of several that go into the bronze reactor. The bronze reactor is useful in other technologies as well. The bronze reactor is what will be used to neutralize the toxins of bio-warfare, if that happens.

287

THE MEETING

May or Early Summer, 1996

I was transferred from the small ship to a larger ship. I saw about one hundred humans on that ship, along with other entities, including the Greys. I saw many of the humans I had been working with, and the human scientist as well. I saw Raytheon, Winsha, and the mean Grey (whom I also call the mean doctor).

It seemed that each human was put alongside their hybrid child, with two Greys on either side of the human. I was given Winsha to hold. I realized that she had gained some weight because she felt heavier than before. She put her thin arms around my neck and began making vocal sounds to me.

Raytheon was on my right and the "doctor" was on my left. We were lined up in a large circle along with all the other humans. All of us (humans) had a look of fear on our faces. The entities and the human directors knew what was going to happen, but we (the abductees), were not told what would occur.

We were finally told that a large door would open and we were to walk down a ramp and follow the people in front of us. We were told to stay in line. The room was filled with anticipation and many of us humans were fidgety. I was toward the front of the line.

I felt a gust of fresh, cold air as the lights in the room dimmed. I looked ahead and saw a large door opening. People began to walk slowly and when it was our turn, we walked through the door to the outside. At first, I did not know where we were going, if we were on Earth or what. My entourage, consisting of Raytheon, the doctor, and Winsha, who was holding onto my neck, walked down the silver, metal ramp onto ground that seemed to be dirt. Thank God! Earthly dirt!

I felt cool air hitting my face and body. I looked up and saw a full moon in a dark sky with no clouds. The area we were in was lit with bright lights, making it possible to see. There appeared to be a cleared pathway for us to walk upon. We seemed to be in a desert. I saw small cacti, dried yellow grass, small and large rocks, and desert terrain. I tried to turn around and look behind me but was told by either Raytheon or the doctor not to turn around, just keep following, and stay in line.

The area was well-lit with large, free-standing, tall lights. The noise from the generators woke up our sluggish heads. Outside the roped area were many green camouflaged, army vehicles, large guns, army tanks, and some helicopters. With the reflection from the lights and with the aid of the full moon, I was able to see surrounding mountains or high hills.

Cool, brisk air touched my face. Winsha's sparse, straggly hair was blown into my face as she tried to quietly mutter something to me. We continued to walk inside the roped-off area and I began to see people as we approached.

The first person I saw was a man whom I recognized as President Bill Clinton. He was standing there with an astounded, quizzical look on his face. He was wearing a light-beige trench coat. Standing next to him were former Presidents of the United States, Carter, Bush, and Reagan. Carter also had a light-beige trench coat on. I saw the awe-filled and puzzled expressions on each of their faces. Standing next to them was Yelsin, from Russia, and leaders from Japan, China, Iran and Iraq. I believe a representative from every European country was there as well.

They all stood outside the roped-off area. Their faces were stern. The shock of seeing us (humans, aliens and hybrids) was evident on some of their faces. Intermittently, I saw military men dressed in green camouflage, holding large rifles, standing as if ready to attack.

The women abductees were dressed in their night clothes. The men abductees who did not have on night clothes were given a pair of dark-colored pants to wear.

As we were paraded around the circle, I was able to see what we had been transported in. I saw a large, dull-silver-colored spaceship. I was able to see that some Nordics, as well as the taller Greys, were there along with some humans that wore dark blue uniforms. I did not know who the humans were, but they were the "leaders" at the beginning of the parade.

To the right of the spaceship were some large tents. We were marched into the tents and kept there. In the large tent were many folding chairs and some long tables and chairs facing the audience. The tent was also very well-guarded with camouflaged military men holding rifles.

All the government dignitaries were then led into the tent. It was quiet as they filed in and took their seats. Each one stared as they passed us. One of the humans who wore a blue uniform, stood up and introduced himself as having something to do with a "Federation." He welcomed the crowd. We were then dismissed and paraded back into the ship.

When we entered the large room on the ship, I saw small cushions on the floor. We humans were asked to lay down on them. I handed Winsha over to Raytheon. To this day, I can still feel Winsha's small arms tightly holding onto my neck, and I believe she was trying to kiss me on the cheek to say goodbye. The doctor came and touched my forehead and the sides of my head.

I found myself lying in my own bed, early the next morning. I was awe-struck, feeling my experience had not been a dream, but an actual event that had taken place the night before.

Where had the meeting taken place? My gut feeling told me it was either a very secluded area of southern New Mexico, or a secluded area in Arizona.

What made me feel good about the experience was knowing that, out of one hundred humans who had been taken that night, more than one had come back with the memory of what had transpired when they awoke the following morning. They also remembered what I remembered.

August, 1996

Michelle and I took a trip to the Oregon coast. We stayed in a condominium where we met some old friends. During our vacation, we went to some seaside towns. On two particular days, while in two different coastal towns, I noticed an older lady with short, white hair.

The first day, we continued to bump into her as we went through the various shops. I did not think anything of it. The second day, we realized the white-haired lady was once again in the same town as we were. But this time, two people in our group felt as if she was following us. We sat in a small grassy area by some shops, and so did she. She ate at the same restaurant as we did for lunch.

She seemed to be there by herself. I spoke to her and she seemed to be quite nice. Perhaps she simply felt safe being around us.

Ralph Nader

October 10, 1996 Thursday

I had heard the day before that Ralph Nader was a candidate for president of the United States on the Green Party ticket. He would be speaking at the University of New Mexico Law School. I called Karen and told her he was going to be in Albuquerque. I told her I needed to attend his lecture to verify whether or not he had been the man who had abducted me. Karen said I should go but to take someone with me and to be careful.

Fred and Michelle were the only two who knew of my suspicions about Nader and they were both busy the afternoon he was scheduled to speak. I had no one else to go with, so I went alone. I made sure I had my cell phone, just in case I needed it.

I was filled with anger toward Nader and my anger gave me courage. It made me mentally strong rather than fearful or nervous. I had to confirm the identity of the man, to see with my own eyes if he was the same person who had drugged and interrogated me. I knew there was no way he could hurt me. He was on my territory now.

I arrived early so I could get a good seat. I carried a black leather folder with paper for taking notes, so I would not look out of place in the lecture hall. I found an aisle seat in the fourth row. I would have a perfect view of the speaker. I hoped no one would try to strike up a conversation with me about Nader as I knew very little about his politics. I decided to simply listen and act interested in his cause if anyone engaged me in conversation about him. Fortunately, no one did.

Mr. Nader entered the large lecture hall with a younger man who sat in the front row. The first thing I noted was Nader's red tie and black suit. His face; the color of his skin; the size of his body; his dark, graying hair; the bald spot; everything about him was as I remembered from my abduction experience. The only exception was that he wore no eye glasses the day of the lecture.

I scanned the audience to see if there was anyone present I might know. The young man who had walked in with Nader was also scanning the audience and writing in an open book. He seemed to be looking for specific people. He continued to do so throughout Nader's speech. The young man looked directly at me, then wrote something in his book. I thought that was odd so I glanced in his direction a few times. He continued to look directly at me with a stolid look on his face. On three occasions, he looked at me, then wrote something down. The man made me feel quite uncomfortable.

Nader sat at a table, looking down, until he was introduced. He stood up and walked to the podium to begin his speech. Ralph Nader had, what I call, "devious, quick eyes." You could not tell if he was looking straight at you or not. I remembered his eyes from my abduction experience.

I felt fear as I sat in the audience. Hearing his voice sent a cold chill down my back as the terrible memories flooded back into my mind. Nader's mannerisms and personality were exactly as I remembered them. He was an intimidating, strong willed, and dominant individual who liked to point and wave his finger. He had done that to me during my abduction.

While he spoke, Nader turned toward each side of the circular room, making eye contact with people. Several times, I thought he had noticed me because he looked in my direction frequently. He seemed to pick me out of the crowd. I felt as if he was speaking just to me.

At 12:45 p.m., my cell phone rang. I quickly fumbled through my purse and brought it out to answer it. I heard the voice of an older lady on the line and she called me by name. I did not recognize her voice so I told her she had the wrong number. I disconnected and put the phone back into my purse.

The lady called back. This irritated the men who were sitting around me. I spoke quietly into the phone as I asked what number she was dialing. The lady had the same accent as Mr. Nader when she answered. She was trying to dial my cell phone number. I told her she had the wrong party and turned off the phone.

The phone call could have just been a wrong number, but the lady's voice bothered me. I didn't think I was being overly sensitive to the situation. When I got back to the office, Fred told me he had tried to call me on the cell phone at 12:45 p.m. (the same time the older lady had called me). Fred said an operator had answered, saying there was a disruption occurring with the service on my cell phone.

When I could concentrate on the campaign speech, I found Nader interesting. When the speech ended, I immediately left the lecture hall with all the other people. There were many TV and radio-news reporters in the common area outside the lecture hall.

Attending Nader's campaign speech had allowed me to positively identify my abductor. I wondered if the Greys had simply been providing a "screen memory" for my benefit. As I stated earlier, the entities have been known to wipe out (or screen) an actual memory (of an abductee) and replace it with another memory that may or may not have happened. Had I actually been abducted by Nader? Or was I the victim of a screen memory? My gut feeling was that the abduction had been a real experience.

November 21, 1996 Thursday

On Wednesday (the day before this entry), something unusual happened when I arrived at the office. Fred had gone to Los Alamos that morning. I was to open the office at 10:00 a.m. When I got to work, there was a dark-blue, GMC truck parked on the northeast side of the parking lot that was close to our office. Sitting in the driver's seat was a man with black hair and a moustache. He appeared to be of medium build and could have been Hispanic.

I opened up the office and went to work moving boxes from our warehouse into the office area. I was up and down as I worked at my desk. I had not paid much attention to the truck once I started work, but had the feeling someone was watching either me or the office.

Awhile later, I looked out through the glass door and was surprised to see the man in the truck still sitting in the parking lot. He was staring directly at me. Our office front had large glazed windows. I checked every ten minutes to see if he had left. Each time I looked out, the man seemed to be staring in my direction. I felt uncomfortable about him sitting there in his truck all morning. I wondered if he was casing the place for a robbery.

Michelle arrived at 12:00 p.m. with a sign we were going to hang on the door of the restaurant two doors down from our office. As we came out of the office, headed for the restaurant, I looked at the blue truck and its occupant. The man inside pulled down the sun visor, I thought, to hide his face. What I noticed instead, was a small black box on the front of the visor. It apparently was pointed toward Michelle and me. The man was doing something to the black box.

As the two of us walked down the sidewalk, I turned several times to look at the character in the truck. I wanted to be sure he wasn't trying to break into our office. Each time, he appeared to hide his face in the shadow so I could not see him.

The owner of the restaurant, whom we knew well, drove up and parked directly behind the blue truck. John got out of his car and walked over to where Michelle and I were standing. We were laughing because we had gotten caught, red-handed, hanging up our funny "Turkey" sign on his restaurant door.

We walked toward John and he came to meet us, laughing at our prank. We met in front of our office door. I faced the blue truck, hoping I could see the man inside. I asked John if he had noticed the man in the blue truck. I told him he had been parked there all morning. I also asked him if he knew the man in the truck. He answered "no" to both my questions.

I told John the truck had been parked there since I had arrived at work early that morning. He turned around to look at the truck. As he did so, the driver bent down in the seat so he could not be seen. John came into our office to make sure Michelle and I would be safe. He wanted an inconspicuous place to get a good look at the truck and it's driver, in case we had a problem with him.

John stayed with us about half an hour, then said he was going to run over to the restaurant and come back. We walked to the office door with John. I was going to lock us in when John left. As John walked out the door, the blue truck sped off to the north. The time was 12:40 p.m.

John told us to keep the door locked and only let in customers we knew. He said he would come back and check on us and have someone from the restaurant call to check on us. He also thought the situation was unusual and that maybe we were being cased for a robbery.

This event brought back a forgotten memory. In October of 1996 (exact date unknown), a similar occurrence happened in our parking lot. It may or may not be relevant to what happened on November 21st of 1996. It might simply have been an innocent activity.

Once the restaurant closed at 2:00 p.m. each day, there was no traffic in the parking lot of our small business complex other than that from our own customers. There was always parking available in front of our business so our customers rarely parked in the diagonal spaces away from our office.

At the beginning of the week, I noticed a blue Geo Metro pull in and park in one of the diagonal spaces. The time was 4:00 p.m. The driver was an older white-haired lady. At that time of year, the sun went down around 5:00 in the evening. I would normally leave the office at 5:30 p.m.

Every afternoon that week, the white-haired lady in the blue Geo Metro would arrive right at 4:00 p.m. and park in the same space. She would remain parked there until I left the office at 5:30 p.m. Our parking lot had no lights, so the area was dark when I left the office.

When I put my car into reverse to back out of my parking space, I noticed that the lady in the Metro was reading a large, white book. How could she be reading a book when the parking lot was dark? The times I left the office and she was not reading, she appeared to be watching me as I got into the car and drove off. We reported her to the police, but she continued doing this for one week.

December 4, 1996

Wednesday at 10:30 a.m., I was on my way to work. I had to stop at the post office before continuing on to work. The post office was about 2 ½ miles from the intersection of the streets I normally drove to get to our office.

I was driving in the middle lane and was going to change lanes in order to turn into the small strip mall where the post office was located. I checked my rearview and side mirrors so I could change lanes. I saw a white car about a block behind me. I was traveling about forty miles per hour.

When I looked in the mirror again, the white car appeared to be exceeding the speed limit because it caught up to me very quickly. The car did not pass, but tailgated me. It was riding right on my bumper. I checked my side mirror and verified the fact. I thought the car was going to rear-end me.

I looked in the rearview mirror again and thought I recognized the same older lady with white hair that had been camping out in her Geo Metro in our parking lot! This time, however, she was driving a white car and she wore large, dark sunglasses. It was the same lady who had spent a week watching me leave work every day!

I wondered what her problem was. I wanted to hit the brakes and let her ram my car. I wondered if she realized she could cause a serious accident by doing this. I began to feel very uncomfortable at that point, so I increased my speed to get away from her. She matched my speed and continued to tailgate me.

As I approached the turnoff to the post office, I slowed down to twenty-five, then twenty miles per hour. I stopped to make the turn into the strip mall. I thought I would lose her, that she would continue on, after I turned. When I looked in the rearview mirror, I saw her turn in just as I had. I searched for and found, a parking space near the post office. The white car drove past as I pulled into my parking space. I had planned to say something to her if, in fact, her destination was also the post office.

I sat in my locked car and tried to calm myself. Surely, all this was just my imagination! No. I was convinced it was not my imagination. I sat in the car for about five minutes because my intuition told me not to get out just yet. There were a lot of people around, so I should be safe.

When I was ready, I checked to see if it was safe to exit the car. I was nervous as I got out of the car. I looked around to see where the lady had parked. She was in the same row I was in.

I thought to myself, "Well, maybe this was not the same lady who had parked in front of our office," though she looked like the same woman I had seen in October. I walked quickly toward the post office, checking over my shoulder to see if the woman was going to follow me inside. She stayed in her car and continued to watch me. I did not see her leave her car.

I finished my business at the post office and got back into my car. The lady was still watching me. I started the engine and pulled out of my parking space. As I straightened out, the lady suddenly pulled out right in front of me. I hit the brakes. She made a right turn onto the main street and stayed in the right lane. I immediately pulled into the left-turn lane, headed for the bank on the next corner. I was relieved that the woman had to make a right turn because that meant she would be traveling away from me in the opposite direction.

I went through the drive-up window at the bank, then headed north, on the main street toward the office. I was glad the woman was no longer following me. I wondered why she was harassing me. I had certainly given her no reason to do that to me. I couldn't figure it out.

I drove in the right-hand lane. I had passed several businesses when I happened to look to my right. There was the white-haired lady, parked and facing the main street I was on! She stared at me as I went by. I did not like what was happening and feared she would soon be following me again.

I moved into the center lane and exceeded the speed limit to get as far away from her as I could. I turned on the first north/south street and blended into traffic. I checked the mirrors constantly to see if she was behind me. No lady following. I felt better.

I wondered if she knew I was a MILAB (military abductee). I wondered if it was her job to intimidate or harass me, for whatever reasons. I had a gut feeling she would be waiting in the office parking lot when I got there.

Fortunately, I was wrong. She never showed up at the office parking lot that day. I watched the lot like a hawk all that day. I felt very paranoid, intimidated, frightened and angry.

THE SHOWER AGAIN!

January 15, 1997

I was in the shower. It was 8:30 p.m. I was about to turn off the water when I heard a loud electronic noise. It sounded as if a microphone had been turned on. I heard the voices of a man and woman speaking to one another through a microphone. Because I was startled, I did not immediately pay attention to what they were talking about.

I turned toward the bathroom door and heard the man call out my name two times. Slowly, he said, "Gloria. Gloria." He called out my name in a loud, clear voice. Then I heard static, like the kind you hear on a radio. I thought Fred had come home from work early and turned on the TV in the bedroom.

I put a towel around myself and opened the bathroom door. I hollered at Fred. The male voice continued to speak to me, but I paid no attention because I thought it was the TV I walked into the bedroom. The TV was not on. I heard the front door open as Fred came inside, home from work. I asked him if he had gotten off work early and would this be the second time he had come into the house. He said, no, he had just gotten home from school.

As I talked to Fred, the male voice continued speaking to me. I paid no attention to what it was saying. I told Fred that I was hearing a man's voice in my head and that I had not been paying attention to what it was telling me. Oddly enough, the voice sounded familiar to me, but I could not identify the owner.

I went back into the bathroom, not hearing Fred's response to my statement. As I put on body lotion, I tried to concentrate on the sound of the man's voice rather than on what it was telling me. I recognized the voice of Ralph Nader. No sooner had I finished with the lotion and put on my nightgown, than I heard a low-flying helicopter. It was coming closer to the house, making it vibrate.

Suddenly, the male voice quit speaking to me. I ran to the balcony door and looked out through the glass to see if I could locate the helicopter. I was afraid to open the door, as the helicopter seemed to be very close by. I was filled with fear, even though Fred and Michelle were home. I was the only one upstairs and I did not want to be upstairs in my bedroom with a low-flying helicopter circling the house.

I quickly put on my robe and ran downstairs to join Fred and Michelle. I asked them to turn down the TV so they could hear the helicopter. They did not seem to be interested in the helicopter. Fred said it was just passing over, and he and Michelle turned their attention back to the video they were watching.

Was this incident simply my own paranoia? Or was the male voice I recognized and ignored, connected to the helicopter that was shining its light onto our balcony? This was not the first time a helicopter had shone its light on our balcony. The helicopter made three passes over the house and left. I stayed downstairs until Fred and Michelle finished watching their video. I felt safer there than upstairs.

January 20, 1997

The Albuquerque Journal Business Outlook section carried an article which I read on the Local Update. The title of the article was, "*Mr P'*.to Keynote Quality Conference." I thought it interesting that the former chairman of the Joint Chiefs of Staff was going to be the keynote speaker for the 1997 Quality New Mexico Conference. He would also be present for the New Mexico Quality Awards Ceremony on March 6th and 7th at the Albuquerque Convention Center.

I wanted to attend the conference to see retired army general, Mr. P. in person. I wanted to see if he was the same person who had abducted me. Unfortunately, travel plans and other commitments conflicted with those dates. I would be in New York at that time. Still, I found it quite interesting and strange that Mr. P. would be in Albuquerque.

PHONE TAPS?

January 28, 1997

I did not know what a tapped telephone line sounded like when someone was listening in on your conversations, but I came to realize that my phone line most probably was being tapped. It was Karen who educated me to this fact. She taught me what to listen for when I was on the telephone. The perplexing thing was the frequency of intrusions. It seemed to happen most often when I was talking to Karen.

On the evening of January 28th, 1997, I was talking on the phone to my cousin. I heard clicking sounds on the line. I asked her if she was doing something to her telephone to cause the clicking. She said no, she wasn't. When I spoke into the phone it sounded like I was hearing an echo or talking in a hollow room. Other times, it seemed as if I was talking to myself and I could not hear the other person on the line. Then I would hear a tone over the phone that I recognized as the sound I occasionally heard in my ears!

I also sensed the presence of a third person on the line. It would sound as if someone was constantly tapping on the other end. Other times it would sound as if someone had picked up an extension phone and the person I was speaking to would sound very far away. This was accompanied by static interference on the line. Several times we would hear someone breathing over the phone line. The phone would also suddenly disconnect while I was talking to someone.

HYPNOSIS SESSION WITH KAREN IN NEW YORK

March, 1997

I traveled to New York where Karen hypnotized me on the first Nader abduction. My memories of the abduction had been verified, along with more memories that were revealed through hypnosis.

301

I evidently used some type of word blocker as a mind-control element when I was asked certain questions. The words that came out of my mouth were "RA CHOL BRA." I had no idea what they meant. I apparently used those words several times during the interrogation by Ralph Nader. I also hollered out those words periodically, during my second experience with Nader.

I conducted my own personal investigation into the meaning of those words. I found out that "RA" was the name of the ancient Egyptian sun god. "BRA" (to me) was a brassiere. That still left the mystery of the word "CHOL." At a later date, I was given these words: "MA TU SU TU."

After several of those abductions, I would actually freak out and feel a lot of fear when I heard the name Saddam Hussein. I did not know why until that memory surfaced through hypnosis.

During hypnosis, the following words came out of my subconscious mind: "Watch out for Saddam. He's working with underworld. His substance is getting out of control. Will destroy to gain his power. Will affect universe severely!! MUST STOP HIM. Specific entity working against Higher Power." The meaning of those words was revealed to me during a later abduction.

In the March hypnosis session, I began to name countries such as Russia, Japan, China, Nova Scotia, Canada, and the United States. I also named certain military bases in the United States. I will not identify those bases here. They were bases that worked with the entities to conduct experiments. In case of accidents, those bases were the secret storehouses of antidotes. The personnel there were also aware of the green substance and K-LITE. (I have no conscious memory of the definition or description of K-LITE.)

During the hypnosis session, my unconscious memory revealed the following:

I found myself in a large laboratory. I was in the large laboratory with some of the Greys and other humans. We worked

302

along side a human scientist working with nuclear fission/fusion and the green substance.

I came up with a chemical formula that I drew on paper after the hypnosis session. As I drew the chemical formula, I began to repeat this sentence: "What does it mean when you take a particle away from nuclear energy and a laser beam splits an atom." Little did I know at the time, that nuclear energy is released by reactions within an atomic nuclei by using fission or fusion. Seeprevious Illustration.

Through hypnosis, I saw, on a table in the laboratory, a model of a nuclear weapon diffuser. The model was small, round, and bronze colored. There were many shielded windows around the model. Through the windows, the inside units would shoot off white laser beams that contained other "vehicles" within the laser beams, to neutralize nuclear activity.

There were other laser beams that our governments (U.S. and alien) had developed. I had worked on the larger diffuser and its size was extraordinary. It was one-half the size of a football field.

RALPH NADER RETURNS

May 3, 1997

Nader came back to the University of New Mexico Law School to officially launch the newly incorporated, New Mexico Association for Public Interest Law. The reason for his Albuquerque visit was to support the Appleseed Center for Law and Justice in New Mexico.

Appleseed was founded by Ralph Nader to support public-interest law centers across the United States. The Association was a coalition of public-interest lawyers and representatives of organizations who advocated for children, disabled persons, immigrants, women, poor people, and racial, ethnic, and religious minorities.

Nader spoke in the same lecture hall as before, at 2:00 p.m. There was a variety of people attending the lecture; about seventy-five in all. I was there to seek confirmation of the identity of my abductor. It was suggested that I attend to see if he could identify me. I sat in the second row, in front of the podium.

I was talking to some women when a young Caucasian man entered the lecture hall. He looked very familiar to me. I thought he might be the same man who had accompanied Nader on his October visit. He looked like the man who had been surveying the audience and writing in his ledger book during the lecture.

The young man sat behind me and one seat over to the right. He looked at me as he sat down, then said hello. I must have had a strange look on my face. Perhaps that was what prompted him to say hello to me. The man was dressed casually. He had on light brown Dockers and a white, short-sleeved sweater.

He asked me questions about Mr. Nader. During our short conversation, I was certain he was the same young man. However, he had shaved his head since the last time I had seen him. Either that, or he had a twin brother that had been with Nader in October!

Peter Cubra introduced Ralph Nader. Nader walked down the aisle to my right, onto the lower floor, where he would speak. He wore a black suit, maroon speckled tie, and a white-striped shirt. I had a perfect view of him as he began his speech. Nader talked about how law schools could and should do more to prepare graduates to battle big business. Nader appeared to be more relaxed than the last time I had heard him speak.

I suddenly had a strong impression that someone was staring at me. I tried to ignore it, but the sensation would not go away. I turned my head and looked around. Everyone was focused on Nader. The sensation grew stronger as I sat there quietly. I turned so I could see the back of the lecture hall, thinking maybe there was someone present that I knew. When I turned my head, the young man was staring directly at me. I quickly turned back to the front, but Nader also appeared to be staring straight at me.

Seeing his small, beady eyes sent a cold chill down my back. It brought back memories of the abduction and his forceful questioning about the entities. I wanted to get up and leave, but I felt intimidated and frightened by Nader. I sat there waiting for the ordeal to be over.

Nader spoke about the fact that few law schools offer courses on government contract vs. no contract, relevant to federal, state, or local contracts. He also spoke about corporate attorneys and corporations. I could not concentrate on the speech. Or maybe the content of the speech was too technical for me to understand.

I gazed around the lecture hall and saw a man with a video camera aimed directly at me. I put my head down and turned toward the front of the auditorium. Nader was staring at me again.

As the man continued to video tape me, I moved my chair directly behind the man sitting in front of me in an attempt to hide behind him. I wrote in my book to remind myself what had transpired during the lecture. When I looked up from my book, Nader gave me a hard look, but I kept writing, as if taking notes on his speech.

The feeling of being stared at made me so uncomfortable that I turned around again. The man was still staring at me. He smiled. Nader spoke about NAFTA, Mexico, missiles, congress and the UN; the disarming of Russian missiles, the United States, poverty and health insurance; large corporation contracts, Intel contracts, tort issues, and General Motors.

Nader gave me another hard look, which I returned. His demeanor on the podium was pleasant as he joked throughout his speech. I looked up again at the table and the man was pointing his video camera at me again. I was not being overly sensitive about the man with the camera. I quickly began to write in my book.

Nader made another joke and the audience laughed. He appeared to look straight at me and I stared back at him.

The question and answer period gave me an opportunity to turn around and look at the people who were asking questions. My reason for turning around was to get a better description of the young man. He was about thirty or thirty-five years old. He had the same physique and mannerisms I remembered from before. He smiled at me again as I turned away.

Mr. Nader's speech ended as soon as the question and answer session was over. The audience applauded. The people in my row stood up. I gathered up my belongings and walked toward the center aisle so I could make a fast exit. I was detained at the end of the row, waiting for the rows behind me to leave the lecture hall. Before I knew it, Nader passed within inches of me, speaking to the Hispanic woman who had been audio taping his speech.

I was surprised to see him leaving with the audience. The last time, he had left through a door behind the podium. When the row behind me emptied and it was my turn to go, I let people pass by me and stood waiting. I did not want to be that close to Nader. I walked up the steps, taking care not to trip and fall. I made sure there were people around me.

As I got closer to the doors of the lecture hall, I realized I was right behind Nader and the Hispanic woman. She was still interviewing him and taping his responses. She used a long microphone and she wore a head set. I could not figure out how I had caught up with the two of them.

As I left the hall, I had a memory flashback. In my mind, I was back in the hallway of an office, feeling drugged, and following a man wearing black pants. The man walked me down the hall into another room where the floral couch was. The room had large windows. The thing that triggered the memory, was looking down as I left the lecture hall, and seeing Nader's black pants.

At that moment, Nader suddenly turned around. Momentarily, we were very close, facing each other. I was frightened and as if I had been drugged. I avoided making eye contact with him. I just wanted to run away and escape his presence. But another part of me wanted to scream out loudly at him, "Ra Chol Bra!" The feeling was so overpowering, I had to fight to hold back the words. Karen's words came back to me, "Don't approach him and don't speak to him. It could be dangerous for you, Gloria."

I stopped, realizing I could not do that in front of all those people. I stepped to one side to avoid confrontation with him. I literally pushed myself through the surrounding crowd. I was upset with myself for not paying attention and for getting caught in that situation.

Finally, I was outside the circle of people. I wanted to run out of the room, get in my car, and leave. As I left the crowd, I happened to look to my left. Walking alongside me was the bald young man! I walked faster. So did he. I needed to cross over to get to the other side of the corridor in order to reach the outside door. I was uncomfortable because I knew he was watching me and following me.

I crossed over in front of him and went through the exit. I saw a group of people and walked fast to catch up with them. I joined the group and walked alongside them. When I turned around, the young man was still following me. I left the group of people at the stairs and ran toward my car. I turned around to look and the young man was running down the stairs also.

I had my car keys in hand. I unlocked the door, jumped into the seat, and locked myself inside. I started the ignition and began to back out of the parking space. The young man was not in sight behind me. As I prepared to exit the parking area, I looked in the rear view mirror and saw him walking toward the back of the building. He turned and disappeared behind the building. There was a side door there and I suspected that was where Mr. Nader would be exiting the building.

AM I BEING WATCHED?

May 20, 1997

As I turned into our cul-de-sac at 5:00 p.m., I passed a white truck parked between our neighbor's driveway and ours, making it impossible for me to pull into the driveway. I saw a man in the driver's seat so I thought he was ready to drive away. I figured he would circle at the end of the cul-de-sac and leave. He did not move his truck, so I pulled up in front of our house.

I thought it unusual for him to be parked between two driveways like that. I thought he was a repairman, though the truck had no identification on the driver's side door. I collected my items from the passenger seat. A strange, uncomfortable feeling came over me. I did not want to get out of the car.

I looked in the rear view mirror to see if he was leaving. If he was, I would stay in the car and let him pass by me. I saw him watching me. I thought maybe he was waiting for me to get out so he could drive past me. I did not feel safe, so I pretended to be doing things in the car until I felt brave enough to get out. I opened the car door but did not lock it, in case I needed to get back in quickly.

As I walked around the back of my car, the front of the man's truck caught my eye. He started up his engine and seemed to be keeping an eye on me. Instead of circling the end of the cul-de-sac, he backed up his truck all the way to the end of the street and into the driveway of a house that *faces* our cul-de-sac! He turned off his engine. I thought this was a very weird thing for him to do, although in retrospect, it *did* prevent me from seeing his license plate.

I wondered if he had a partner who was robbing one of the homes, maybe my home! I wanted to see what that character was up to so I checked the mailbox, pretending to look through the mail. I turned my head slightly to keep an eye on him. He faced straight ahead, still watching me.

I was even more uncomfortable and concerned for my safety. I was hesitant to walk up to our front door because it was shielded by the wall of the garage. I did not know what I might find inside the house. I unlocked the front door and felt a presence inside the house.

I stood in the entry way for awhile, just listening. I heard nothing unusual. I went in and checked the ground floor for any kind of disturbance. Everything seemed to be okay. I did not go upstairs, but instead, went back outside. I peeked around the corner of the garage in time to see the man in the truck drive off in a hurry. I knew that Fred or Michelle would soon be home. I decided to wait for their arrival before going upstairs.

When Fred got home, I went upstairs to our bedroom. When I entered the room, it felt as if someone had been there. I checked the bedroom closets and the bathroom in case someone was hiding there. I found no one. The feeling of an intruder was particularly strong just inside the doorway to our bedroom.

That feeling stayed with me for many months afterward. I felt "violated" the way you do after a burglary. It felt as if someone was constantly watching me dress, undress, and go to sleep in my own bedroom!

I later spoke to two of our neighbors about the man in the truck, asking if either of them had called a repairman to their homes. They both said no, but one of them did see the white truck and thought it was strange that he had backed up all the way out of the cul-de-sac.

HYPNOSIS SESSION WITH MR. BUDD HOPKINS

July 3, 1997

The July 3rd hypnosis session confirms this event I experienced and awakened other stored memories about it after the session was over. I knew about "the reactor" and about using uranium ore, laser energy and control-fuel rods. I also had knowledge of equalizer reaction with energy particles being split. The entities also used krypton (I spelled it criton). Criton may in fact, be the correct element name and spelling.

A question that had been bothering me, was how I had been transported to wherever I was taken to be interrogated. Under hypnosis, re-living the night the two camouflage men woke me, I remembered seeing a bright, yellow light.

When I realized it was not the Greys who were taking me, but humans, I wondered if I was awake or dreaming. I felt the actual movement of my limbs as they grabbed my arms, held my back, and turned my legs, forcing me up out of bed.

As they lifted me off the bed, one of the men made sure my eyes were fixed on the yellow light. He covered my mouth with some kind of cloth as he held the back of my neck. The cloth had some kind of chemical on it that took my breath away and made me feel listless. The force of the man's hands on the back of my neck caused pain. He was strong, and I could not get away from him.

The men forced me out onto the balcony. I tried to fight them off but they held my arms. The pain was intense. I cried within myself and thought I was crying out loud for Fred to help me. Where was he?

As they maneuvered me out onto the balcony, the men looked up into the night sky. I felt the hand release its hold on my neck. I looked up as well. I saw the black underside of something. I did not immediately recognize what I was seeing until I saw blades going around. The thing above us was a medium-sized helicopter. I did not understand why I couldn't hear its motor. The helicopter was completely silent!

I saw a net of some kind being lowered down by another camouflage man. I realized that the bottom of the helicopter was open. The two men who had forced me outside picked me up. I was put into the net, face down, and lifted into the helicopter.

As I was lifted upward, I saw our balcony and the furniture on it become smaller. When I reached the helicopter, two men pulled me inside and placed me on what felt like a cushioned pad. Just before they injected me, I saw a Grey standing opposite where the pilot sits. The men covered my eyes. Everything went black as I felt the sharp sting of a needle enter my right arm.

During this same hypnosis session, my memory of a substance called "K-LITE" was confirmed. I had worked with the substance and had been told that it could be found deep within our Earth. K-LITE is not a known element on Earth. It is (or works with) an acetic acid (not vinegar).

I had also been introduced to a green substance that could be used for many purposes, including medical, chemical and nuclear projects. The green substance was also deep in the Earth, but so far, was not a known element.

Various components of the green substance could be mixed with other chemicals to produce potent bio-warfare substances that could be introduced into our air. A small vial of the green substance in its concentrated form, in the wrong hands, could spell disaster for planet Earth.

THE VIAL

Date Unknown

Speaking of dangerous substances landing in the wrong hands, I came back with this memory after an abduction with the Greys and military/government people.

After working my allotted time in the laboratory, we (the abductees) were undressed and made to shower. Then, we were walked through a unit with a bluish beam across its doorway. Once inside the unit, we stopped while the beam scanned our bodies from head to toe. This was to make sure all chemical particles remained behind and that we were not carrying or hiding any small vials of the elements we had worked with.

On the other side of the unit was a human male. His job was to re-check the insides of our mouth and ears. We were then transferred to the other side of the unit and walked to

311

another room to get dressed again in the clothes we had arrived in.

It was in the dressing room that I encountered a small man of Japanese or Chinese descent. He was already dressed in shirt and pants and was walking away by himself. He bent down and coughed, holding his hand over his mouth. As he straightened up, a vial about one or two inches long, came out of his mouth. He quickly showed me the vial. It contained the green substance we had been working with.

I don't know how he was able to hide the vial from the unit that scanned our naked bodies. I don't know why he showed the vial to me. Maybe he was just a smart aleck trying to get away with something. He laughed as he left the room, and threatened me by saying if I ever told anyone, it would mean my life.

As far as I knew, he was able to take the vial with him without further checks from the Greys or the military/government people.

The next time I was abducted to work in the laboratory, word was out that a person had escaped with a filled vial. I was not told how they knew, or if they knew who had taken it.

During yet another abduction, working in the laboratory, I heard that the Asian man who had stolen the vial was dead by the hand of Saddam Hussein. It was also said that Saddam had a vial of green substance, that he was hiding in water, and that he had the capability of creating the green substance.

A HOLOGRAM TEST?

July 9, 1997 Friday, 4:30-5:00 a.m.

I thought I had wakened from a restful night's sleep, but felt very nervous. I had a strong sense of having some kind of duty to perform. I also felt anxious. I had an urge to turn on the television because I knew there would be an emergency broadcast on TV and radio.

I did not bother to get out of bed to turn on the TV. I had a feeling that I'd just been brought back from being with the Greys. The memories then began to flood my conscious mind.

There were two scenarios to this experience.

Scenario #1

It was mid-afternoon. Michelle and I were at home. We were watching television when an emergency broadcast interrupted "Oprah." The message was a warning about a large and unusual storm of great magnitude. The storm resembled a tornado and had caused devastation and death in California and Arizona. It was a fast-moving storm.

Authorities believed the suspicious cloud was spreading an unknown poison through the air and it was killing people. The origin of the poison was unknown. The winds were so powerful they had left devastation equal to an A-bomb or H-bomb explosion.

We were told to find cover inside a building immediately. We were told to take shelter in an inner room, such as a closet or bathroom, and to stay away from windows and doors. We were to turn off all gas stoves, heaters and electrical breakers. The message was repetitive.

Then the wind began to blow, softly at first, then harder. As I stood in the middle of our great room, looking outside through the windows, I saw the sun disappear and the daylight became darkness. I tried to call Fred and the rest of the family, but was unable to get through on the phone line.

I was standing in the kitchen, about to hang up the phone, when an unbelievably strong wind hit the house. Through the kitchen windows I saw trees breaking and bending. I saw roofing materials flying through the air. Michelle and I ran quickly into the downstairs bathroom. We heard the sounds of buildings breaking up.

This is the end of the memory.

Scenario #2

Fred, Michelle and I were at the office. It was mid-afternoon. We were listening to some pleasant music on the office radio. The music was interrupted with the same emergency broadcast *(as Scenario #1).*

The front of the office was all windows. As we looked out, the sunshine disappeared and the day became dark. A forceful wind came up, the likes of which, we had never before experienced. The three of us ran and hid in the bathroom. Fred thought we would be safer in the basement of the building across the parking lot.

We ran across the parking lot as fast as we could, but the force of the wind held us back. As we crossed to the other building, we noticed that traffic was at a standstill. Cars were screeching to a halt and hitting each other.

We encountered much confusion on the way. Many people were leaving their cars and running inside whatever building was nearby. When we got inside the building we were headed for, everyone was in a panic to find shelter. The wind was much stronger. As we opened the glass doors, a rush of people crowded the entrance to the building. We knew how to get down to the basement so we quickly headed for the stairs.

Much to our surprise, the hallways in the basement were already filled with people. There didn't seem to be room for even one extra person. People were in a panic and we heard screaming and saw people pushing and shoving each other.

As we stood by the stairs, we heard loud screaming from the upper floor. The lights went out and we were plunged into darkness. Suddenly, everyone got very quiet. We heard the monster wind shattering glass and tearing up walls above us.

Without warning, I heard a familiar electronic voice in my ear. The voice told me to prepare and take action as I had been programmed to do. I instantly knew what I had to do. I told Fred to help me get to the small kitchen which was about 20 feet away from where we were standing. We pushed and shoved our way through the crowd.

314

Once in the kitchen, I opened some of the drawers, not even sure what I was looking for. Then I found it. Plastic wrap. I told Fred to wrap me tightly in the plastic wrap. Inside one of the drawers was also a box of aluminum foil. I automatically wrapped myself up in the foil as well. I knew that my "outfit" was only a temporary measure until the Greys came to get me and take me to their ship to be outfitted properly.

I heard more screaming. The electronic voice told me to turn around and look up. A Grey was there. He floated me up and out of the broken building. I saw dead, burnt people. Others were hardly alive. I was floated up to a spaceship that hovered above us.

As I entered through the bottom of the ship, I continued to float to the floor. Waiting for me there were several entities who stripped off my make-shift outfit. There were some humans along with the Greys who dressed me in a silver-colored suit.

While on board the ship, I was briefed by the human scientist and the Greys. I was told that many of the diffusers (the bronze, round units) had been projected to specific places in the United States to begin the process of neutralizing the poisoned air.

The vicious storm was being propelled by the jet stream, thus headed for Texas. The storm would cover most of Texas and go through many states before it finally hit our nation's capitol in Washington, D.C. At that point, it would either go out to sea, or turn toward New York. Evidently, the United States was the only country that was affected by the bio-warfare.

This devastating incident was the result of the green substance falling into the wrong hands. A relatively powerless, foreign government was poisoning our air. With the knowledge and technology of the green substance, it would now be easy for that government to take over the world. I was given the name, Saddam Hussein. His was a terrorist attack to gain power.

I was taken down to the ground in a small ship, along with other humans who were to help the people that were barely alive. My job was to put a breathing apparatus onto their mouths. Within the square, black unit I carried, were pills that would neutralize the poison in the water and food they would consume for survival. I poured liquid green medicine over the victims' burnt skin. The green liquid would heal them.

Had these scenarios been a holographic test given to me by the entities and the military/government? Were they preparing some of us (abductees) for a potential terrorist attack on the United States and/or other European countries?

I wondered exactly what the BIG PICTURE was here. Over the next few years, I found out that some of the information I had been given that night was actually true.

TRIP TO ARIZONA

July 12, 1997

Fred and I had been in the Phoenix area for about two days. We were traveling west on I-10 early in the afternoon. In the distance, I noticed a pink building on top of a round hill, off to the right of the highway. As we got closer to the pink building, I realized it was a large water tank... a water tank I had seen in one of my experiences!

I thought, if this was the same tank I'd seen in my experience, then there would be dark buildings with lots of windows on the other side of the tank. We drove around the tank. There were no dark-colored buildings with lots of windows.

We returned to I-10 and continued on toward our destination. As we approached the pink, water tank again, I had an impulse to look to my left. There, on the left side of the road, across from the water tank, sitting high on a hill, were the buildings I had seen in my dream! I had been in those buildings! Some humans and Greys had taken me into one of those buildings!

The area looked very familiar to me in the daylight. The buildings were set next to a hill that almost looked like a mountain and they were built on different levels. They were single story and had many large windows. The buildings appeared to be offices. As we passed them for the third time, I was unnerved. As hot as it was that day, I felt chilled. I had an eerie feeling as I remembered the night I had been there.

We had met someone in a room in one of those buildings. I was sure of it. The incident had happened about six months prior to our visit to Phoenix. I remembered having been forced to sit in a chair next to a large window that overlooked the lights on the highway. I saw the reflection of the pink, water tower.

I don't know the reason I was taken to that building, or by whom. In my mind, I again saw the faces of Ralph Nader and Mr. P., and heard their directions to me. I suspect I was flown in an alien space craft that night, to Phoenix, Arizona.

MAKING NOTE

July 19, 1997

I had been reading The Secret School by Whitley Strieber. I was reading page 133. Without turning the pages back, I realized I was re-reading page 111. I did not know how this could have occurred.

I looked at the page and it was page 133, so I began reading again. Before I knew it, I was re-reading page 111 once more. I checked the page number without turning any of the pages. The page number was 111. What I was "made" to read again was this paragraph:

Modern science is beginning to corroborate this radical view. In the August 13, 1993 issue of Science, a remarkable discovery was detailed by Dr. Asish R. Basu. What he and his colleagues discovered was that these lava fields contain quantities of helium-3, a primordial gas

317

associated with magma from very deep in the Earth. "We are proving definitively that it's from the core-mantle boundary," Dr. Basu said. Is what Dr. Basu discovered the same or close to the discovery of the "green substance"?

STRANGE ILLNESS

August 7, 1997

It was 7:00 a.m. I woke up with my left eye covered with thick, green mucus. I got out of bed and immediately washed the eye with warm water. The washing did not seem to help as the eye was again quickly covered with the thick, green mucus. My eye felt as if sand paper had been rubbed over it. The whole eye hurt.

I had not been up more than fifteen minutes before my right ear and the right side of my head became severely painful as well. I also had pain in my right cheek and the teeth in the right side of my mouth. The left side of my back and chest also felt uncomfortable.

By 8:00 a.m., all my symptoms were worse. I continued the warm- water eye washes. The eye was completely covered with very sticky, green mucus. The eye had turned dark red. By 10:30 that morning, my symptoms were even worse. I thought it unusual, since I had been well the night before. I literally felt as if a freight train had run over me.

I called my doctor and made an appointment for 3:00 p.m. By then the eye was swollen shut and beet red. The green mucus was literally running down my face from the eye.

The doctor was puzzled about what was happening to me. He said I had every symptom that ended with "-itis." The question was, where had I picked up this type of infection? I had a bad ear infection, sinusitis, bronchitis, and severe conjunctivitis.

I was not sure if I had been abducted to work in the laboratory the previous night. I also could have picked up some type of bug at the hospital my dad was in.

Two weeks later, my face and eye looked as if I had been in a street fight. My face was swollen with red strips and patches of dark red on it.

August 13, 1997

I was awakened by a human, male voice calling out my name. While my eyes were closed, it felt as if I was in a standing position. I opened my eyes and I was standing straight up. I felt very confused and not quite awake.

In front of me, about six or seven feet away, was a human male whom I recognized as Bill Hamill. He was dressed in a very clean, white, starched, laboratory coat. I was still somewhat fuzzy, yet it felt as if someone was standing very close behind me. I felt hands tightly holding onto my neck and head to prevent my turning in any direction. Bill Hamill was speaking to me, but having just awakened, I could not immediately understand what he was talking to me about.

Suddenly, the person or being behind me, forced me to walk closer to and around the small wooden desk where Bill Hamill was sitting. On the desk was an open book. Hamill picked up a black pen and seemed to make a check mark after some writing. I thought he may have checked off my name in the book. After he did that, he told me I was going to need two pairs of "jeez" suits. I was instructed to go to a nearby cubbyhole and pick up two of the jeez suits.

More awake now, I moved my eyes toward the right side of my head to see what else might be in the cubbyholes. I realized the wall was covered with different-sized cubbyholes and that some of them seemed to be about ten inches by ten inches. The cubbyholes were gray and held various different items.

I touched my face and could not feel that I had my glasses on. How, then, was I able to see Bill Hamill and recognize him right away? At that moment, whoever was controlling me, forced me to step to the left and around Bill

Hamill. My neck, head, and upper back were in pain from whoever was holding me so tightly.

I was directed to walk toward the rack that held silver, body suits. The rack was located in front of the cubbyholes. I knew I had worn those suits before. I removed two of the body suits from the rack. The suits hung on large, wide, black hangers. After removing the silver, body suit from the hanger, I automatically threw the suits down to the floor with my right hand.

I picked up the first suit that was to go on my body. I took the sleeve of the uniform and crumpled it tightly in my hand. I wanted to feel the texture of the strange material because I did not recognize the material it was made of. I noticed that even the weave of the material was strange looking. It appeared to be a tightly woven, chain link. It puffed out a little at the neck line. The material was very lightweight, and its silver color reminded me of aluminum. I was told to stop fooling around and get dressed. They did not want me to examine the material of the suit.

I was already nude. I did not know who had undressed me or when it had happened. I put my weight on my left leg. While the suit was on the floor, I pulled it up over my right leg. Then I put my left leg into the uniform. The uniform did not have buttons or a zipper. The material reminded me of spandex. As I pulled hard on the uniform, it seemed to take the shape of my body.

I felt nervous. I was all thumbs and my fingers would not function properly. By that time, I thought I was going to fall to the floor in fright. Whoever was holding my neck and head was still back there, preventing me from turning around. I guess I was taking too long to get dressed because Bill Hamill told whoever it was behind me to help me.

As "we" pulled the suit up around my neck the material felt as if it was going to strangle me, it was so tight. I was then told to pick up the other suit. The second suit was also silver-colored, but shiny. I again took the sleeve and crumpled it in my hand. The crumpling left a strange, triangular wrinkle pattern on the material. The first suit had not wrinkled at all. The second suit made a crinkle noise as I crumpled it in my hand. Even with the chain-link effect of the first suit, both suits felt very smooth.

Bill Hamill called out the name of Peter and suddenly, I had the second suit yanked out of my hand. I saw dark-skinned arms as the person began to dress me. The second suit also had feet in it. The second suit did not feel as tight as the first one. There was immediate confusion as Hamill spoke excitedly and loudly, giving directions to Peter. He said something about timing.

Before I knew it, I was standing very straight and had something put over my head. It was a helmet with a square, glass-covered opening on the front. I was able to see very clearly. Peter adjusted the helmet and connected it to the stiff, rubberized collar of the suit. He locked it into place. It felt as if it was locked with Velcro or some kind of tape that was put around the inside locking device.

The helmet rubbed against my nose, but with some adjustment from the outside, that was remedied. Inside the helmet, I heard and felt cool air rushing against my face. I was able to breathe. My whole body felt very hot. I did not know what was happening to me or where they were taking me. I did not like not knowing! I felt large gloves being put onto my hands. Then, I was walked through another door into...where?

My memory fails me as to what happened next or where I was taken. I woke up in my own bed and immediately woke up Fred. I asked him what the time was and he looked at the clock and said it was 5:30 a.m.

I felt so confused! I was disoriented and tired. I felt as if I had worked all night long with no sleep at all. I asked Fred if he had ever heard of a jeez suit and he said no. He wanted to know why I was asking, so I told him about my experience.

I know I have been dressed in this fashion many times before and taken into a bio-chemistry laboratory. I believe I was working on the diffuser, using various chemicals.

As I mentioned before, the "diffuser" is a large, bronze-colored, round object that carries an antidote for any type nuclear or bio-warfare agent that might be used by an enemy. The diffuser contains "elements" to diffuse the hazardous chemicals of bio- and nuclear warfare. The diffuser has a sound to it. The only way I can describe the sound is a constant, pulsating hum of high and low pitches.

The diffuser is the entities' technology. They are hoping the diffuser will not ever have to be used, but they are prepared for its quick deployment, nevertheless.

August, 1997

I woke up on a table somewhere, either in an underground base, or on an alien ship. Anymore, I didn't know where they were taking me. A male, dressed in what appeared to be a brown Air Force uniform, roughly guided me to a room. I walked through the door that had the beam of blue light that checked your body when you entered. This did not make sense to me.

I recognized familiar people along with the taller Greys. Sitting at a table at the far end of the room were two men in white lab coats. I was walked over to the table. Mr. Bill Hamill was sitting there with another man. I was told to go and get dressed.

We walked over to the rack that held the protective uniforms (the jeez suits) that I wear when working in the bio-lab. I noticed other familiar faces of abductees before their helmets went on. I was advised to hurry so we could all enter the bio-lab together.

I noticed light gray arms behind me, helping me into the tight-fitting outfit I had come to call the spandex uniform. I looked over at Mr. Hamill. I had been told by the other abductees that Bill Hamill was not his real name. His real name was Edwin Aldrin. They called him "Buzz." He was an astronaut.

I did not believe what I had heard. Mr. Hamill was always present when I was brought in after being abducted. I was not certain what his status was in working with the entities and the government. I knew I would see him in the biological laboratory and also in the large room with the panels that eventually go inside the diffusers and reactors. I did know that he had been retrained.

Bill Hamill-- Buzz Aldrin

After I was completely dressed, we walked out of the room and into the bio-lab. The other abductees and I were, at times, able to have short conversations. But we were supposed to remain silent and work with our microscopes or the vials containing the green substance.

Another door out of the bio-lab led to the large room that holds panels we used to help bend the tubes the green substance flows through for the diffuser and the reactor.

August 27, 1997 1:30 a.m.

Michelle had come into our bedroom to show us an unusual insect she had caught. After we all examined the insect, she went to bed. We turned off the lights. I felt very restless.

After awhile, I began to hear the electronic voice in my ears. It kept instructing me to go outside.

I told myself to stay in bed and go to sleep. The electronic voice insisted that I go outside. I felt as if someone was watching me to see if I would get out of bed and go outside. I became quite curious, but before looking out the door, I used the bathroom. Then I walked over to the open bedroom door and went out onto the balcony.

Looking up into the northeast night sky, I saw two, round, flashing lights high in the sky. I went back inside, walked over to the nightstand, and grabbed my glasses so I could see better. The lights looked familiar.

The lights were to the northeast and appeared to be in front of the Sandia mountains, but higher up than before. They were pulsating with colors of green, peach, purple, and blues.

I went back inside and got out my binoculars, thinking I would be able to see the lights better. I felt eerie and afraid, so I retreated into the house, throwing the binoculars on top of the entertainment center. As fast as I could, I jumped into bed.

I don't remember falling asleep, but I woke up at 6:00 a.m. feeling just as restless and full of anxiety as I had when I went to bed the night before. I had the feeling I had been taken by the Greys or the government, or a premonition that they were going to come soon.

I started my day early and as the day wore on, I became nervous and the symptoms got worse. Around 2:30 p.m., I suddenly realized that the symptoms I was experiencing were the "day after" abduction symptoms. This time, I was left with no memory of what had transpired during the night.

THE BLACK HELICOPTER

September 26, 1997 Friday 11:25 to 11:45 a.m.

My mother and I were about ready to leave the house. I was going to drive her to the hospital to visit with my dad for the afternoon. I was in my bedroom when the telephone rang. I was on the phone about four minutes when I heard a helicopter approaching from the south. I did not pay much attention to it. Just another helicopter.

As the helicopter got closer and passed over our house, the walls and windows began to vibrate so hard I thought the windows were going to break. The noise from the helicopter was deafening. It seemed to be very close to our house. It made so much commotion I wondered if it was going to crash in on us.

I hung up the telephone and ran to the bedroom window to look out. I saw a low small, streamlined black helicopter flying in the arroyo just the other side of our east wall. The helicopter was just about level with our upstairs balcony! It circled around our home twice. It was so close to the house, I said to myself, "My God, it is going to crash into the house!"

When the pilot in the helicopter saw me, the chopper turned east and gained altitude. It rose high enough to clear another two-story house, then moved over the neighborhood, traveling east toward the Sandia mountains. As the helicopter moved off, I felt safer about venturing outside onto the balcony. I wanted to see what was going on. As I watched, the chopper did not seem to gain much altitude and I thought it was going to crash into the mountain.

It did not crash, but turned south, circling the area in which I had seen two spaceships a couple of years back. The helicopter circled twice, then headed straight west and back toward my house. It seemed to travel faster than other helicopters I had seen before. As it approached, I ran inside and locked the bedroom door.

325

I heard the walls and windows vibrating again. I was frightened because I did not know what was going on. I thought someone was going to jump out of the helicopter and try to come into my house! I ran through the house closing and locking outside doors as quickly as I could. Then I ran back upstairs. My seventy-year-old mother who has dementia, was in her bedroom by herself. I did not want to leave her there alone.

After checking on my mother, I went back into my bedroom and looked out the window. The helicopter was hovering near our balcony. Next, it proceeded north, away from our house. My heart was pounding so hard I thought it was going to come out of my chest. I was overcome with fear. I wanted to run and get away. I had no idea what was going to happen or what the helicopter people were after.

I grabbed my purse, grabbed my mother and hollered to her, "Let's go, NOW." We fled down the stairs as fast as we could go. I thought we would encounter whoever was in the helicopter trying to gain entrance to our house.

I opened the garage door and got my mother situated in the car. I walked over to the trash can by the garage door to deposit some trash. I looked out toward the street. There, in the middle of the street, about twenty feet from our driveway, was a small, late-model red car. The car was blocking the street. The hood of the car was up. A tall man with white hair was standing in front of the car. The man did not look old. He appeared to be working on the car engine. He turned his head as I stood there by the trash can, and stared in my direction. I thought it strange that he was working on his car in the middle of the street.

I got into my car. When I turned my head to back out of the garage, he was standing up straight and still staring at us. I had not yet pulled all the way out of the garage when my intuition kicked in, telling me to make sure the car doors were locked. As I finished pulling out of the garage, I noticed he was still watching us. I was already feeling uncomfortable about the helicopter and now there was a stranger in the middle of the street, watching us.

I wanted to let someone know what was happening in case safety was an issue. I used the cell phone to call a close friend of mine who was an abductee and lived close by. I spoke with her and with her husband. I told them what had taken place. Her husband wanted to come to our rescue. They both felt that something was not quite right. I convinced them not to come over, but they insisted we drive straight to their house. They wanted me to call every five minutes while en route.

While I spoke to my friend, I kept an eye on the man in the street. He did not take his eyes off us. I closed the garage door with the automatic opener. I slowly backed out of the driveway. The man slammed down the hood, got into his car, and sped off. Because I was looking the other way as I backed out of the driveway, I did not see which way he turned at the intersection. He disappeared. I thought he might have taken the short route to the main street, but did not see him anywhere.

The man may have been an innocent coincidence, but my gut feeling told me otherwise. I still felt as if someone was watching my movements. I just wanted to get away from my home. I approached the main highway and turned left. I made the second phone call to my friends, telling them that we were safe and that the incident seemed to be over. They still wanted us to come by their place and to keep calling as we traveled. After driving about 3 ½ miles, I felt quite safe even though we had to stop at every traffic light.

I approached the east-west main highway to make a left turn that would take us to my friends' house. The last thing I remember was looking down at the black pavement of the road. I don't remember if I stopped at the traffic light or if I drove through the intersection. The next thing that happened was I "woke up" and I was driving west on Interstate 40. There were no other cars on the freeway. Mine was the only car until a black Bronco with very dark tinted windows suddenly appeared and drove right up against the side of my car.

I was still in a stupor, not knowing how I had gotten onto I-40. How could I have fallen asleep and yet still driven to where I was? The sudden appearance of the black Bronco, the oddity of no other cars on the freeway, and the dubious intentions of the Bronco driver totally baffled me. I could not explain any of this.

All those thoughts went through my head as I tried to figure out what I was doing on the freeway. I had to concentrate on the black Bronco and try to understand what was happening. The Bronco was in the left lane and was keeping pace with my car. Then it slowed down and dropped back, moving directly behind me. The Bronco was tailgating me.

Next, he changed lanes, sped up and passed me, cutting in front of me. Something was not right about the situation and I decided to take the first exit off the freeway. The sun shone through the Bronco at just the right angle to allow me to see through the back window. There appeared to be only the driver in the Bronco. He had long, ratted hair that stuck out from his head. He seemed to be a large person.

My exit was coming up fast. All I could think about was my mother's safety. I looked over at her and she seemed to be in some kind of numbing trance. I checked the speedometer to see how fast I was going. Seventy miles per hour. I knew I had to slow down quickly to be able to exit and get away from the person in the Bronco. I stepped on the brake to slow my speed. The Bronco did the same.

As I approached the exit, the Bronco moved into the right lane and dropped back even with me, preventing my exit off the freeway. I nearly rammed him. Okay, so I missed the exit. I knew the next one was about two miles down the road. I moved into the far left lane, increased my speed, and passed the Bronco. He seemed to be having trouble controlling his vehicle as a result of blocking my exit.

I do not know how fast I was traveling, but I managed to stay ahead of the Bronco. There were still no other cars on the freeway. I reached the next exit and got onto it without a problem, but I couldn't slow down fast enough to stop at the red light. I ran the light, hoping and praying I wouldn't hit anyone. I saw the Bronco behind me. He had to turn in the opposite direction.

I drove faster than the speed limit, thinking that the Bronco would soon catch up to me if I didn't. Finally, I came to a main street. I made a right turn and kept an eye on the rearview mirror. I never saw the black Bronco again.

I came to an intersection and stopped for a red light. Right behind me was a small black car with dark tinted windows. The car seemed to be following me and tailgating me. In the rearview mirror I saw a lady driver with large sun glasses and long straight hair. She saw me looking at her and dropped back. As I sped up and passed other cars, the lady did the same.

When I reached the intersection that would take me to the hospital, I noticed the black car about a block behind me. If I moved into the right lane, so did she. Somehow, I was able to lose her when we got close to the entrance of Veterans Hospital.

I was surprised to discover the time was 1:00 p.m. when we arrived at the hospital. Normally, the drive takes less than thirty minutes. We left the house at 11:45 a.m. That morning, the trip took an hour and fifteen minutes - almost three times as long as it should have taken!

When I got back into my car to drive to the office, I tried to call my friends. The line was busy. Several times I tried to call them, and each time, the line was still busy.

When I reached the office, Fred had not yet come back from Los Alamos. I finally got through on the phone to my friends. They had been worried sick about us. They had been getting ready to start searching for me. Instead, my friend came and stayed at the office with me.

We talked about the black helicopter. She suggested we call the police. She said they had a helicopter, though she didn't know what color it was or how big it was.

The Albuquerque city police said they did have a helicopter that was black, but the side of the aircraft had police markings and numbers on it. The police department checked the flight schedule of their helicopter and told us it had not flown at all that day. They also checked through the computer link with Federal Aviation. They found out that a helicopter was up at 11:49 a.m. but had not flown over the northeast section of Albuquerque. The chopper that had flown was not black.

While my friend was still at the office with me, we figured out that I had about twenty minutes of missing time from the intersection where I was about to turn toward their home until I found myself on the freeway with the black Bronco. Everything in between was just blank.

I wanted to find witnesses to the black helicopter event. I found my witness next door. My neighbor told me her house and windows had been vibrating very hard and that she hadn't known why that was happening. I had not yet told her about the helicopter. She had not gone outside because she was ill. She said she knew it had to be a helicopter from the noise it was making. She became frightened when she noticed it circling our homes several times.

Another witness who lived close by told me that there are government helicopters in a special area out at the base. Those helicopters are black and they work undercover. He knew this because he worked at Sandia Base. He also told me that one of the helicopters was small, sleek in design, and black. It was also unmarked and fast. He said only one government person is put on alert in the tower, day or night, when he has flying orders for that particular helicopter. That person was on alert the morning the black helicopter flew over our houses. His orders come from the government.

I tried to question him about which department gave the orders for that chopper to fly, but he could not tell me. Only a few military men are even aware of those helicopters.

My neighbor did not know about my abductions or that part of my life. He was curious as to why the helicopter was in our area and in the arroyo next to my home. He said he was going to check the flight schedule and get back to me. I never

330

did hear anything else from him with regard to this subject. I felt as if I may have put him in jeopardy.

DIAMONDS IN THE SKY

September 29, 1997

I went out onto the balcony before retiring for the night. Fred had already gone to sleep. I saw objects pulsating with hues of orange, blues, and greens. I had given them the name of my "diamonds in the sky."

That night, my diamonds were high up between the Sandia and the Manzano mountains. The month before, they had been in the northeast sky and close to the Sandias. On this Sunday night, I stayed outside, staring at the diamonds in the sky. I don't remember coming inside the house to bed.

I awoke the next morning (Monday) at 7:00 a.m. in our bed. My left forearm was hurting. I looked at it and discovered two very red puffy fingernail scratches about two inches long. The scratches appeared to be infected.

Later that morning, I call another abductee friend. I asked her if she had been abducted during the night, and if so, did she have any scratch marks on her. She said that she had no scratches, but did find about fourteen needle marks on her right arm. However, she had no memory of an abduction over the weekend.

On my arm were also other fingernail marks along with scratches where the skin had been pulled back. My abductee friend and I had made a pact that if we were together on an abduction, we would scratch each other so we could confirm that we had been abducted together. The infected fingernail scratches disappeared within three days.

THE GRID BRUISING

October 4, 1997

I went upstairs to our bedroom at 5:00 p.m. to change clothes and clean up. We were going out to dinner. I was sitting on the bed to get dressed when Fred walked into the bedroom. As he entered the room, he looked at my undressed backside and ran over to me, hollering, "What is that on your back?" When he inspected my back, he said I had an unusual looking bruise in a unique pattern.

I got up and ran to the bathroom where there is a large mirror. I was shocked to see that my entire lower right back, near the spine, was covered with a unique square pattern. I saw dark blues, purples and reds. It was as if a grid had been laid out on my back. Also on my back were eight different, large, needle markings in a circular pattern. When softly touched, they produced a sharp pain that shot deep into my body.

On my right thigh, I found an area about 1 ½ inches long that had needle marks within three circular bruises. The circular bruises were about one inch apart from each other. To the right of the circular bruises, was a long, straight-line bruise, 1 ½ inches long. About two inches below that was a larger circular bruise. Near the bruising, we noticed an indentation of the letter "V" that remained on my skin.

I had no memory of an abduction or of how I had gotten the strange markings on my body. Fred took pictures of my back.

On Sunday, October 5th, I went to visit some other abductee friends who have a video camcorder. They took video footage of my back. By the 8th of October, the dark markings had completely disappeared. They left behind a lighter skin color and residue pattern on my back. It looked as if I had had surgery in that area.

The leg bruising disappeared on the fourth day. I thought it unusual that, for as bad as the bruising had been, the injuries had disappeared so quickly. Normally when I got a

332

bruise (from running into the corner of a desk, for instance), it would be visible for over a week.

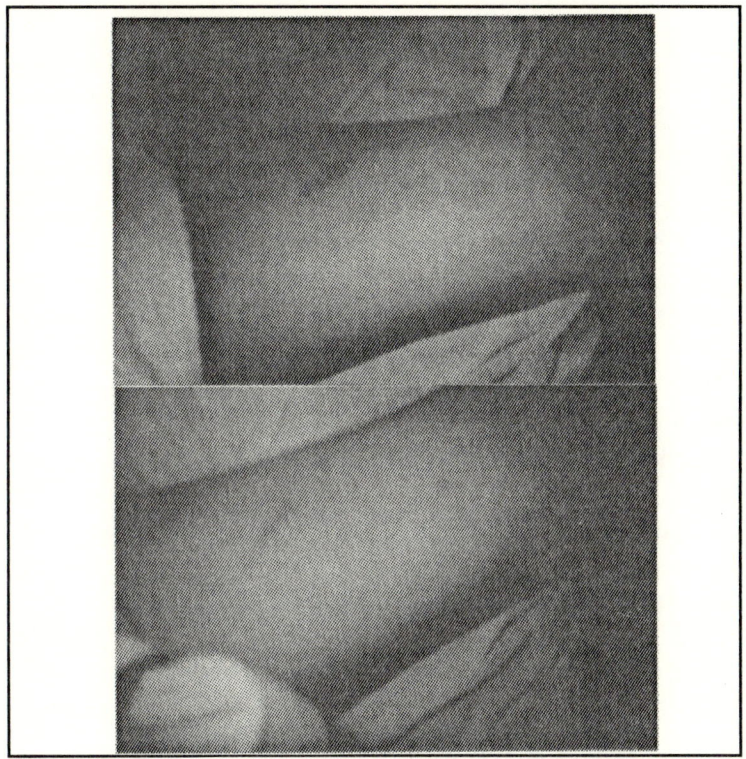

Bruises on my leg

THE HOTEL ROOM?

November 2, 1997

This dream had a strange beginning. I woke up, thinking I was in my own bed, only to discover that I was not. I also was not alone in the room as Fred was there, too. The room appeared to be a hotel room. Fred and I got up from the unfamiliar bed we had been lying on. There was another bed in the room. Michelle and someone else were lying on that bed.

When Michelle woke up and got out of bed, I recognized my oldest daughter, Debra as the other occupant! I was so surprised that Debra was there, too. Debra got up and walked with difficulty over to a chair that was close to the bed. Not yet fully awake, she did not say one word as she sat down. She seemed very tired and unaware of her surroundings as she looked around the room.

From where she was standing by the bed, Michelle walked toward a white door. She walked as if she were drunk and unstable. None of us knew where we were. Fred and I also walked to the white door as if we were drugged. We thought the door would lead to a hallway. We tried to open it, but it would not open.

Michelle, Fred, and I were standing by the door when we thought we heard human voices on the other side. Michelle turned and brushed up against me as she headed back to bed. Fred had either sat down or fallen to the floor. He was trying to look through some open slats on the bottom of the door.

The sound of voices was getting closer. I looked at Debra and thought it was unusual for her to be sitting so still in that chair. I too, knelt down on the floor to see if I could peer through the small open slats. I wanted to see what was outside the room. We were trying to figure out where we were and how we had gotten into this predicament.

The voices were just outside the door when Fred jumped up and secured the chain and turned the doorknob lock. We didn't know how they had locked us in, but we locked ourselves in, against whoever was out there. Fred told me to get the other chair or something to block the door. I felt as if I was moving in slow motion. Right at that moment, someone was trying to turn the door knob to enter the room.

Fred braced himself against the force of the door being opened and I helped him push on the door. Before we knew it, they had broken the door in two and pushed the wood away so there was an opening. They reached in and unlocked the door.

334

Two men in green fatigues walked in! There was a lot of shouting and Fred and I fought the men to keep them from coming any further into the room.

They overpowered us. One of the men grabbed Fred and locked his arm behind his back. The other man grabbed me and held me. To my surprise, Ms. A, dressed in a dark blue suit, walked through the broken door!

The man who was holding me forced me to walk. I tried to fight him but he held my arms even tighter and dragged me. Ms. A was not as sweet or nice as before. Her tone, when she spoke, was terse. I was literally dragged down a dark hall and into another room. My throat hurt from screaming so much. All I could think about was what was happening to Fred, Michelle, and Debra.

The room I was taken to was dimly lit. I saw ten to fifteen men and women. Two men were trying to put me on a steel table that had a mattress, pillow, and leather restraints for my hands and feet. I fought hard. Ms. A joined the men who were trying to restrain me. They succeeded in getting me onto the table. They bound my hands and feet with the restraints.

Ms. A then told me they were going to administer a SISK or SICT test. (The spelling of this test may be incorrect. I have spelled it as I heard it pronounced.) I was given an injection on the inside of my left arm.

I quieted down and began to survey my environment. I recognized some of the men who were there. Ms. A then stood at the foot of the table and held a brown, legal manuscript book. A heavy-set man who had been standing next to the table, went and sat down at a table holding monitors and computers. I recognized some of the computers as ultrasound equipment.

The man began typing on the keyboard and I saw graphs on one monitor. I did not know what I was looking at on the other monitors. A blue beam was moving across the table I was lying on. It was slowly scanning my body from feet to head. This was done twice.

At that point, I was becoming groggy and listless. Before I blacked out, I heard a man's voice tell me they were going to find out once and for all, if I was an alien abductee, and find the implants I had inside of me. Some of the implants had to be removed because they held important information. The blue beam would locate the implants. He said, instead of using more injections and hypnosis, they had another "better" method of getting the information out of my head.

I remember the blue beam stopping around my midsection. Then I blacked out. As before, when I had been injected, I heard a lady talking back to a man as if she was being interrogated. The lady was not very coherent as she answered the questions. I felt as if I knew the lady's voice.

Whatever else transpired that night, is unknown to me. I woke up the next morning in my own bed with Fred lying next to me. Michelle was in her bedroom and Debra was in her own home with her husband.

Fred experienced much pain in his back, neck, and arms. He told me he felt as if he had been in a fight. He had no memory of an abduction or of anything that had happened the night before. He stayed in bed that morning because of the pain. I lay there in a groggy state, with both my hands hurting around the wrists. My ankles hurt as well. I also had stomach pain.

That day, we were all argumentative with each other and not feeling well. If Fred, Michelle, or Debra had any memory of this episode, it was never mentioned between the four of us. This experience was just as real as normal everyday life for me. I do not know if this event was a real life happening or not.

I don't know why Fred, Michelle, and Debra were involved and I don't know what happened to them. I pray that one day, perhaps, their memories will come back and we will be able to sit down and discuss this. Much healing needs to take place.

November 7, 1997

It is rare that I watch CNN news. I was switching through cable channels and caught mention of Ms. A. For some reason, I felt as if I was supposed to see that segment.

As she entered the room and walked toward the podium, I was shocked and upset to see her wearing the same dark blue dress she'd worn on November 2, 1997, when I'd been abducted. I was very afraid. I did not understand why this was happening and I just wanted to cry. Her hair was combed the same it had been during my abductions. I heard her voice as I had during the abductions.

I sat glued to the chair for some time, not realizing that the topic had changed and something else was being discussed. I was convinced that I had seen Ms. A in some of my abduction experiences. This was the same woman!

December 28, 1997

By now I should have been used to hearing and waking up to noises in our bedroom, but I was not. As I woke up to these strange noises, I felt someone touch my face. It felt like a human hand. Someone stood near the head of our bed on my side. As the entity (human or alien) was rubbing my head, it made a muffled sneeze. The muffled sneeze sounded as if it came from a female.

I was afraid to turn my head toward the entity. I remained very still, frozen in place. I heard movement, as if someone was walking, then the usual sound of "venetian blinds" that are being rubbed and separated. It was the sound of Greys or military people going through the wall. Whoever it was had gone through the wall.

I fell asleep again and woke up in a dark room. I realized I was no longer in my bed or in my bedroom. I woke up with strength in my arms. My arms were moving above me as if I was protecting myself by fighting. I was trying to keep three people away from me and seemed to be fighting for my life. Three humans were trying to force me to lay down on a table and I did not want to. Evidently, I was given an injection. I went to sleep not knowing what was done to me that night.

The next morning, I had large bruises on both my legs down to the ankles. I had four small, bruised needle marks on my upper thigh. The needle marks lasted for more than three days. When I come back with bruising from the alien entities, the bruising only lasts three days.

I still had these bruises on 01/03/98, indicating to me that I did not get them from an alien entity, but from a human being. This was the appearance of the "dots" needle marks looked like this: (..

January 2, 1998

I woke up in a darkened bedroom and realized I was in my bed in my own bedroom. I heard footsteps. Whoever it was, walked through the wall by my bed. I turned to see who it was, but was too slow to catch a glimpse of them.

March 30, 1998

I was in a well-lit room, standing among male and female humans dressed in dark blue, military uniforms. One man, whom I did not know by name but looked familiar, walked over to me and put an item into my hand. The item was known as a "yina." This yina was different, though. This yina lit up. The two dots that are separated by the curving "S" within the circle were lit up with a blinking red light.

The yina vibrated in the palm of my right hand. I wished I could remember what its purpose was. Another military/government abductee said she was also given something similar, confirming my own recollection. She also confirmed that Mr. P. was involved, as well as the man at the top that I already knew.

THE IRON LUNG?

April 6, 1998

Both alien and human governments are not allowing a lot of conscious memories of abductions. I have realized a lack of conscious memory since January (1998), but have had cuts, bruising, and needle marks with unexplained memory of these wounds.

I had been taken the previous Saturday night because when I got up Sunday morning, I felt very disoriented. I passed it off as having gone to bed late on Saturday night.

Sunday morning, I put my contact lenses in. About two hours later, I nearly passed out from a horrible burning pain in both eyes. The feeling of wanting to pass out did not go away for awhile. I remained seated in my chair for at least twenty minutes, until I could see and the feeling of faintness went away. It was unusual for this kind of thing to happen.

I thought about the disk needing to be replaced in the contact container I put my lenses into for the night. About a week prior, I had put a new AO Sept disk into the unit. The burning lasted for about three hours after the initial burning sensation when I first inserted my lenses. I was somewhat disoriented the rest of the day. Other than the feeling of disorientation, the day went smoothly.

Sunday night, I had a dream. After the dream I woke up to familiar noises in our darkened bedroom. In the dream, I was taken by someone in a dark military uniform into another large room where I saw three or four other humans dressed in the same uniforms. I did not know where I was or how I had gotten there. I did not remember everything I was told, but remembered some things of great importance.

To my left and in front of me, was where the other men were standing. The men were standing by a very large, long, round, silver and white object. The object reminded me of when polio victims having trouble breathing had been put into a lung respirator/filter/decompressor unit (iron lung).

The unit in this room was used when an accident occurred in the chemical laboratory. Some of the chemicals that were being developed into gasses to use for bio-warfare and medical purposes would invade the lungs. This unit was built out of some kind of steel. The inside had two different levels where patients would lay. The unit was white and silver and had four round windows at the top so the patients could be viewed. In the front of the unit were two silver-colored, small, round wheels that could be opened, closed, and locked.

The lung respirator/filter/decompressor was in use when I was in the room. I listened intently to the pumping; air pressure and life-sustaining gases were being inserted into the unit. The pulsations of high and low pressure seemed to indicate that the unit was helping to sustain the life of either a human or an alien entity.

I looked into the iron lung and saw a man lying inside. I am fairly certain that I was also put into the iron lung that night.

I woke up after this dream and could not go back to sleep. I became very restless, irritable, and concerned. I tossed and turned. I did not feel comfortable. I went to sleep and slept later than my usual time.

When I got up the next morning, I sat on the side of the bed because I was disoriented and dizzy. I began to tremble and felt as if I wanted to pass out. My legs were shaking. I heard a tone and vibration in my left ear. My whole head was in pain and I wanted to cry. I was experiencing "morning after" abduction symptoms.

LEARNING TO FLY A HELICOPTER?

July 20, 1998

I awoke in a familiar concrete-looking room. There were two other women whom I recognized. I knew their names while I was with them, but when I was brought back home, I could no longer remember them. The two women had been

340

taught with me at this facility for some time now. Prior to that, they had been taught about helicopters. They had helped build helicopters and knew how to fly them.

The women had been instructed to give me lessons on flying a helicopter. When the session was over, we were taken back into the facility. The human teacher came over to me and stared into my eyes. His warning to me was "Look, and go with the people who come to get you in a silver and black helicopter." He repeated the statement over and over again.

Silver and black was stressed in his statement. I was to go. I didn't know what this meant or when it was to happen. I did not know what I was to be a part of.

July 21, 1998 (Repeat)

I met with friends, Carrie Satter and Sharon Klein at my home for dinner. Sharon and I discovered we had other mutual friends, Mary and Ray Rowlison, whom she had not seen for at least two years. We had met briefly at Mary and Ray's home three or four years prior. Neither of us could remember the exact date.

After dinner, Sharon and I spoke about our experiences/dreams. We found that we shared some of the same information and experiences. Sharon also told me she knew about a green substance that can also be converted for medical, nuclear, and bomb uses. She also talked about the wayward Asian scientist who had stolen some of the green substance.

Sharon knew and shared the same feeling I did about Saddam Hussein. She also experienced fear, beginning about the same time last year, as I had; from the end of October (1997) until April or May of 1998. She did not trust Hussein either.

I never did discuss those things with Carrie, since I had just met her in May (1998). That information was very private as far as I was concerned.

A CONFIRMATION

August 3, 1998

A mutual friend introduced me to a woman named Cindy who was also an abductee, living in Albuquerque. My friend thought I should get to know her because Cindy also knew of the green chemical substance.

Cindy told me that her knowing about the green substance was more like a psychic "hit" rather than interaction with the entities. She knew that it glowed an iridescent green and that it was very toxic. She also knew that there was a possibility it was in the wrong hands, or at least in danger of being so.

She said there were those involved who understood the power of the green substance and were committed to protecting the secrecy of the element until we, as a species were more evolved. She said that the substance could also be used to accomplish incredible good in the world.

Cindy did not really know how she came by this knowledge of the green chemical substance.

August 7, 1998

I had not been sleeping well for the past three nights. I would wake up anywhere between 1:00 a.m. and 3:30 a.m. each night. On the night of August 7th, I could not fall asleep because of the feeling that something was going to happen. I tossed and turned until I finally fell into a kind of half-sleep.

I was rudely awakened around 3:00 a.m. I heard a noise coming from the bathroom. It sounded as if someone had dropped something onto my mirror tray. I felt a strong presence in the room, but was unable to see any human or alien form in the dark. The presence walked between the bathroom and the bedroom. I became very fearful and full of anxiety.

Suddenly, I felt excruciating pain in my right ear. The pain traveled down the right side of my face and down the right

342

side of my neck. As I grabbed my neck and face, I realized I was outdoors! We were outdoors. How did I get outdoors? Where was I? I was uncertain about who the "we" defined.

It seemed to be close to dawn because the sky was getting a bit lighter. Either that, or there was another light source that made it appear that way. I saw a military man standing in front of me. To the left and the right, I saw two other military men. All three were dressed in camouflage uniforms.

I did not know what was happening, but there was a sense of excitement. There was thick fog or smoke in the air that had an odor I could not identify. I felt very nervous and I was shaking inside. I didn't know where I was, why I was there, or what was going on.

The intensity of pain in my ear, neck, and face grew worse. The pain seemed to overwhelm me. I remember being led off by two of the military men. I may have blacked out. I don't know what happened.

I woke up at 6:30 a.m. My ear, face, and neck still hurt, but not as badly. I felt very sluggish and began to experience the symptoms of having been abducted. I was barely able to get dressed. I was in slow mode, but made it to my hypnotherapy class on time.

As I sat down at the table, my friend Kathryn, who was sitting on my left, turned and asked what was the matter with me. She had observed my appearance and the condition of my neck. Sandi, a new friend, was sitting at the end of the table. Together, both women exclaimed, "What happened?"

Before I could even explain, Kathryn was examining my neck. It was swollen and red. Both women saw two round circles like puncture marks on my neck.

I began to tell them how I had been abducted the night before. I told them about the presence in the bedroom and the pain in my ear, face and neck. I told what I remembered. (Kathryn and Sandi knew about my history of abductions.) They wanted me to go see the doctor and I told them I would if the swelling was not down by afternoon.

Some of the swelling did go down, but by evening, my neck was swollen again. My primary-care doctor knew about my abductions. Budd Hopkins had me tell the doctor in case there would come a time when I would need care after being mistreated by my abductors.

The next day was Saturday and my doctor did not work on Saturday. I was very apprehensive about seeing another doctor. How would I explain the whole scenario of abductions to another doctor? I could not bring myself to do that.

On Saturday morning when I woke up, I had some memory of the previous Thursday night abduction. Re-living the experience, I saw myself standing and holding a device in my right hand. The device looked like some kind of communications radio. Toward the top of the radio was a round speaker where I could speak to others. The device also had five other odometers that had a white background with black lettering and black dials on it. The device had a button on the top right side of the unit that I would push in. The noise it made sounded like something dropping onto my mirror tray in the bathroom!

I don't remember what I was saying or who I was calling on the radio, but I felt as if I was guiding or destroying something with the unit. Was I being used as a guinea pig? I drew a picture of this unit.

THE HACKER

October 6, 1998

I had been storing my abduction documentation on the computer. The computer I used also had internet access. The evening of October 6th, I found out what a hacker is and just what kind of damage he can do.

I had been on America Online in the private area of an abductee support group that I belonged to. I was answering emails. Suddenly, the monitor went black and I heard sizzling noises coming from the inside of my computer. I quickly turned it off but the crackling noises continued. I turned the computer on, but got no response from the machine other than the crackling noise. The computer seemed to be completely shut off.

That night, Fred began his investigation to resolve the problem and get the computer up and running again. No such luck. He could not understand why the computer would act as if it had crashed. He had just installed new parts the week before.

Fred began testing the various components over the next couple of days. He went through the mother board, modem, and hard drive. All showed no activity! Along with the other components that had gone down, the situation was very suspect. But to what? There was no way to obtain the lost programs or documentation. Everything was simply gone.

After a week of frustration, Fred set up a newer computer to replace the damaged one. Again, we connected to America Online. I was able to get back into the support group site. I was informed that two other abductees' computers had also crashed on the same day and at the same time mine had gone down!

When we were finally able to get back online together, we compared notes. We discovered that the same components in all our computers had been lost. They too, had the same sizzling, crackling noise that had destroyed my computer. They too, had lost programs and documentations as well.

As a result of this incident, some of us in the support group began to ask questions as to what might have occurred. We questioned the possibility of invasion by a hacker. It was known that abductees were not immune to this type of violation.

Many of us abductees think we are part of a genetic enhancement experiment and are monitored for our unique differences and loyalties. Some abductees may be monitored more than others, possibly, by a military operative who does this type of thing.

A couple of researchers in our group, along with the majority of the group members, felt this situation should be researched. This incident had affected three people in the same group, so perhaps a hacker had been able to find a way "in" because no firewall had been used for protection. I felt that maybe I was the one being targeted because of my military/government abductions.

An investigation was begun by the researchers in our group. They did not share their sources or contacts with us for security reasons. During their investigation, the CIA, military personnel, military bases and other government departments were checked out. Some of the information that was shared with us confirmed that there was no apparent involvement by the United States government, their departments, or military.

Three people were located as suspected hackers. They had been using a specific internet service in the Springfield, Virginia area. The outcome of the investigation was successful. I did not recognize the names of the three men who were caught, or their internet addresses. My thought was, who is to say those men were not government or military connected personnel?

The whole episode made me much more cautious about my surroundings. These hackers had been able to get into my computer and take my personal files as well as the files I had on government and alien abduction experiences. They had also gotten my personal notes and communications from various UFO investigators regarding government abductions.

I felt the invasion and theft of files was particularly aimed at me. The men who were caught were working out of a location that was very close to the government people I had accused of abducting me! I felt so violated! I was appalled that someone could do this and invade my privacy in this way. What upset me the most was the fact that yet another person had invaded my private life.

I wanted to expose the people who were abducting me. I did not want to get back into the support group, because I wanted to protect them. However, because of their entreaties, I re-joined the group.

As I stated earlier, I had been taught what to listen for on the telephone when a line is being tapped. During the two weeks of the hacker investigation, I heard evidence of my phone being tapped. At other times, I heard another person breathing loudly when no conversation was taking place. When the person I was talking to, for instance, would put the phone down and walk away to do something, I would hear breathing on the line... breathing that did not come from *my* mouth.

I also had trouble with long distance calls. When I would talk to investigators long distance, the phone line would suddenly go dead with no dial tone. We would be unable to re-establish phone contact until the following day.

October 8, 1998 Thursday

I was contacted by a researcher indicating to me that I may already know another government/military abductee. She seemed to be having the same kind of experiences as I was. Her description fit the description of one of the women who'd been inside the helicopter with me. She also described the instructor who was teaching the two of us how to operate and fly the helicopter. We had been given turns at the controls of a gray military helicopter.

The other woman, I found out, had also been trained to parachute out of helicopters. I was never given her name. She had evidently come back from an abduction with a very lucid memory.

A DISCOVERY?

October 9, 1998

I thought I had a wonderful discovery late on the morning of October 9th. I had gone to a metaphysical book

347

store with a friend of mine. As we walked into the book store, two women were standing at the counter. I stopped at the entrance and closed the door slowly. I stared at the woman because she looked so familiar to me. She, in turn, stared back at me in awe.

She said she recognized me and began to make light conversation with me. We tried to figure out were we had met before. She brought up the topic of UFOs and the memory came back to both of us. She told me where she knew me from. We had been on a Greys' ship together! She and her family were also abductees. I asked her if she wore red glasses and she said that she did. We both recalled the incident where we had met.

My documentation of our meeting is titled "The Family." I had drawn pictures of her family. We both were exhilarated but tearful at having found each other.

The following week, I showed her my drawings. She was astounded to see that I had drawn her family and herself wearing her red glasses. She confirmed that her daughter had night clothes like the ones I had drawn.

I wanted more confirmation than my drawings, so the following week, she brought in pictures of her daughter at age six, and pictures of herself. I was saddened by the possibility that her daughter had not been the same little girl I had seen. Maybe this was not the mother I had seen on the ship, documented in "The Family."

As of October, 1998, her daughter was fourteen or fifteen years old, which would have made her too old to have been the little girl in the November 18, 1994 abduction. The small girl I had seen was about six years old, which would have made her ten in October of 1998. I felt confused because at the same time, on the local news, I had seen a small girl, age ten on TV She was identical to the girl in my memories.

If only I could have seen the girl from TV in real life, along with her mother, then I would certainly have known if this was the same family.

The mother knew me because we had shared at least three experiences together. She confirmed a couple of the experiences I had written about. She believed we first met on the night Raytheon walked me up to where they had been standing by the tables. We planned to get together at her home in the near future because she wanted me to meet her family... the family I had drawn.

Weeks went by and I tried to contact this woman by phone. I even visited the book store, but she had been busy with customers. She worked at the book store as a psychic. Time went by and our renewed friendship seemed to dissolve.

October 12, 1998

An unusual day. I had received a message from one of my investigators to stay off the computer for awhile until they caught the hacker. He told me that, because of my military involvement, I might possibly be the target of this hacker.

I had been on long distant calls and had been cut off twice from my party. The telephone had just gone dead again. After that incident, there were many times I would hear breathing or a clicking noise on the phone.

Another incident happened during the day, which may or may not be related, but I found it strange. Telephone cables with our prefix had been accidentally cut. It was not known how the cables were cut. We did not have phone service until late the following day.

I guess when you are being watched, have helicopters and airplanes circling your home, and strange phenomena occurring all around you, you begin to wonder about your safety. You also wonder about the strange incidents that happened that day.

October 14, 1998

At 11:30 p.m., Fred was still reading in bed. Before turning off the light, he got up to go to the bathroom. I turned over and faced the open balcony door and east window. I saw white strobe lights in the dark sky. I heard no unusual noise. I fell asleep after seeing the strobe lights. I awoke the next morning with three, odd-looking bruises. I had no memory of an abduction during the night.

At the request of one of the investigators, I had contacted Mr. Derrel Sims at the first part of the year. Mr. Sims and his team of scientists wanted to analyze the suspected implants that had come out of my ears. They also wanted to analyze the orange substance Fred and I had found one morning next to our bed.

At the last minute, I decided I could not mail those items to him. For some reason, I just could not let them go. When Mr. Sims had responded to my initial contact, he had told me to get the orange substance to him quickly because evidence like that would soon be "discovered" and would disappear from my house.

As it turned out, that is exactly what happened. I'd had the orange substance hidden. It disappeared the day I saw the tall Grey in my home. I saw him go into the room where I had hidden the substance. I did not think at the time, that he would know where I'd hidden it. It didn't occur to me that had been the reason for his visit.

I thought I still had the substance on the day I was asked to contact Mr. Sims again. I had asked him about the possibility of taking the items to the New Mexico Institute of Mining and Technology in Socorro, New Mexico. I had read and had been told by others that he had done work with someone at the Institute.

I too, felt the need to have the items analyzed, but in order to do that, I needed to hand-carry them and take care of them en route. I simply could not let them out of my possession and I did not understand why I felt that way.

Mr. Sims was quite upset with me for not following his instructions and for not trusting his judgment and his scientists. I found out later that I had been wrong about his having worked with someone at the New Mexico Institute of Mining and Technology.

Mr. Sims told me that he would be glad to help, but that I had underestimated the alien presence (as the reader may have figured out by this time!). He told me that as long as an abductee knew where something was, the aliens knew it too. It was that simple. He went on to say that, with him doing the tests, I wouldn't know where the items were.

He then told me that it was up to me. Obviously, if the entities wanted the items, they could get them as long as I knew where they were hidden. Why tempt fate? It had already happened once. Why chance it again? As it turned out, this was good advice from Mr. Sims.

AM I BEING ABDUCTED OR WHAT?

November 1, 1998

On Sunday morning, I found two bruises with needle-sized marks inside of them. The bruises were located on my right inner thigh. I had been very tired the night before. Perhaps this was why I had no memory of an abduction during the night. However, I did experience the day after abduction symptoms on Sunday morning.

I began to doubt myself when I had no memory of an abduction; but when I would discover bruises, needle marks, and cuts on my body, I would realize that I had been abducted during the night. I'd had none of those marking when I'd gone to bed the night before, and could come up with no other reason for their appearance on my body.

MORE CONFIRMATION?

November 6, 1998

The headlines on November 6th read: **BIOLOGICAL-ATTACK ANALYSIS LAB PROPOSED FOR LANL.**

LANL is the abbreviation used for Los Alamos National Lab. The article seemed to fit some of the knowledge I had retained from working in the laboratory, either on the alien ship or at some military base I had been taken to. The article gave the description of a location within Tech Area 54.

The article described a building that would be built and inside the building, yet another building. The executives at LANL thought the new lab would help guard against terrorism. The people there would be working with biological agents.

Disease researchers call this kind of facility a biosafety level 3 or BSL-3 lab. BSL-3 labs are a standard facility at major U.S. universities and pharmaceutical firms. Two such facilities are already known to exist in New Mexico.

Inside the facility, scientists would use cutting-edge genetics to fingerprint the DNA of pathogens such as those that cause anthrax and botulism. The article seemed to hit home with me because of the work and/or the analysis I'd done on the green substance under the direction of the entities and government. The green substance could be used as an element for medical, bio-warfare agents.

On the same day, I was downloading some files that had been sent to me regarding an unknown radio signal that had been picked up in our galaxy. A researcher I knew, who had been closely monitoring the signal (along with other scientists), had sent me a file on this.

I opened the email, got into the file and proceeded to print copies of the radio signals and articles. I was printing an article from Japan about the radio signals, when I noticed a one inch by one inch white square flashing on the left hand side of the monitor. In the center of the white flashing square, I saw something that resembled a black circle. The white square flashed five times. Then, for some reason, I was thrown off the internet and into the directory of my computer!

I was able to get back onto the internet, but the file I'd been copying had disappeared. I searched for the email and the files, but could not recover them. I had never noticed that flashing white square before. Had someone not wanted me to have those files? Had my computer been invaded again?

The next day, November 7th, I was out doing errands. Once again, a black vehicle was following close behind me. Everywhere I went, the large black vehicle tailed me.

That night, I awoke to the noise of the wall vibrating. I was surprised that no Greys or military men had come through the wall. I had no memory of an abduction the next morning, but Fred had fierce pain in both of his legs. Was this an indication that perhaps, he had been abducted?

A SECOND DISASTER DREAM

November 22, 1998

During this second disaster dream, I was given a formula. I did not know what it meant. The formula was:

X Y V V (the V's have an attached line on the top left hand side) and this: X X Y Y 2 2.

"CORNBREAD"

December 6, 1998

We woke up at 4:00 a.m. Something was wrong with my nose. I felt it and it began to bleed. There was a lot of pain, as well. My right leg (the one that had been affected by post-polio syndrome) was hurting badly. It felt as if I'd done some extensive walking or climbing. Those activities always adversely affect my right leg like that.

Not only did my leg hurt, but my body, as well. I felt tired, as if from working hard, then realized I had not done any hard or heavy type work during the week. The memory came back to me then. I had been abducted by the government that past night.

I was lying on a cool concrete floor inside a large concrete building when I woke up. There were about four other abductees already standing up or in the process of getting up from the floor. I noticed some men dressed in camouflage and others in white lab coats. They were yelling directions at us. Directly in front of us were several rows of stacked yellow boxes. We were instructed to pick up the boxes and carry them carefully. We were told, "Don't you dare drop any of them! Get them outside to the truck."

We were not told what was inside the yellow containers. As my vision adjusted, I was pulled up from the floor and told to get my ass moving. I walked close to the first stack of yellow boxes and picked one up, thinking it would be quite heavy. I was amazed to discover that it was very light. The box was about 1 foot by 1 ½ feet. The boxes were not made of cardboard, but of a sponge-like material.

I was yelled at and told to get in line and get those boxes moving and get them into the truck. I was curious as to what was in the containers. We were not to ask what was inside and were told to shut up and not talk.

As we walked in unison, carrying our containers, someone told me to think of cornbread… that we were carrying cornbread. We walked through a doorway large enough for a truck to drive through. I felt a cool breeze hit my body as I walked through the doorway. It was not cold outside, even though it was December.

Parked outside was a large, gray, panel truck with black numbers. I remember some of the numbers being 432. There were no other identifying marks on the truck. Inside the bed of the truck was a large Caucasian man with dark brown hair. I believe his arms had freckles on them.

There were lights on outside. The concrete building looked like a military warehouse. We handed our containers to the man in the truck. He stacked them neatly and tightly in the padded truck. I don't remember how long we worked, carrying the yellowcornbread containers.

Since we had to be quiet, we were able to hear the men yelling that if they did not hurry, they would be found out and they had to meet the deadline. There was a lot of excitement in their voices. I did *not pay much attention to what the men were doing. just remember seeing men running and rushing about.*

I recognized some of the other abductees as people I had worked with in the chemical laboratories. I had an idea of what we were carrying. I think we were carrying vials of the green substance that we had analyzed.

I was not sure of the location of the warehouse or where the cornbread containers were being taken. I did not know most of the men I saw that night. We finished our job for the night. I don't remember much of anything else.

I woke up the next morning in my bed. I could hardly stand up! I felt as if I had worked all night long. I was so tired, my body ached. I had bruises on my arms and legs. I noticed needle marks on my arms. Whenever I am injected with whatever they inject us with, I always have a pounding headache afterward. I felt nauseated and had dizzy spells.

It takes awhile to focus on life after one of these episodes.

MY TONGUE

December 17, 1998

In this abduction experience, I was with two other women whom I had been working with before in the laboratory and in a school. One of the women was an older, gray-haired lady. The other one was around my age and had dark, shoulder-length hair.

We were in a gray brick room where we had been many times before. We called the room our school house. Our teachers seemed to be the same human males who had taught us before. The room was guarded, inside and out, by military men in camouflage. They carried large rifles. Our male teachers always wore white lab coats. They appeared to be in their late forties or early fifties. One was bald on top and had light brown hair around his ears and the back of his head. The other teacher had blondish hair. Both men appeared to be strong and somewhere between 5'8" and 6'0" tall. They wore light brown uniforms under the white lab coats. Both men had stern personalities.

Usually, we "woke up" sitting next to each other in folding chairs at a long brown table. There were many of these tables and chairs in the large room with no windows. A large green chalkboard hung on the wall.

At the beginning of class, the bald man came over to where I was sitting at the table. He told me that I had been "talking." I said no, I had not been talking to anyone. He said that was not what he had heard. He said that he was going to fix that to where I would not talk anymore. Then he motioned over the men in camouflage.

The other teacher walked toward me with a hypodermic needle, and the bald teacher began to force my mouth open with his hands. I fought him and turned my head back and forth, but he was stronger than me. One of the military men held my head and they forced my mouth open by pressing on my chin and my jaw.

I felt the needle go into my tongue. At first my tongue felt quite painful, then numb. My body suddenly felt hot. The men stepped away from me with angry looks on their faces and told me they had warned me not to talk.

I felt my tongue swell and I tasted blood. I told them I needed to go to the bathroom, then became frightened when I realized I could not feel my tongue or hear any words come out of my mouth! They apparently knew what I wanted because they instructed one of the military guards to walk me to the bathroom. He held onto my right side because I was very weak.

I walked into the filthy bathroom and locked the door behind me. I felt faint and felt blood building up in my mouth. Something strange was blocking the inside of my mouth. I didn't know at the time, how swollen my tongue had become. I thought my mouth had swelled. I bent over the commode and threw up blood. I didn't bother to flush the toilet. I stood up and turned toward the sink. As I turned on the dirty faucet, I hoped at least, clean water would come out.

I rinsed my mouth and my face and saw that the water was bloody. My mouth felt full and my tongue hurt. I wanted to look in the mirror to see what they had done to me and to find out what was wrong with my tongue. The small mirror was so worn with age and dirt, it was hard to see anything. I found a spot on the mirror I could look into.

I saw blood, around my mouth, face and neck, that I had not completely washed off. My mouth felt so full! But full of *what*? I opened my mouth and nearly died from what I saw. Dear God, my tongue had swelled two and a half inches larger than its normal size. My tongue looked as if it had split apart! The skin was dark bloody red and pink, serrated, and literally pulled apart! It did not look like a tongue.

I felt hot tears streaming down my face and heard myself crying. The military guard heard me crying and began banging on the bathroom door for me to open up. I ignored his angry outburst. I was *not* going to open that door! I stood there in shock, wanting to collapse. I grabbed the front of the filthy sink and held on as I stared into the mirror. My tongue looked like a piece of boiled beef that has been cooked too long. When you pull the beef apart, you can see the serrated, pulled meat.

The guard broke the door down and pulled me out of the bathroom. The other two women were in tears as they saw me pushed and pulled to my seat. The dark-haired lady stood up and tried to console me. She wiped my face and I opened my mouth to show her how they had so cruelly disfigured me. The guard pushed her back into her chair.

The bald teacher walked over to me and stated that he had no antidote and to let this be a lesson for talking about the project. He said we would be taken to the other area and there would be doctors there. Hopefully, someone could help me. He informed us that we were already late for the other area, "So quit your crying and get out the door!"

I was shaking and crying. Both women held me up as we walked out the door. The guards kept trying to push them away from me. They were told horrible things about what would happen to them if they did not leave me alone. They said that "I was a big girl."

The older woman was pushed into the back seat of a strange- looking jeep. I later realized it was a camouflage Humvee. Then I was pushed inside by the guard. The younger woman's anger got the best of her and she pushed him back. At that point, one of the teachers stepped in and scolded the guard. He was told to quit pushing.

The younger lady helped me into the back seat of the vehicle. The older woman was trying to buckle me in. I saw, what appeared to be, my painful tongue, hanging out of my mouth! I had no feeling in my tongue, yet I was in a *lot* of pain. I tried pushing my tongue back into my mouth, but it would not stay there. Finally, on the third try, it stayed inside and I was able to close my mouth over it.

After the younger woman was buckled into her seat, she pulled me over onto her shoulder and began to softly rub my face. The older woman rubbed and massaged my arm and shoulder. I felt the wetness of their tears of concern. I remember hearing the motor of the vehicle and feeling movement as I blacked out. I do not know where we were taken or what antidote I was given.

When I woke up, I was repeating the name "Abrigale." I didn't know if that was the name of one of the women I'd been with that night or not. I felt the need to search for and find her.

I was in my own bed and my tongue felt stiff and extremely painful. I remembered what had happened to me. I got out of bed and went to look in the mirror. My tongue was back to its normal size but appeared to be more red than usual. There was no blood in my mouth or on my face.

As I examined my tongue, a strange feeling came over me. I grabbed at my tongue and pulled hard on it, trying to tear it out of my mouth! I don't know what stopped me from doing that, but the sensation went away.

I went downstairs in an unusual state of mind. I made breakfast. When I opened the knife drawer, I picked up a sharp knife and stuck out my tongue to cut at it! Again, I don't know what stopped me from doing that.

The week wore on. The pain in my tongue diminished to where I had a large bump on the tongue and a burning sensation. The feelings of wanting to destroy my tongue continued. Mentally, it was very difficult for me to control those feelings that week. Many times, I tried to tear at or rip out my tongue. Fortunately, I never succeeded in doing so.

THE LONG FACES

March 9, 1999

I had a question for the special support group I was in. I had also asked the same question of a couple of UFO researchers and investigators. My question was this: Had there been any reported entities that looked like humans but had very long, narrow faces, long noses, and dark, shoulder-length hair? I did not know how tall they were, but there were at least four or five of these characters.

No one could answer my question about the "Long-Faced beings."

Last night (Monday), I woke up and sat on the side of the bed. Then I found myself outside, on our large bedroom balcony. I was looking toward the Sandia Mountains. I knew I was not by myself. The same long-faced beings I had been with the previous Saturday night were there.

I was lifted up by them and put into a small, square wire basket. The basket did not support my back and my legs hung over the side of the basket. I remember holding onto a rope, of sorts. I remember that the beings (or humans) were talking very fast and moving quickly to get me into the basket. There were two or three of them.

I don't know where I was taken or what happened. There was a heavy odor of sulfur. I half-way woke up, and saw nothing but darkness. I heard a rustling sound, as if fabric was

359

rubbing against something. There is a type of fabric that makes this kind of sound. I can identify it. It is not a smooth material.

I felt someone's arms moving me around and putting me into something else. I could not see anyone or anything, the darkness was so complete. I think I may have been blindfolded.

I heard voices saying, "We have to hurry, be quicker!" They repeated this over and over again. I felt my legs and knees being drawn up to my chest. My arms and neck were bent and tucked into my chest. I felt as if I was put into a small compartment.

I woke up later that night in my own bed. I woke Fred to ask him if I had been in bed all night. I looked at the clock. It was 5:00 a.m. I told Fred about the dream and asked him what chemical smelled like heavy cigarette smoke. He did not answer. My body hurt all over. I was somehow able to go back to sleep.

Waking at 7:30 a.m., the word "sulfur" immediately came to mind. I believed that was the heavy chemical odor I had smelt. Or had it been cigarette smoke?

I stood up from bed, using my right arm to push myself up. I experienced a very sharp pain in my right arm. There was a place (about the size of a quarter) on my upper arm that felt as if someone had driven a large nail through it. The pain was so intense I had to draw my arms up toward my chest.

On the left side of my body, below the waist, I also had a very sharp, intense pain. There was pain in the left side of my throat as well. I went to use the bathroom. For some reason, when I stood up, I looked down at the commode. My urine was dark yellow, almost red.

Later that morning and throughout the day, our telephone had a consistent popping noise to it. The phone line seemed to have been disrupted. Again.

PLEASE DON'T LET THIS DREAM BE TRUE!

March 30, 1999

I don't even want to think about this dream, because if it is true, I am a murderer. I pray that this did not happen. Perhaps, this is the reason I no longer have complete or recoverable memories of being with the Greys since this date. This experience is just as real to me as all my alien and government abductions are.

> *I woke up during the night and quickly bounced out of bed because there was something by the side of my bed. It ran towardthe door that leads to the stairway. I followed. It ran down the stairs, and so did I. As we fell to the floor in the living room, I heard myself yell to the entity, 'I caught you! I caught you!" I was on top of a small entity.*
>
> *I felt my fingers go around his neck. I strangled it. I looked into his large eyes and his face as the entity made a squealing noise. Finally, there was no noise at all. I don't remember much more than that, other than the fact that I killed it.*

No alien body was discovered lying on the living room floor the next morning, but the horrible memory of that act lingers yet in my soul and mind. Since then, I've heard that same squealing noise twice, coming from an unknown source within our home. Fred has also heard the two squealing noises. He said it was possibly a cat, outside.

I fear I may have killed an entity. I say the words, "I am so sorry" with my heart and soul, because this was one of God's living creatures. Or, if you believe in a Higher Power, as the entities do, the being I killed was a living creation of that Higher Power. If I did do this, and I pray God I didn't, then I ask my God's forgiveness for the act. Again, I must ask myself, was this another psychological test for me?

THE LETTER

October 20, 1999

Dear Budd,

I do hope that you remember me, Gloria Hawker from Albuquerque, New Mexico. You put me through the process of hypnosis while I was in New York and when you came to Albuquerque and Roswell in 1997. Budd, because I do value your opinions and have trust in you, is why I am writing this letter, a plea for help from you regarding my ill health. As of this date, there has been no resolution in determining a medical diagnosis as to my lung problems and I am now resolved to believe that maybe my lung problems may be caused either by the entities who have abducted me for years. I do feel this is a medical emergency for me, as at one point I was told that I may have just three to five years to live. Please bear with me as I explain to you what has been going on with my health. Last week, I completed a series of tests with an immunologist/allergist who was my last hope of finding out exactly what is the cause of my lung problems. All the blood work and special lab work that was ordered including many skin tests all came back negative, thus I do not know what other tests could be next as it seems all relevant tests have now been performed. I have been under the care of six specialists regarding my health since January, 1999. On Monday, August 23, 1999, I had a right thoracoscopy surgery. This is a lung biopsy. I was fortunate to get away with three large incisions on my back. The various diagnoses from the lung biopsy has been interstatial pneumonitis, and idiopathic pulmonary fibrosis, and hypersensitivity pneumonitis. The right lung was much worse than the left lung. I had been using only the top half of both lungs. The diagnosis before the thoracoscopy was idiopathic pulmonary fibrosis (meaning the doctors do not know where I picked up an unknown virus or disease in my lungs) and hopefully, there will be a cure. I was asked many times by these various doctors if I had ever been out of the country. I could not bring myself to tell all, but my primary-care doctor knows that I am an alien abductee.

Several years ago my primary doctor and I did discuss this phenomena of abductions occurring in my life.

On September 1st, we received a verbal diagnosis from the pathologist who was definite on one of the findings, which is the interstatial pneumonitis which is in agreement with the surgeon's and pulmonary doctor's diagnoses. Originally, the pathologist could not come to a conclusion or cause of my lung problem and gave the diagnosis of "inconclusive findings" (meaning they do not know the cause of what has happened to my lungs). Fred and I were sitting in the pulmonary doctor's office when we received this verbal pathology report. The pulmonary doctor was not satisfied with this diagnosis from the pathologist and therefore, strongly influenced the pathologist to change and/or include on the report, the diagnosis of "hypersensitivity pneumonitis." I resented the intrusion of the pulmonary doctor into the formal diagnosis decided upon by the pathologist. This was not giving me an explanation or understanding of my symptoms. My lungs were very infected, inflamed, along with a large majority of scar tissue due to the infection within the lungs. The infection has persisted since I have been on the medication Prednisone, since September 3rd. I am presently decreasing the dosage of the Prednisone and we are all waiting to see what is going to be the outcome as the medication leaves my body. The immunologist is now trying to connect the constant, open sores in my nose to the condition of my lungs. The surgeon that operated on me remarked to Fred and me, that the lung tissue that was removed was "fleshy" and "strange looking," not normal-looking tissue. Even though the lung tissue that was removed was infected, evidently it did not look typical to the surgeon. He was also concerned about the color of the lung tissue, as normal lung tissue is pink in color. The surgeon was quite concerned about the texture of the lung as he had not seen lung texture such as mine. During this last nine months, there have been many chest x-rays, CT scans, pulmonary functions tests, and it seems like weekly blood tests; not to mention having to go through surgery, with its extra pain, and associated difficulties which took me back to the emergency room. Then, having an infection in one of the incisions that had

363

to be reopened, without any pain medication, and then packed and redressed twice daily for six weeks. After the incision infection, I was abducted and woke up lying on a table in a familiar room. Two Greys were staring at me from only a few inches away. Their eyes looked sad. I do not know what they did to me.

The history of this lung condition began in May of 1998 when I started to cough and began to self medicate it. The cough was very persistent and I did nothing about it until January, 1999 when I began to experience a horrific, breath-taking cough and pain across my chest. I thought I was having a heart attack. My primary-care doctor, Dr. G. Davis, began to treat my cough with medications that did not work. Each proceeding month the cough would worsen, as did my immune system. I was taking two naps a day and could not walk even short distances or barely climb stairs. I also had a very bad rash around my neck and arms. X-rays, blood tests, urine tests all came back negative, until the first of August.

During this short history of illness from 1998 to 1999, I did have some experiences with memories of either the Greys or another entity who looked or took the form of a human being. Entities who appear human, and who wear the military outfits and also wear the white medical jackets. I am holding on to a memory which concerns me. It occurred last December, and dealt with these human looking beings who injected my tongue. My tongue swelled one to two inches. I felt pain in my tongue for the next several days. In this memory, I was allowed to use a bathroom where I did vomit up blood. The bathroom had a dirty mirror. I looked into the mirror to see what they did to my tongue, as my mouth felt numb, swollen, and full. I nearly died on the spot, as I stared in shock at my tongue. The only way I can explain it is to boil a small portion of roast beef, and have a look at the serrated "strings" when you pull away at the roast and you will see what I saw in this mirror. These "human beings" did this to me as punishment for talking about their activities. They threatened me by saying, " This would only be the beginning...and I'd better remember this..." In 1998, I also have memories of being dressed in special suits and having a helmet put over my head for protection, and taken to the lab to do work. Recently, the Greys and these other entities do not let me have the visual memories that they would normally let me have, but I awake with the normal bruising, cuts, etc. all over my body and experience the symptoms of an abduction the next day.

Fred, my children, relatives and friends, all keep asking me the same question: "Have these entities caused this lung condition?" Now I find reason to ask myself the very same questions. Is it possible, what have they done to me? Is my life expectancy shorter now that the doctors cannot find the cause and will therefore be unable to treat me? Budd, I am scared, I cry now every day, wondering if the Greys or these other entities are the cause, and why have they not healed me the way they healed me with the post-polio syndrome. I want to live a long and healthy life. I am so filled with anger in knowing that maybe they did this to me and yet, just not knowing.

Budd, can you help me now with some kind of an answer to my dilemma? Because you may know many medical doctors who do work in the UFO field and because of your contact with many unusual, medical, alien abduction cases, I pray you can help me to heal and understand my condition. I also pray you will contact me. Right now, I feel that you may be my only answer in this distressing situation. Could you please, please, Budd, contact me either way. Even if you do not have an answer for me, it will be a help to me to just speak with you. If you ever recovered the videotape I sent to you, yes, I have had the same type markings again on my back.

Thank you, Budd, for listening to me. Please feel free to call me collect (505) phone number. After five days, if it is not a bother for you, I will also try to contact you, if I have not heard from you by then.

Thank you for your time, Budd,
Gloria A. Hawker
Albuquerque, New Mexico

Budd did call me regarding my letter. He was quite upset about my lung problem and said that he was not aware of this having happened before in connection with any UFO phenomena. During a second phone conversation, when I asked Budd if he could give me a yes or no answer as to whether the entities, or our military, or the government could have done this to me, his response was that he could not say "yes" or "no." End of answer. He did ask me to stay in contact with him regarding my health.

October 21, 1999

I woke up during the night and felt a liquid running out of my nose. I thought I just had a runny nose and did not bother with it other than to use a Kleenex. I fell back asleep, but soon woke up again with the same problem. I wiped my nose, then blew it. I felt comfortable and fell asleep.

In the morning, I woke up in a puddle of wet blood. The blood had soaked through the sheet and down through the mattress cover. I had worn a white night gown to bed the night before. The front of it was covered with blood. My face was also covered with blood. I had no memory of having been abducted. I do not know why I lost so much blood that night.

December 27, 1999

I had been taken again during the night. I woke up during the night and went to the bathroom. On the way back to bed, I stopped and looked out the bedroom door. Feeling okay, I went back to bed. I don't know what time it was, but it was very dark outside.

When I woke up at 7:30 a.m., I felt very weird. I had pain in my left lung. Fred was sitting in his chair and I asked him how long he had been up. He told me he had been up for an hour.

I blew my nose and it was bloody. I got up and went to the bathroom again. Returning to bed, I felt something come down in my nose and block my right nostril. I blew my nose and a lot of thick blood came out of the right nostril. This is the nostril I'd had a problem with in the past.

I had a lot of pain in the back and front of my left chest. The pain scared me. I also had a shooting pain on the right side of my forehead and sinus cavity. I was very weak and lightheaded. I asked Fred if I had been in bed all night and he said he did not know. The lightheaded feeling stayed with me. The pain in my forehead got worse. It spread to my scalp, then down, covering the right side of my face, and back to my ear. The pain stayed with me for most of the following week.

I had not discovered any bruises but there was a strange-looking mark on my legs. The mark resembled a triangle with the bottom line missing. The texture of the skin on both my legs looked strange as well. There were no adhesive patch marks. I noticed two, small scoop marks on my right leg.

During the week, both legs seemed to vibrate hard when I would sit down. When I walked around and the legs were vibrating, it felt as if I had needles stuck into my feet, penetrating upward to the legs.

December 29, 1999

Fred had turned off the bedroom light around 11:00 p.m. I had not fallen asleep and was quite restless and full of anxiety. Every time I tried to close my eyes I heard a noise in the bedroom and bathroom. I heard the clinking of glass and someone going through a Christmas bag I had sitting behind a chair in the bedroom. The bag contained blouses I was going to return.

I thought I had only laid there ten or fifteen minutes after the light went off. I became agitated and decided to look at the clock on Fred's nightstand. The clock read 1:00 a.m.!

I don't know where the missing time went. I felt as if I had not been asleep because I remembered being awake and turning my body to stare out the bedroom window. I

367

remembered lying up against Fred's body. The whole thing was very weird!

The memory of the dream I had was this: I awoke, and found myself lying face up on a table with two human males standing near the table. One was dressed in a blue military uniform. The other was in camouflage green. The two men were trying to hold me down on the table. I began to fight the man in blue, hitting him and trying to scratch him. As I lifted the top half of my body to get up, I noticed that the man in camouflage was holding down my legs. I was also trying to kick.

The man in blue called out to someone else and another person came and pulled me back down onto the table. I was given a shot. I blacked out immediately.

I woke up in a well-lit room with two women that I recognized. I knew the blond lady's name. She had shoulder length blond hair and appeared to be older than my daughter, who was also there. The blond lady had a medium build and was about as tall as my daughter. She had light-colored skin. I was certain I knew her from somewhere on Earth, but I didn't know where.

The other young lady that I recognized was either Michelle or my other daughter, Vanessa. I felt comfortable and safe knowing they were there with me.

The two women were standing opposite each other, at the end of the table I was lying on. They were talking about both my legs. I heard them say that I had round Band Aids covering both legs. They noticed that I was awake and they asked me if I could sit up and look at my legs.

I first tried to lift both legs in order to see them, but could not do so. Weakly, I raised up the top part of my body and supported myself with my elbows, so I could have a look. As soon as I propped myself up, I saw that I did not have my pajama bottoms on.

Both my legs were covered completely with white round patches. The patches were half-inch rounds that either had a hole or something black in the center of them. The patches reminded me of the electrode patches the nurses had put on my chest before the lung biopsy. The same type of patches are also used on patients to monitor their hearts during surgery.

The patches on my legs felt hot. It felt as if electricity was going through my legs. I did not know who had put the patches on me, or for what reason.

March 2, 2000

I woke up with no memory of abduction. I had bruises and unusual sores on my right wrist. There was a bruise that covered the entire calf of my right leg, right down to the ankle. This was no small bruise! The entire leg was blue.

I don't know why they are not allowing me to come back from an abduction with the memories. They had allowed it in the past. I know I have been abducted because I wake up with bruises, needle marks and the feeling of having worked all night.

March 3, 2000

When I woke up, I smelled a strong odor. It was the odor of sulfur and another disgusting chemical I could not identify. The odors remained with me most of the day. I could not seem to locate the origin of the odors. The reason I mention this is because of the possibility that these were the body odors of the entities. Do entities perspire?

The bruising on my right leg (from the day before) had just about disappeared.

A CLIENT'S STORY

July 12, 2000

A hypnotherapy client informed me that I had been abducted the night before. He had seen me on the small ship,

369

sitting on a bench with six other people. The entity (human or alien) my client had been standing with, was evidently quite upset about which person was helping him. My client was supposed to pick out that person. He would not tell me if the entity was human or alien. My client described what I was wearing that night and the color of my garments. He said my hair was messed up.

I had no memory of that abduction, but I did have the "day after" symptoms. I did in fact, have bruises on my arms and legs when I woke up the next morning.

THE CIRCULAR WIND

August 7, 2000

I am not sure if this experience happened on this night or if it was a flashback of a recent memory.

For some reason over the past six months, Fred had been closing the inside bedroom door to the small hallway, at night. The night of August 7th, I woke up to the sound of something being dropped downstairs. Then, I heard someone walking up the stairs. The footsteps drew closer to the bedroom door.

Fred heard the same noise I did and quickly got out of bed. He quietly opened the bedroom door. I heard a rushing wind coming from outside the door. It entered our dark bedroom. I asked Fred what was happening and if he had seen anyone. He said he'd seen nothing. He was pushing against the door, trying to close it.

I felt a strong circular wind above me. It made a humming sound, like that of a rotating motor. I was lying in bed on my stomach. Before I knew what was happening, the circular wind was pulling my body up from the mattress! I grabbed the bottom sheet and held on tightly, but the sheet itself was being pulled off the mattress.

I hollered to Fred that the wind was pulling me upward. I hollered for him to come and help me. He ran back to the bed and was trying to hold me down. I blacked out. I don't know what happened after that.

August 9, 2000

I woke up with a small bruise and about thirty smaller, scattered bruises on my upper left arm. I have had this type of bruising many times in the past. When I rubbed the area there was a needle-type pain in my arm. I showed Fred and Silva the bruises. I had no memory of an abduction, but was very tired and just wanted to sleep that day.

WHERE WILL IT ALL END?

Included in this book are just a few samples of the alien and government experiences I have lived through. I did not include articles of experiences with the Nordics, Reptilians, or the entities I call the Praying Mantis.

Much of my documentation conveniently "disappeared." There were other times when I was abducted repeatedly during the week and simply did not have time to update my documentation. Somehow, I thought I would remember each incident. I was traumatized by my abductions. Having to deal with that while going through it was bad enough. So at times, the thought of documenting and re-living the experience was not a pleasant thought.

It is common for an abductee to live each day with feelings of being insane. This is particularly true if the abductee does not believe there are other living species in the universe. I was administered psychological tests by the psychiatrist who worked with the first hypnotherapist I saw. The tests proved I was indeed, sane, normal, and possessed high intelligence.

That first hypnotherapist I saw terminated my sessions because I would not continue seeing the psychiatrist he had recommended. He said I had anger management issues that needed to be resolved. I felt I had no anger management problem. I was working in the mental health field at the time and my colleagues had told me I had no problem with anger management. Therefore, I did not see the need to continue with the hypnotherapist's recommended psychiatrist.

I have been told that the majority of alien abductees, experience some type of ongoing trauma in their lives - trauma that often begins in childhood and continues on through adulthood. The trauma might be a dysfunctional family, severe financial problems, physical or sexual abuse. My life has certainly fit into that profile.

Writing this book has been one of the most difficult things I have ever done. With each telling, I again went through the pain; but with each telling, came healing and freedom. Doing this was worth the price I have paid because I have now fulfilled my goal of telling the story, at last. I leave behind, a small history for my siblings and their children, my own children and theirs to come, and future generations in our family. It is my hope that this will be helpful to them, the telling of my extraordinary "secret life" and how I learned to accept and live with the reality of what was happening to me.

During the many years of learning about these new species who had invaded my life, I have gained a lot of knowledge about them. Through the teachings of investigators, researchers, and other abductees, I am now able to share that knowledge with others who may find themselves in this situation.

I did not choose to live this way. The choice was made for me because of my genetic make-up. There is nothing one can do to rid oneself of these universal entities. After enduring panic, fear, pain, and feeling insane, literally hating and not accepting the mistreatments from these two entities, (alien and human) because of the disrespect shown by them towards another creation in our universe. With the traumatic reactions my mind and body have to the experiences, I had to come to terms of my own as I am only a compassionate human living on this earth. I am responsible for my own happiness and conscience in my lifetime. I had to reach an understanding (of sorts) with the entities.

372

We can learn from them. After awhile, the physical and medical mistreatment seems to change character. The abductee is then accepted and taught by the entities. They are given knowledge in the advanced technologies of medicine and the different sciences. Also included in the abductee's education by the entities, is knowledge of nuclear and bio-warfare.

The hurting side of this extraordinary experience for me was when I also realized that humans were abducting me. I still don't understand why this was necessary or how it connects to alien abductions. Repeatedly, I ask myself, WHY? It is heart-breaking to have to live with mistreatment coming from another human being on our Earth, in these United States. I cannot understand a government that would allow this to happen.

Only a handful of MILABS (Military Abductees) are known to researchers. Perhaps there are many more out there, not wanting to come forth because they fear for their lives. They or their loved ones have been threatened against speaking out, as I was.

I have been told by some well-known researchers and investigators, that the governments of our world are not involved with the entities. The hurtful experiments performed and the mind control used on alien abductees by these governments, are strictly their own doing.

To briefly sum it up, how about screen memory; shape-shifters, trained to speak our languages and appear to us as top leaders of our countries? Are the leaders of our countries being "used" by the entities? Or is this, in fact, a case of abuse of citizens of the world by their elected governments?

This is the first time I have spoken out about this, other than communications between family and close friends. I do so now because of my desire to help others who find themselves in this situation; and because our great country guarantees freedom of speech.

At this point in my life, I blame certain departments within our United States government and rogue military units for what they did to cause disease and fibrosis in both my lungs. (These people know who they are). It is unknown how long I have yet to live. They cannot hurt me any more than what they have already done. Therefore, I feel I can speak out now by publishing this book.

Many names have been changed for my family's and my own protection. Out of respect for (and protection of) the people within the UFO/alien abductee field, names have also been changed or eliminated from this book. These wonderful, caring people have helped and guided me. They have walked with me down this "secret" road I call my life.

There are some very special people in my life who believed in me from the very beginning of these experiences. Because of their loyal friendship, they know of my "secret life" and have stood by me and supported me, my husband Fred, and our four children. I mention these other special people by first name only. Linda and Don, Kathryn, Juanita, Silva, and Christine M.

My wish for all alien abductees and MILAB's is this: Never give up hope, have faith in the Creator who made you, and face every new challenge with patience and forgiveness. Because only then, will you be able to love yourself and find true healing in your lives.

My "Secret Life" is No More............
Gloria

About the Author

Gloria Hawker is a native of the Land of Enchantment. Born and raised in Albuquerque, New Mexico, she grew up in the northwest valley. She attended Valley High School and went on to attend business school after graduation. Throughout the years, she also attended many classes at Albuquerque Technical Vocational Institute and has worked mostly in the medical and computer fields.

Ms. Hawker is of Spanish-Irish descent, and has one brother and one sister. Gloria has been married for thirty-six years, and she is dedicated to her four children. She enjoys spending time with family and friends. Since the beginning of her ordeal, Gloria has found emotional support in the most unlikely places.

Ms. Hawker is a certified hypnotherapist who now helps other abductees, through therapy, counseling, and friendship. She recently started a support group for abductees in the Albuquerque area.

Printed in the United States
881600002B